ACCESSIBLE AMERICA

P9-CFI-933

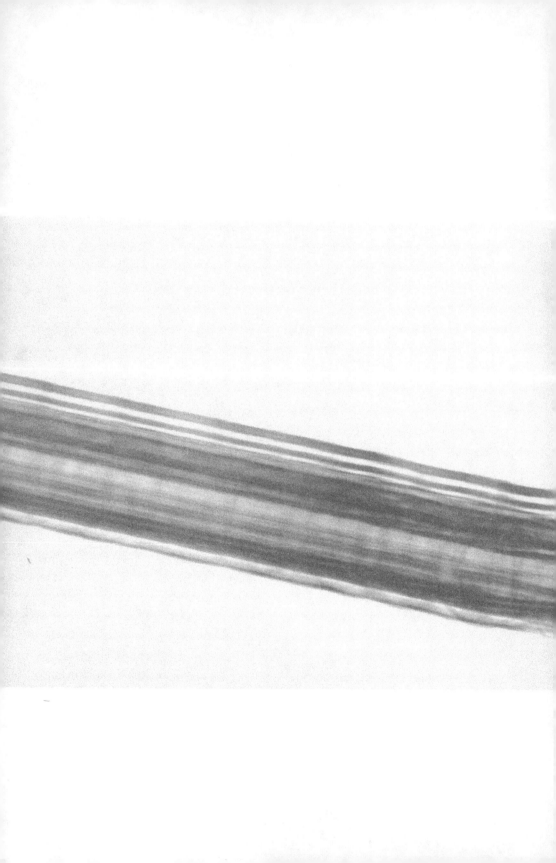

Accessible America

A History of Disability and Design

Bess Williamson

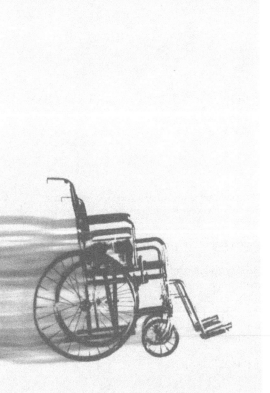

NEW YORK UNIVERSITY PRESS

New York

NEW YORK UNIVERSITY PRESS
New York
www.nyupress.org

First published in paperback in 2020

© 2019 by New York University
All rights reserved

References to Internet websites (URLs) were accurate at the time of writing. Neither the author nor New York University Press is responsible for URLs that may have expired or changed since the manuscript was prepared.

Library of Congress Cataloging-in-Publication Data
Names: Williamson, Bess, author.
Title: Accessible America : a history of disability and design / Bess Williamson.
Description: New York : New York University, 2019. |
Includes bibliographical references and index.
Identifiers: LCCN 2018012212 | ISBN 9781479894093 (cl : alk. paper)
ISBN 978-1-4798-0249-4 (pb : alk. paper)
Subjects: LCSH: People with disabilities—United States—History. | Barrier-free design—United States. | Universal design—United States.
Classification: LCC HV1553 .W55 2018 | DDC 362.4/047—dc23
LC record available at https://lccn.loc.gov/2018012212

New York University Press books are printed on acid-free paper, and their binding materials are chosen for strength and durability. We strive to use environmentally responsible suppliers and materials to the greatest extent possible in publishing our books.

Manufactured in the United States of America

10 9 8 7 6 5 4 3 2 1

Also available as an ebook

In Memory of Philomene Asher Gates

CONTENTS

Introduction

Disability, Design, and Rights in the Twentieth Century

Every day in my city, I use the things I write about. I am not disabled in any conventional sense of the term, but I use curb cuts, feeling under my feet concrete grooves and rubberized bumps that signal a shift in terrain. I see parents pushing strollers, travelers wheeling bags, and street vendors and movers with hand carts all using curbs and ramps to go about their daily tasks. Returning an armful of books to the library, I hip-check the large metal button that opens the automatic door. In a crowded bus, I look up at the LED words telling me (if they are working) which stop is next. As a historian of design, I can even note a few relevant works from design history: the long, smooth ramp of Frank Lloyd Wright's 1943 Guggenheim Museum, not designed explicitly as a wheelchair ramp but suggesting alternative means of traveling up and down a grand building; the round Honeywell thermostat, easy to read and rotate, designed by ergonomics pioneer Henry Dreyfuss in 1948; and the black rubber-handled OXO Good Grips vegetable peeler, developed in 1989 by Betsey Farber, who had arthritis, with her husband, Sam, a product designer. Some sites surprise me with unconventional approaches to accessibility, like the gentle bird-chirping and wind-chime sounds piped in to mark key pathways on the campus of San Francisco State University, or the light displays along quiet underground walkways between terminals at the Detroit Airport that provide a break from the audio and visual overload of the rest of the airport. More commonly, features of accessible design seem to materialize the decades of struggle that it took to put them into place: subway elevators reeking of pee or out of order; accessible toilets repurposed for storage or inexplicably locked.

"Accessible" design—design that is usable for people with physical, sensory, and cognitive disabilities—is a ubiquitous part of the contemporary built environment in the United States and, increasingly, the world. Over the last half century, legal and social mandates for disability inclusion have brought about changes in nearly every public space in the country and influenced a new range of forms in office equipment, household products, and personal technologies. Initial efforts to address physical barriers in public spaces came in the 1940s and 1950s, partially in response to the return of disabled veterans from World War II and the well-publicized effects of the polio epidemic.[1] Congress passed the first federal law requiring accessibility in government buildings with the Architectural Barriers Act of 1968, and followed with a series of mandates that culminated in the 1990 Americans with Disabilities Act, calling for accessibility in all aspects of American life, including private businesses. Along with these legal measures, a growing segment of consumer products responded to variations in the body, from ergonomic keyboards and large-text reading material, to bright and colorful walkers and wheelchairs, to customizable audio and visual features built in to electronic devices. While design cultures around the world give attention to disabled and elderly populations in different ways, the notion of "access" as a civil right has distinctly American roots. The United States was the first country to establish architectural access as a national law, and its statutes form the basis of global declarations such as the United Nations Convention on the Rights of Persons with Disabilities, which includes a commitment to ensure access "to the physical environment, to transportation, to information and communications, including information and communications technologies and systems, and to other facilities and services open or provided to the public."[2]

The objects and architecture we describe today as "accessible" are artifacts of a period in which many Americans revised their perceptions of disability and the place of disabled people in U.S. society. The idea that disabled people could and should participate in public life took hold in the medical, legal, and social mainstream of the twentieth century in a shift that Henri-Jacques Stiker refers to as making disability "ordinary": rather than pitied or reviled, Stiker writes, in this new era the disabled were to be "folded into the commonplace" through rehabilitative efforts to normalize.[3] Design played a significant role in this task of normalization. The resulting designs, however, were often controversial or ineffective. Often these features were added reluctantly, as technical afterthoughts, or were difficult to use, requiring people who needed them to ask or search for supposedly accessible services. Regulations on access addressed only a limited segment of the disabled population when they prioritized physical mobility more often than other concerns such as communication, comprehension, or social dynamics.

This history finds in the concept of "access" a story of twentieth-century design politics. As Langdon Winner wrote in his 1986 essay "Do Artifacts Have Politics?," the political implications of technologies are as likely to be a product of their circumstances as inherent to their design. In contrast to the most overt of political technologies, such as large-scale systems that are compatible with strong, centralized authority, the politics of what Winner calls "technical arrangements" are less apparent, seemingly minor details in the construction of everyday spaces and things.[4] With "arrangements," Winner is really discussing details of design—elements such as the clearance height of highway overpasses that restrict public buses from driving on scenic highways, or the openness of university campus plazas that might minimize student demonstrations.[5] The accessible design we know today became a part of the norm in American material life because of a public acknowledgment that these technical arrangements had a direct relationship to the rights of people with disabilities—the right, as Jacobus tenBroek wrote in 1966, "to live in the world."[6] The means by which these arrangements became rearranged was highly political as well. Initial legal measures had little material effect when accessibility requirements were rarely followed or enforced. It was not until citizen activists pushed for specific and stringent enforcement that meaningful change began to appear. Once in place, the artifacts of access took on new meaning, particularly for opponents who saw accommodations as moves of a "nanny state" intervening in private life and business. As Winner might point out, advocates of access and their opponents shared a deeply political reading of everyday design.

Access became a measure of new priorities in design of the twentieth century. Design, a catchall term for the many practices of shaping and organizing human tools and environments, has often been deployed within modern agendas of organization and standardization.[7] Whether in reform of public housing and industrial work conditions, or in more recent plans to improve environmental performance, mediators suggested that design was a tool of social improvement. When it came to disability, as medical professionals, veterans' advocates, and community activists pointed to stairs, buses, parking lots, phone booths, and everyday appliances as barriers to inclusion, they defined the social experience of disability through the material world. Through this line of thinking disability itself could be seen as a product of design, and design the potential maker of an inclusive society.

Efforts to improve access contributed a new sense of the social potential of design, but also revealed deeply held American beliefs about technology, space, and society. From the start, conversations about access touched a sensitive nerve in American political discourse—namely, the bias against collectivism and shared resources, rather than private property and individual economic power. Throughout the late twentieth century, advocates favored approaches that centered on an individual, economically mobile actor rather than a figure representing general social welfare. These concerns recall other design histories in which U.S. government agencies and consumers have favored approaches that center individual rather than collective participation. This preference did much to shape the realities of the American home and its gender roles. In the early twentieth century, efficient, modern conventions such as commercial kitchens and laundries lost favor in a consumer culture that painted ideal middle-class households as spaces where an individual woman performed housework using her own appliances.[8] The same biases worked to reinforce a strict definition of homeownership as the purview of individual, white, heterosexual households in the post–World War II housing boom. Investors rejected designs that suggested greater communal support, hewing firmly to racially redlined maps and blocking plans for neighborhoods proposed to include social services such as childcare or even shared yard space.[9] As the first three chapters of this book show, this normative household image also shaped prescriptions for the kinds of accessible design that should be developed—namely, that which maintained expectations of race, class, and gender roles.

In the case of disability policy, American design conventions favoring the individual, autonomous user merged with the equally powerful bias against social safeguards as a threat to individualism.[10] Proposals for and against improved access both invoked core American ideals of independence and autonomy. For advocates of access, design could create pathways to individual choice and expression. In disability protests of the 1980s and 1990s, activists who could not walk dragged themselves up stairs or onto inaccessible buses, making a striking statement that it was not their physical impairments, but the built environment that kept them from public life.[11] Meanwhile, critics of accessibility efforts pointed to the very same ideals of individualism and autonomy as reasons not to require design change. Federal mandates signaled the worst of bureaucratic generalization, a "death of common sense" for critics who saw these regulations as favoring the concerns of a few over the cost to the many.[12] Even apart from architectural codes, automatic, robotic, and ergonomic technologies of the later twentieth century seemed to many to portend a weakened human state. The 2008 Pixar film *WALL-E*, for example, projects a future in which people simply give up on walking, lifting, or other physically taxing activities. Instead, in the dystopic future world of the film, people simply float around on carts, being delivered food and drink on voice command.[13] The very inventions that promised freedom and mobility to some represented constraint to others; or, read another way, biases against physical impairment and technological reliance persist even after the successes of the disability rights movement.

Disability and Modern Material Culture

This book explores the ways national ideals of individualism and rights came to shape the material environment, often with unexpected consequences. Scholars have explored the rich connections between people and their material surroundings, tying, as Bruno Latour puts it, the knot that interweaves nature and culture, objects of science and technology with workings of human society.[14] Historians of material culture remind us that the seemingly banal objects of daily life, the "small things forgotten" that archaeologists find in the corners and trash piles of historic sites, play significant roles in human lives and rituals.[15] When it comes to material traces of disability, objects such as canes, splints, and eye patches preserved over time remind us of the persistence of physical variation as well as its social nature. The circa-1880s Marks adjustable folding chair (figure I.1), for example, is an artifact of a past disability culture. The iron lounge chair, with a moveable back, folding legs, plush cushions, and fringe, was advertised as "a Parlor, Smoking, Reclining, or Invalid Chair, Lounge, Full Length Bed, Child's

Figure I.1. Marks Adjustable Folding Chair Company, folding armchair, ca. 1877–1897. An iron multipurpose reclining chair, advertised as an "invalid chair." Pictured here with its adjustable footrest up and a replacement cushion. Metropolitan Museum of Art, New York.

Crib, Combined in one Article."[16] The chair captures the cultures of novelty and domesticity that coexisted in the nineteenth-century home, but also suggests that physical impairment and illness were visible in the nexus of refined social life: the parlor.[17] By contrast, the brightly colored, lightweight sports-inspired wheelchairs of a century later no longer fell into the category of domestic furniture, but instead trumpeted the cultural values of speed and lightness.[18] The changes in wheeled chairs over time reflect shifting expectations of flexibility, portability, and terrain. These are more than just shifts in material experience of disability, as they also influence visual forms such as the stick-figure International Symbol of Access that reinforces public notions of disability as a static, and visible, phenomenon.[19]

The physical objects and environments associated with disability have often been ignored or discarded from the historical record. As disability studies scholars point out, disability remains taboo despite being among the most common of human experiences.[20] We inhabit vulnerable bodies, prone to temporary and permanent ailments; we nondisabled are TABs—"temporarily able-bodied." These realities are not always evident in the writing and collecting of history: wheelchairs, canes, and other equipment were often hidden in photographs, removed from personal records, and unlikely to be preserved in historical monuments.[21] These traces, when they can be found, represent a physiological reality at odds with assertions of autonomy and self-reliance as the core characteristics of the citizen in Western democracy. Disability poses a direct challenge to declarations such as Ralph Waldo Emerson's, that when we are free, "we are men . . . not minors and invalids in a protected corner," or constructions of a universal "body politic" and the citizen's right to "property in one's person" in the U.S. Constitution.[22]

If objects related to disability are often invisible in official accounts of U.S. history, personal narratives and ephemera reveal disabled people's experiences accommodating themselves to worlds not designed for them. The American essayist Clarence Day, who had trouble walking due to arthritis, commented on the grand stairways of public buildings in a 1921 essay entitled "Legs vs. Architects." Day decried "the debonair habit architects have of never designing an entrance that is easy to enter." Any "dignity and beauty" in a grand stair, he found, was a "hardhearted" kind.[23] Day took readers on a revisionist architectural tour of the New York Public Library, where "some architect has built the thing like a Greek temple . . . mounted on a long flight of steps." He looked for a side entrance, but found more steps; he sent in a young friend, but the book was in the reference section, and could not be taken out.[24] The presence of people like Day in spaces planned for the sturdy-legged recalls Dell Upton's assertion that landscapes are "fragmentary," with overlapping but distinct experiences for different groups who use and inhabit them.[25]

Disability narratives of public spaces provide the missing fragments of an architectural history usually told from the perspectives of architects. Objects, too, document histories not covered in written texts. Katherine Ott defines the category of "disability things": "artifacts owned and used by people with disabilities and those that are used upon them."[26] Ott has accrued a collection of these things in her role as curator of medicine and science at the Smithsonian National Museum of American History. Manufactured things such as crutches, glasses, wheelchairs, alongside singularly evocative objects such as a homemade key found at a mental asylum closed for abuses and a glass eye printed with the Chicago Cubs' logo as an eyeball, stand in for myriad undocumented histories of disability.[27]

While disabled people have navigated public spaces not designed for them throughout recorded history,[28] differences of the body took on new significance in the modern era, given the increasing standardization of architecture, equipment, and consumer goods. Sarah Rose chronicles how the modern social category of disability itself was formed in the era of mass production. Rose describes a nineteenth-century industrial world where missing toes and fingers, bent spines, and other forms of physical trauma were common marks of the worker's body in railways, shipyards, and factories. This work took its toll on the body, she asserts, but people continued to work with these impairments. The modernized routines and equipment of the twentieth-century assembly line, by contrast, increasingly excluded disabled people from work.[29] The assembly line also churned out products that separated disabled bodies from the image of a "typical" American worker or consumer. In the cars, radios, furniture, telephones, and other gadgets of the automated and electrified twentieth century, small details of design echoed the assumptions that users of technology were generally spry, and male by default (alternatives might be provided in "ladies'" models).[30]

If modern technology often excluded disabled people through inadvertent bias, some designers made direct links between ideal products and ideal bodies. As Christina Cogdell has documented, designers of "streamlined" Modernist products and buildings in the 1920s and 1930s imagined the smooth surfaces of chrome machines as physical manifestations of the eugenic ideologies of their time. The science of aerodynamics and speed evoked, for some of these designers, the ideal of eliminating the "drags" in the flow of human evolution—including racial "undesirables" as well as people with physical and cognitive disabilities.[31] These ideas circulated not only within the well-appointed studios of New York designers, but through broader efforts to educate Americans about ideals of form and function. Carma Gorman describes educational programs of the interwar period that presented posture and exercise regimes through comparisons to engineering.[32] Cogdell and Gorman's work sheds light on the ways that design culture and designed objects defined certain bodies as preferable to others.

In contrast to these dreams of a streamlined world, design has also played a part in more inclusive narratives of improvement. Nowhere is the enthusiasm for technological responses to disability more evident than in discourses surrounding prosthetics. Prosthetic limbs—particularly when intended for veterans of war—featured in dramatic paeans to the possibilities of technology to restore the body and, in a more abstract sense, a sense of personhood. Following the Civil War, journalists and advertisers linked national Reconstruction and medical treatment, imagining that those who had "save[d] the Nation from dismemberment" would now find reconstitution through prostheses.[33] After both World War I and World War II—increasingly industrialized conflicts—military and government leaders argued for the necessity of developing modern, advanced replacements for lost limbs.[34] As the first chapter of this book describes, Congress's enthusiasm for the prosthetic limb as a tool for reintegrating disabled veterans of World War II led to the first government funding for accessible design when it extended subsidies to cover adaptive cars and accessible housing. Publicity images of amputee veterans learning to drive cars (figure I.2) encompass a postwar technological culture of military-industrial collaboration, with an American vehicle and a high-tech prosthetic hand in a single frame. Given that most of the adaptive tools for automobiles were designed for legless, not armless, veterans, these publicity images staged a fictional version of accessible technology.

Disability things often defy the intentions of their makers—whether that intention is to heal, cure, accommodate, or eliminate disability. When it comes to prosthetic limbs, the actual experiences of limb wearers rarely meet the futuristic fantasies promised by manufacturers or circulated in popular culture.[35] In contrast to publicity images of veterans wearing limbs as they smoked, shaved, or drove cars, for example, post–World War II studies of limb use showed that only 12 percent of arm amputees used prostheses at all, and only 6 percent used them for "work and routine life" as opposed to mere cosmetic purposes.[36] Historical sources further show that disabled people used both accessible and inaccessible design in unexpected ways. Clarence Day wrote of slowly

Figure I.2. Photograph, ca. 1945. Pfc. Robert Langstaff, a uniformed soldier wearing metal dual hook-style prosthetic arms, demonstrates the "special controls" on a Ford motorcar. Science Service Photograph Collection neg. #81912–1, Division of Medicine and Science, National Museum of American History, Smithsonian Institution.

making his way up steps, defying their cruel form of beauty; others with mobility impairments drove cars, rode in wheelbarrows, and even shipped themselves using freight services to access the inaccessible.[37] These experiences of design show the limitation of reading objects and monuments alone as evidence of who used them and how. In this book, disabled people's accounts often document aspects of use that go beyond the plans of designers alone.

Another significant shift over the twentieth century was the increasing participation of disabled people in design processes, rather than as subjects of pity or scientific research. One way to summarize this change is that disabled people became visible in new ways. Modern design and policy had done much to render disability invisible, removed from statistical norms and literally removed from view and into institutions.[38] In early proposals for accessible design, advocates often replicated or at least capitulated to this invisibility by proposing design that was as discreet as possible, "without extra cost," as Timothy Nugent, the author of the first building standard for access, wrote, "without loss of space or function to the general public."[39] As disabled people made their own access, whether at home on their own or through political and design action in public, it was often more obvious and more ambitious. It is notable, for example, that it was not a U.S. authority who proposed an International Symbol of Access, but a British architect and wheelchair user who rejected what he saw as an American-style "secret" approach to access in favor of marking and showing disability in plain sight.[40] In more recent times, disability advocates call for another kind of visibility with the hashtag #saytheword, rejecting euphemisms such as "special needs" or "differently abled" in favor of an unabashed naming of disability and its social realities.[41]

In this book I define access in a very literal sense: in terms of physical usability of architecture, infrastructure, and products by disabled people. As a result, the book joins the many histories of disability that focus on physical disability with little attention to sensory, cognitive, and intellectual disability. This bias partly reflects the emphasis of the disability rights movement itself, many prominent leaders of which were people with physical disabilities for whom "accessible" meant "wheelchair-accessible." It also reflects the logic of an accessible design, in which the very visibility and materiality of basic components such as curb cuts and ramps made useful rallying points for change. These material solutions could also undercut the complexity of disability inclusion by creating the perception that access was "done" when ramps were built. The shortfalls of accessible design as addressed by government and the private sector remind us of the ways technological discourse can make promises "both too large and not large enough," to borrow from Matt Ratto and Robert Ree's writing on humanitarian applications of digital technologies.[42] Promises of an accessible world are too large when they glorify small changes, viewing a ramp or a limb as an activator of change alone. And yet, they are also not large enough when they overlook the complexities of technological change, including the populations left out, the compromises of collaboration, and the out-side manipulation of economic, social, and political pressures.

Design as a Tool of (Disability) Rights

While I refer to this story as a history of design, professional design-ers play a relatively small role. Instead, I approach the history of design as a study of the broader practices of planning and making the mate-rial world, performed by people individually and in groups. The term *design*, as many scholars have noted, is difficult to pin down, encom-passing both actions and products, and spanning the spectrum from seemingly inconsequential widgets of mass production to the luxuri-ous products of consumer society.[43] For my purposes, the definitions of design as, first, a human activity based on intention, and, second, one that shapes the physical environment, are most relevant, and relevant in tandem. Accessible design emerged as a result of a new consciousness about the effects of the built environment on the lives of disabled people. But intention alone does not capture the history of accessible design: the material reality of these things, sites, and technologies is also significant to the story.

This is also a history of design that incorporates perspectives of many actors other than those who plan and make design works. Many dis-cussions of design focus on specific objects—especially attractive, well-functioning objects—with little mention of their lives after they have been made and sold. In accessible design, the gap between intention and reality is hard to ignore: the "handicapped" parking space with a mislaid curb that blocks it, the broken elevator, and the captions that do not sync with their audio counterpart all confront the user with a design intention not fulfilled. As a result, the story of accessible design would be incomplete without attention to the people who used, adapted, and outright rejected its artifacts.

The design focus of this book also refers to the optimistic nature of design, drawing from Judy Attfield's analysis of design as the "material culture of innovation driven by a vision of change as beneficial." Attfield identifies this optimistic move to change as widely dispersed—not just the domain of "good design" but also informing the design world of "poor taste, badly behaved 'trifles,' fancy goods, the kitsch, the fetish, the

Figure I.3. ADAPT, bumper sticker, ca. 1990. A bumper sticker promoting the Americans with Disabilities Act, originally printed in red, white, and blue, features the text "To Boldly Go Where Everyone Else Has Gone Before" in a calligraphic font. To the left of the slogan, the ADAPT logo reads, "Free Our People" with the image of a wheelchair user breaking the chains of handcuffs. ADAPT.

domestic, the decorative and the feminine, the bric-a-brac that exudes unashamed materiality."[44] Disability itself is a challenge to the Modernist progressive mindset that focuses on improvement;[45] disability activism has often called for design change through adaptation, not invention of something new. ADAPT (American Disabled for Accessible Public Transportation) printed a political bumper sticker (figure I.3) in support of the Americans with Disabilities Act and featuring the slogan "To boldly go where everyone else has gone before," a riff on the *Star Trek* tagline and, perhaps, the general American cultural orientation toward the frontier. Seeking to bring disabled people into the realm already inhabited by others, advocates of access did not call for technological or aesthetic leaps, but for inclusion in familiar, typical sites and structures. Given the eugenic history of futuristic design, access to "where everyone else has gone before" presents an alternative to design's focus on improvement through change.[46]

Nearly thirty years later, ADAPT's slogan also seems wildly optimistic, embracing the idea that architectural and technological change would bring about an all-encompassing access to U.S. society. As Aimi Hamraie writes, the idea of design for "all" or "everyone" is an appealing one, with roots in civil rights–era discourse around equal U.S. citizenship.[47] But it also reinforces a neutral ideal of U.S. spatial politics, as if "everyone else" were a unified and equal group that could simply be expanded to include disabled people. The claims for a seamless "design for all" conceal the inequalities embedded in design and space themselves. As Hamraie points out, the primary sites of accessible design development were the most segregated spaces in twentieth-century America: education and housing (a list to which I would add public transportation).[48] ADAPT was and is on the forefront of movements redefining equality and, in its current iteration, places race and class consciousness at the core of disability activism. That this organization adopted a version of "everyone" gaining equal access to spaces and technologies indicates the pervasiveness of this terminology.

The history of access in America shows the many players involved in design, including not only the makers of things but also users, policy makers, medical specialists, and a host of commentators and observers. Chapter 1 reveals the origins of government involvement in the technological culture of the post–World War II era, when a nation fresh from an industrial-military victory embraced the idea of advanced tools transforming human lives. As part of the GI Bill's veterans' benefits, Congress defined measures to rehabilitate disabled veterans through provisions for high-tech prosthetics, customized cars, and house renovations. While veterans' special status helped convince legislators of the validity of these measures, some administrators cautioned that these went too far, and might cause detriment to a character-building process of adjustment. Chapter 2 explores how some of the same contradictions informed medical rehabilitation practices for the civilian population. In an era before any legal requirement, rehabilitation specialists became spokesmen for access. Their interventions into the inaccessible environment were often accompanied by intense pressure on disabled individuals to perform and prove their worth, a contradiction that also inflected the nature of the design measures that the specialists proposed.

Where government and medical authorities defined access in sparing terms, disabled people themselves devised creative tactics within their own communities. Chapter 3 unearths a little-known history of people with disabilities who took a "do-it-yourself" approach to access. As documented in community newsletters of polio survivors and disabled veterans, individuals and families found technological fixes in their immediate environments, and redesigned houses, cars, and consumer products for their own lives. In chapter 4, these individual efforts to create personal access met a new and undeniable change in American culture: a growing sense of civil rights and resistance to the pressures and norms of postwar society. In the eccentric and progressive city of Berkeley, California, students and activists advocated for access in housing and urban space as a means of securing disabled people's autonomy. While their approach was influential on the national movement that emerged in the 1970s, Berkeley retained its own distinctive form of access embedded in a larger anti-authoritarian, disability-centric worldview.

As the U.S. disability rights movement gained a national profile in the 1970s, access became a key component of its agenda, and a shaping issue for its public image. In chapter 5, I discuss access as a visible and controversial representation of the rights cause on the national stage. Arguments over accessibility mandates, I argue, produced a form of public design criticism, as both supporters and opponents of regulations described design's purposes to support their own priorities. Chapter 6 provides a more optimistic view in contrast to the vexed reception of federal regulations, as certain designers embraced disability access and inclusion as a new and promising direction. The notion of Universal Design promised to meet the needs of disabled users while also appealing to a broad audience. Successful commercial products redefined disability within the design world, but in doing so often simplified disability narratives in favor of generalizations about users and markets. The final chapter looks at more recent reappraisals of disability in design. A number of design projects of the early twenty-first century brought elaborate style and an interest in personal expression to the field. Brightly colored wheelchairs, elegantly styled prosthetics, and experimental prototypes in a range of media all provided a contrast to more conventional approaches to access that aimed to blend innocuously into the landscape.

As a relatively new public issue of the last half century, the ideal of access raised new questions about what design can do for people—and what it should do. Design is a hopeful practice, one that looks to improve the current state of things and connect to functionality with a human, creative, sensitive touch. In the period covered by this book, designers and the users of design sought to define access as a practical, legal, or utopian goal. Is access a ramp—a way to avoid steps, even if it is stuck on the side of a building, pushed to the side and possibly the long way around? Is it an open passageway, with no barriers to avoid or markings to distinguish it? Or does it make itself known, as in a bright orange grippable handle or a playground with platform swings for wheelchairs? And how do we define design's successes: by who fits, or who does not?

The design solutions offered in medical, legal, commercial, and experimental arenas over the last seven decades did not offer a definitive answer to these questions, but they redefined relationships between design, the law, and the diverse needs of human beings. Disability itself changed in the late twentieth century, moving from the margins of acceptable discussion to a category of legal protections and a political and cultural identity that challenges core American beliefs about individual autonomy. This change had deeper resonance than we might initially assume looking at the bare bones of access around us. Sidewalk cuts, elevator beeps, and bumpy subway platforms can go virtually unnoticed or can create new material relationships and design conversations. The frequent failures of these designs due to poor planning, neglect, or outright disdain, too, are part of the story of an accessible America.

1

Progress through Prosthetics

Limbs, Cars, Houses, and the American Dream

Public discussions of design and disability often focus not on spaces and objects of public life, but on a very personal, intimate technology: the prosthetic limb. Prosthetics have played a distinctive role in the history of disability, not only as a category of tools that replace the function of a body part (including arms, legs, eyes, fingers, breasts, and even skin), but also as a symbol of the possibilities of technology to replace or extend human capabilities.[1] These limbs have been particularly prominent in discussions of disability during and after modern wars, visibly and tangibly representing both a soldier's sacrifices and a government's response to it.[2] So perhaps it is not surprising that while much of design related to access is of a more public nature—involving architecture, sidewalks, or mass-market products—"artificial limbs" (as they were often called in midcentury America) were central to early policy moves to regulate design and technology for the sake of inclusion and access. As this chapter shows, in the post–World War II years, the U.S. government's support of prosthetic limb research and provision directly led to the first public provisions for other, everyday aspects of design as a means of bridging the gap between disabled bodies and the material world around them.

In a period when American technology and the nation's expanding global power seemed nearly synonymous, prosthetic limbs linked the individual disabled body to technology of a national scale.[3] The Second World War was a showcase for what Henry Ford called the "arsenal of democracy," when civilian industries produced tanks and airplanes to supply the conflict, and then transformed wartime technical innovations into a new crop of novel and convenient consumer goods after the war's resolution in 1945.[4] Government officials, medical professionals, and other observers described prosthetics as tools of transformation from military to civilian life, symbolizing the successful return of all soldiers, including disabled veterans.[5] In news stories, government messages, and popular films, including the Oscar-winning *The Best Years of Our Lives*, Americans saw veterans donning prosthetics with a sense of pride and accomplishment. Congress made this message official through the largest veterans' compensation package in history, the Servicemen's Readjustment Act of 1944 (popularly known as the GI Bill), which extended provisions for medical care to include long-term support to move veterans into stable, productive lives. In the years that followed, Congress also extended rehabilitation coverage to include customized automobiles and house renovations. These policies foreshadowed the accessible design laws that appeared starting in the 1960s in that they engaged government in the everyday barriers that disabled citizens encountered. These veterans' policies also carried a message of self-reliance that would resonate in later moments when policy makers questioned and pushed back against measures that they saw as excessive support.

The prosthetics program incorporated a number of principles that shaped the later development of access in the United States. First, prosthetic limbs, cars, and houses all started with the individual veteran. While cars and houses may be used by more than one person, the explicit goal in government support was to support a veteran in occupying the role of head of household. Second, this was a distinctly masculine individualism in which both medical technologies (prosthetics) and domestic ones (cars and houses) assured one's freedom from dependence on caretaking women. In future policies, this gendered aspect of technology was not always made explicit; however, advocates often raised the specter of dependence as a point of argument. Third, in each of these areas of technological support, veterans were given the freedom to choose for themselves among available options, acting as consumer-citizens in constructing lives of middle-class masculinity. In succeeding decades, as access became linked to a broadening agenda of disability inclusion, these characteristics of individual focus and consumer orientation remained present even in public forms of design.

A fourth and final aspect of political discussions of veterans' technological benefits was the underlying oppositional argument. As some members of Congress moved to expand measures for disabled veterans, others expressed concern about an excess of social benefits. Even for the most honored members of society who had been injured in military service, there was a feeling of hesitance around government support, particularly when these programs seemed to have any hint of luxury and excess. The fear that providing cars and houses would give an unwarranted "bonus" to veterans enters these technological benefits into the longer history of skepticism, surveillance, and denial when it comes to public benefits for disabled people.[6] In these early moves of support for accessibility, the figure of the independent, masculine user of technology was always balanced with the figure of a lazy or coddled disabled person, a threat to the best of American citizenship rather than a figure of accomplishment through rehabilitation. Much of the history of creating access in America can be found in the narrow space between these polarized figures.

The GI Bill and Prosthetic Policies

In the economically powerful society of post–World War II America, technological support for disabled veterans aligned with the overall goals of the GI Bill to grant returning servicemembers access to the best of American society: jobs, education, and houses in model middle-class, mobile, and self-directed lives. Whereas previous veterans' entitlement programs had provided medical care, job training, and occasionally housing, the GI Bill included previously unheard-of measures to pay for education and provide home mortgages.[7] In the robust economy of postwar America, Lizabeth Cohen argues in *A Consumer's Republic*, the GI Bill was a component of a new form of "consumer citizenship," in which access to consumption became a proxy for democratic inclusion. The bill also reproduced or magnified existing inequalities, as people already on the margins of society were doubly removed from the bill's benefits: African American veterans had few opportunities for mortgages, education, or job mobility, particularly in the Jim Crow South; women faced difficulty obtaining mortgages or entering upper-level job training; and soldiers who had been revealed as gay carried dishonorable discharges that precluded them from eligibility.[8] For those disabled veterans who were able to claim the benefits of the GI Bill, measures of technological and consumer access were constructed within clear categories of race, class, and gender.

Public discussions of prosthetics in the post–World War II era reflect the power of the prosthetic limb as a symbol—as well as the material realities that depart from that ideal.[9] As disability scholars have noted, the science-fiction view of a magic prosthetic limb replacing and surpassing human function has little to do with the actual material experience of acquiring or wearing one.[10] Artificial limbs tend to be cumbersome, failing their human users in a variety of mechanical and material ways: simultaneously heavy and fragile; sweaty, smelly, or chafing; requiring attention in movement and in rest. Further, choices about what aspects of prosthetics to enhance through design research often reflect ideologies about what a body does. Prosthetic limbs after World War II, David Serlin has written, were developed in an era of almost constant effort "to correlate the male American worker with the qualities of a certain brand of normative masculinity: independence, reliability, efficiency, resiliency."[11] These characteristics linked veterans' capacity to return to society as men to their ability to make things work for themselves. Indeed, from the start, discussions of prosthetics circled around veterans' special status, on the one hand, and their responsibility to fend for themselves, on the other. Congress, in hearings and statements, warned that with too much assistance, disabled veterans might not complete the process of rehabilitation by struggling through the barriers society presented them.

Twentieth-century rehabilitation, Henri-Jacques Stiker writes in *A History of Disability*, contained a "flagrant contradiction" in its practices of labeling and goal setting. As a new approach to disability of the twentieth century, rehabilitation was a part of a rupture with past views of the disabled: rather than the permanently designated "infirm, invalid, incapable, impotent" came a new view of motion and progress, or the idea of a "return" to a previous state.[12] Rehabilitation is a "passport," Stiker writes, a labeling system that simultaneously allows the disabled person access to the world of the normal—to be "like the others"—and yet labels them, stamping their history and identity as disabled into this passport.[13] The prosthetic limb is a particularly visible aspect of the disabled experience of being "designated, pointed at, and pointed out," but this assessment could also apply to many forms of accessible and rehabilitative design that call attention to disability even as they also present normative values of imperceptibility.[14]

As the U.S. government established programs to support disabled veterans beyond the hospital, its efforts followed Stiker's definition of rehabilitation in terms of the return to an imagined "prior situation." As subjects of constant attention and functional fascination, prosthetic limbs helped authorities, as well as the disabled themselves, fine-tune the very definition of "normal," specifying new qualities such as smoothness of gait, convincingness of handshake, or ability to perform a range of social and personal activities associated with American masculinity as markers of success. When Congress extended prosthetic limb subsidies to cover cars and houses as well, it clarified that the end goal of rehabilitation was a normative middle-class home life. By continuing to frame these things in terms of "prosthetics," lawmakers also reinforced that even when it included a technology not literally attached to a body, rehabilitation was still an individual process designed to produce an independent, self-reliant person.

Prosthetics and Postwar Rehabilitation

The history of prosthetics follows the modern history of war and recovery from war. Just as each generation of policy makers renewed efforts to support veterans of their era's wars (however they defined "support" for their time), each war spawned a new industry of limb designers and makers sure that they would be the ones to conquer problems of design, distribution, and ultimate function for injured servicemembers.[15] When it came to the end of World War II, Americans once again focused on the problem of limbs and whether veterans were receiving equipment commensurate with their heroic status. Veterans' groups expressed concern over the quality and supply of prosthetic limbs from the beginning of the war, as returning soldiers encountered an industry of scattered, small producers and overall poor design.[16] Many manufacturers had adopted weaker metal alloys during materials rationing, creating limbs that collapsed under their wearers' weight.[17] Prosthetic arms of the period were heavy steel contraptions with either a cosmetic hand or a "split hook"— two curved "fingers" that opened and closed (figure 1.1)—that moved through a manipulation of cords threaded through a shoulder harness.[18] Specialists lamented the disappointments of these devices. Dr. Howard Rusk, one of the foremost advocates for rehabilitation, described shortfalls

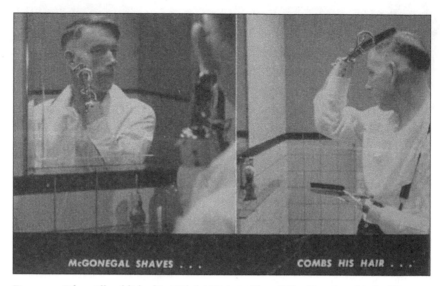

McGONEGAL SHAVES . . .   COMBS HIS HAIR . . .

Figure 1.1. Film still published in *Helpful Hints to Those Who Have Lost Limbs*, War Department pamphlet, 1944. World War I veteran Sgt. Charles McGonegal, captured looking into a bathroom mirror, shaves and combs his hair using split-hook prosthetic hands. U.S. War Department.

in the prosthetic supply as unpatriotic. "A common remark," Rusk wrote, was that "it doesn't seem right that a nation capable of developing the atom bomb and radar shouldn't be able to develop better artificial legs and arms."[19] Dr. Henry Kessler, a prominent surgeon, recounted the shame of hearing parents say, "My boy has given his arm [or leg] for his country, and you have done nothing for him" (original bracket).[20]

The GI Bill specified that "any veteran entitled to a prosthetic appliance shall be furnished with such fitting and training . . . whether in a Veterans Administration facility . . . or by outpatient treatment."[21] This language referred to concerns about the long-term well-being of veterans: rehabilitation, policy makers asserted, would entail not only "fitting" with a prosthetic, but long-term "training" that would improve the chances of success in adaptation. In military hospitals as well as private contexts such as Howard Rusk's Institute of Physical Medicine and Rehabilitation, this training focused intensively on practical skills, often accompanied by a message that equated bodily recovery with psychological improvement. Rusk described the many real-life activities that servicemembers performed as part of their therapy, from practicing climbing stairs to striking a match, using the telephone, and getting on and off buses and streetcars. These practical tasks, he suggested, had the added benefit of instructing a patient "to look upon his disability objectively and realistically."[22]

Popular culture of the World War II era also focused on the process of "fitting and training" of disabled veterans. From Army-issue pamphlets to Oscar-winning dramas, upper-limb amputees, in particular, became visual representatives of veterans' recovery through re-encounters with the materials of everyday life.[23] Two amputee veterans, Charles McGonegal and Harold Russell, became prominent figures in shaping the public image of disabled veterans and their rehabilitation: both dual upper-limb amputees, these two men were able to show clearly and expertly the results of rehabilitation by performing everyday tasks such as smoking, shaving, eating, dressing, and working for news and film cameras and before Congress. McGonegal, who had lost his arms in the First World War, appeared in an Army training film, *Meet McGonegal*, in which the camera closely followed every detail of his daily functioning (figure 1.1). A voice-over from a "neighbor" assured the audience that McGonegal performed these seeming wonders "as easily and casually as any other man." He was "not a super man," but "a man who lived normally before the war, and had no goal but to live normally after it."[24]

Charles McGonegal's demonstration of skill and ease with prosthetic limbs was a precursor to filmed performances by Harold Russell, a World War II amputee who similarly sported two split-hook prosthetic arms on-screen. Russell became perhaps the most famous disabled veteran of World War II when he performed in the Hollywood film *The Best Years of Our Lives* in 1946; but first, in an earlier Army training film, *Diary of a Sergeant*, he recapped his rehabilitation process as a time of overcoming both psychological and physical challenges. After opening scenes showing Russell lonely and helpless in a hospital bed, with a nurse writing in his diary and lighting a cigarette for him, a significant transition occurs when he watches *Meet McGonegal* in a film-within-a-film scene. As the camera pans from Russell's hospital bed to McGonegal's on-screen prosthetic hands buttoning his vest and tying his shoes, the veteran describes watching McGonegal use the loops of the artificial hands to do "all the everyday things I thought I'd never do again . . . just the acts of normal living like eating and dressing and shaving himself." Following McGonegal's model, Russell, too, becomes proficient with his new limbs, and gains confidence to return home, register for college, and even ask a girl on a date. Rather than focusing solely on the successful end point of rehabilitation, as *Meet McGonegal* does, *Diary of a Sergeant* presents rehabilitation as a process requiring both the correct medical technology and the psychological fortitude to embrace them.

Harold Russell performed many of the same "everyday" tasks when he was recruited by director William Wyler for *The Best Years of Our Lives,* a film that focused on the "veteran problem" as a moral crisis in American manhood, and in American gender relations more broadly.[25] Like both Russell's and McGonegal's Army films before it, *The Best Years* shows the amputee easily using a modern, split-hook prosthesis to lift luggage, strike matches, hold a glass, even have a fistfight. But rather than emphasizing the "normalcy" of the rehabilitated veteran, these scenes set off darker narratives of vulnerability and danger. David Gerber interprets *The Best Years of Our Lives* as a story of the threat an ill-adjusted veteran might pose to himself and others.[26] For Russell's character of Homer Parrish as well as two nondisabled counterparts, women provide reprieve during a tumultuous adjustment. In the emotional climax of Homer's character arc, he invites his love interest, girl-next-door Wilma, to his bedroom. In the bedroom scene (figure 1.2), Homer stands before Wilma, somewhat exposed in an undershirt and pajama pants. Fully dressed, Wilma presents a more formal figure, a representative of the outside world of gendered bodies and selves. Homer does not bring her to his bedroom to seduce her, but to show her his arms in full—and to reveal that he relies on another person to take them on and off, that he is "dependent as a baby" beneath the veneer of agility. The fully revealed limbs allow not only Wilma but also the audience to stare at the limbs.[27] This moment reveals Homer's tenderness, but, as Gerber notes, this aspect of the plot is an invention: one of the first things Russell learned in rehabilitation training was how to put on and take off his arms alone.[28] The scene uses the arms to create pathos: without this reveal, Homer's rehabilitation would be defined solely in practical terms, by the grip on a pen or the ability to hold a beer glass. The film's dramatic conclusion shows Russell marrying Wilma with the support of their families and friends, including his two fellow veterans.

Figure 1.2. Still from William Wyler (dir.), *The Best Years of Our Lives*, 1946. Homer (Harold Russell) and Wilma (Virginia Mayo) stand together in Homer's bedroom as he reveals to her the mechanisms of his split-hook prosthetic arms. Metro-Goldwyn-Mayer.

The emotional side of these two performances by Harold Russell provides a clue to the motivations of the U.S. government as it moved to expand veterans' benefits beyond prosthetic limbs to include cars and houses. In the film depictions of amputees' adjustment, the most important prosthetic actions were not writing, smoking, or shaving, but touching a woman. Russell's scenes dancing with a date in *Diary of a Sergeant* and inviting Wilma to touch his arms in *The Best Years of Our Lives* portray the problem of adjustment as social and interpersonal, rather than technological.[29] McGonegal, too, provided this part of his own narrative as he toured military hospitals with his wife on his arm.[30] A heterosexual relationship represented the aspects of "easy and casual" masculinity that could not be captured with a hook holding a razor or comb.

In these public images of amputees, the technological wonder of a prosthetic limb was just one part of the transformation of the veteran into a well-adjusted civilian. As Congress took up the question of whether and how to subsidize technologies for disabled veterans, it responded to similar goals of rehabilitation into a "normal" life of middle-class domesticity. The expansion of support, first for more advanced limbs, and then for cars and houses, came directly from an argument that these measures would complete the social adjustment process of rehabilitation. Precisely because they were not a part of the veteran's body, cars and houses provided a sense of normalcy in a way that the individual limb (or pair of limbs, in McGonegal's and Russell's cases) could not.

Congress and Artificial Limbs

The narratives of *Meet McGonegal, Diary of a Sergeant,* and *The Best Years of Our Lives* had real-life counterparts in a series of congressional hearings on prosthetics and veterans' benefits from 1945 to 1948. In these hearings, congressional committees interviewed veterans and limb experts about the practical and personal challenges of adjustment to disability. They also debated the extent to which the government should or could provide for disabled veterans. Would a basic, functioning limb be enough, or should veterans have a choice of a range of options? Likewise, what about other technological aids that did not literally replace the body's functions, but supported mobility and social life? Eventually, Congress took steps to expand veterans' benefits to include cars and houses among the equipment that could be covered under the GI Bill. But the arguments along the way suggest the fraught nature of these extensions. Even given the special status of veterans in postwar society, policy makers held to a strong belief in rehabilitation as a personal struggle, and cautioned that excessive support could interfere in this process.

Arguments over limb design and distribution centered on questions of the relative responsibility of individuals and their technological tools. Depending on their position at a given moment, veterans, their advocates, and policy makers argued that quality prosthetics could restore the body to activity and accomplishment—or, alternatively, that the onus was on the prosthetic wearer to make the limb work for his own body. That these positions were, at times, adopted by both veterans and policy makers suggests the ambivalence surrounding rehabilitation—

the very tension that Stiker raised between the goals of accepting disability and forcing a "return" to an imagined nondisabled state. These conflicting ideas about men and their tools also align with what David Gerber identifies as a "juncture of the discourses of the warrior and of the disabled" in twentieth-century representations of disabled veterans. In media images and policy debates, veterans were given attributes of "toughness, endurance, and a capacity for action," Gerber elaborates, and yet also became targets of pity as disabled people.[31] Veterans encountered this conflicting set of messages as they moved from the victorious end of the war into civilian life, where they often relied on others—especially women—for assistance in daily life.

Congress responded to veterans' groups' concerns about the quality and supply of limbs with hearings in the Senate Committee on Labor in September and October of 1945. While military doctors admitted that there had been shortfalls in the limb supply, they also emphasized the responsibility of veterans to accept the limitations of available devices. Col. Leonard T. Peterson, chief of the Orthopedic Branch of the Army Surgeon General's Office, testified that, when facing the "difficult adjustment to a mechanical prosthesis," a veteran might "[like] to shop around and try different forms to see which he likes the best."[32] This "shopping" approach, he felt, kept the soldiers from learning to use any one model well. Even veterans themselves agreed that some complaints reflected the impatience of new amputees. Charles McGonegal, the same World War I veteran who appeared as a successful rehabilitant in Army films, lent his expertise to reinforce the notion of the hardworking amputee who adapted to available technology. McGonegal spoke of the difficulties in using his heavy wooden arms and metal hooks, estimating that "there has been no real improvement in appliances for the upper extremities for the last 25 years." Still, he reinforced the message that amputees could learn to use and even enjoy these limbs, given sufficient time and the right attitude. He compared his prosthetic limbs to a more familiar wearable device: shoes. "We tell the men that none of them are comfortable to begin with, like new shoes very seldom are," he testified, but he insisted that "if they keep them on until they are accustomed they will find they are making progress just the same."[33]

McGonegal and the other speakers summoned by the Committee on Labor in 1945 spoke with caution about the possibility of a new, standardized limb. They had seen many promises, yet few advances since the end of the First World War. Despite these reserved testimonies, Congress remained committed to the quest to improve the available options. Less than a month after the Committee on Labor hearings, the Veterans Administration announced a new, million-dollar program for research on improved limbs.[34] Under the supervision of the Committee on Veterans' Affairs and its chairman, Massachusetts Congresswoman Edith Nourse Rogers, the limb program took on new significance as part of the project of rehabilitating *veterans*, not the larger population of "the handicapped" who were addressed through the Committee on Labor. In a series of hearings reviewing the research program in 1947 and 1948, Rogers presided over an investigation that delved into the personal experiences of fourteen amputees, thirteen of whom were veterans, who tested new limb designs. The hearings differed significantly from the testimonies just two years earlier, when medical and military specialists had characterized technological problems with limbs as insurmountable, and veterans as impatient and picky, "shopping" when they should have accepted available options. In contrast to the earlier hearings, Rogers and her committee celebrated variety in limb design and connected these variations to the veterans' overall success in domestic and marital life.

As the first hearings in 1947 began, the Veterans Administration mounted an exhibition of new limb designs. In the office space cleared to make room for the exhibition, crowded rows of arms and legs showed that the research programs had produced a variety of options, not a single, cure-all solution.[35] In a photograph from the exhibition (figure 1.3), distributed by the government-sponsored Science Service newswire, a veteran named John Seeley hosts a tour of women observers. Seeley, in an undershirt, holds up his hand to show the wire-triggered mechanism that attached his prosthetic limbs to his shoulders. In the foreground are several varieties of legs, with complete, encased plastic limbs standing across from laced leather models. Gone, it appears, was the ideal of a single, standardized limb for all veterans. Writing in the *New York Times*, Dr. Howard Rusk enumerated the design options on display in the exhibition, including "air sockets, slip sockets, soft leather, cork insert, leather removable, solid leather, solid wood, leather lined and leather cushioned" variations.[36] The greatest technological change

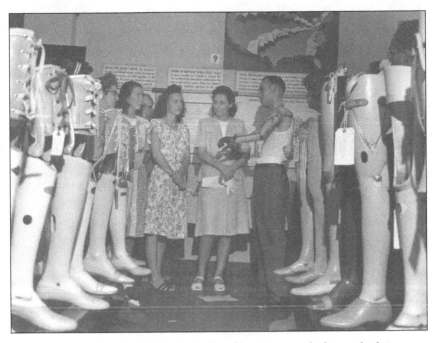

Figure 1.3. "At the Veteran Building a display of spare parts to the human body is enlivened by a demonstration of the use of an artificial arm by John B. Seeley," photograph, 1944. Seeley, wearing an undershirt, demonstrates two prosthetic arms to a group of well-dressed women visitors. Prosthetic legs—some with leather laces, some with metal clips and buckles—are lined up in the foreground. Science Service Photograph Collection neg. #4861, Division of Medicine and Science, National Museum of American History.

came from new materials, such as the "Northrup Arm," developed at Northrup Aircraft, that replaced the rawhide and leather of split-hook arms with aircraft cable and a plastic-encased joint; and new hydraulic joints that helped legs spring back from a step taken.[37]

In these later hearings, researchers and testers highlighted variation in limbs as a positive development because they would be better suited to amputees' personal preferences. The amputees who had tested prototypes of joints, hands, sleeves, gloves, cuffs, and harnesses discussed these parts in terms of their distinct bodies.[38] They noted such subtleties as the feeling of a leg "dropping out from under you" on a hill or stairs; the sharp components of some joints tearing their clothes; and the tension in a joint as, for example, the wearer reached across his chest for his breast pocket. Whereas earlier hearings seemed to dismiss new amputees' complaints as unreasonable demands, the Committee on Veterans' Affairs took a more sympathetic view. Committee Chairman Edith Nourse Rogers and a bilateral arm amputee named Lonnie Carberry spoke of prosthetics as akin to consumer goods:

> CHAIRMAN "Sergeant Carberry, would you recommend that these arms be given at once to the men, or wait a little and try for the other type of arm? I should think that both ought to be given."
>
> CARBERRY ". . . Any man who wants it now should have it, and, as the new developments come out, he should have that. . . . I have talked to a lot of boys and they want to know when they can get it, what is holding it up. I would like to see all of them get this arm, try it, and get their opinion on it."[39]

Rogers's line of leading questions supported her own proposal to move forward with distribution sooner rather than later:

> CHAIRMAN "You do feel that a veteran should have an opportunity to get one, two, or three arms, if one suits them better than the other? . . . And they ought to have an opportunity to select the one they want."
>
> CARBERRY "Surely they should have the opportunity to select. It is like if I am going into a clothing store to buy a suit. I don't want to look only at one suit. Maybe I don't want that suit. Maybe I want another suit."

Comparing the limb to a suit, Carberry classified the limb he wore as a changeable, variable technology, one that a man might select depending on subjective ideas of comfort, fit, and function. In contrast to Charles McGonegal's message to disgruntled veterans in 1945 that a limb might be uncomfortable "like a new pair of shoes," Carberry (with Rogers's support) envisioned a closet with multiple options. Perhaps, to continue McGonegal's analogy, he imagined that the amputee might be able to find a pair of shoes that fit from the start.

In their conversation, Carberry and Rogers implicitly moved prosthetic limbs from a category of utilitarian mechanical objects to consumer goods. Insisting that veterans should have access to the limbs immediately, rather than "wait a little" for future technological development, Carberry and Rogers assumed that veterans could and should choose among a range of choices—like suits hanging in a store—rather than accept whatever limited options the government might provide. Even Charles McGonegal, who had been the literal poster boy for the inner strength and endurance required to make a successful life after amputation, changed his viewpoint. McGonegal attributed new psychological effects to these high-tech limbs. While he had seen little technological change of note for the two decades that he had been wearing limbs, he testified that in the two years of new research he had observed cycles of invention so rapid that a limb introduced six months earlier was already obsolete. He hoped for "another 10 or 15 or 20 [limbs] that will become obsolete through constant research and development" under the research program.[40]

As members of the Committee on Veterans' Affairs interrogated the amputees about the kinds of things they could do with their limbs, they painted an ideal picture of hobby and home life made possible through improved limb designs. Program director Colonel Allen prodded Harold Wyckoff, one of the veterans, to tell the committee how he had driven himself on the four-day trip to the hearings from California. Wyckoff, Allen eagerly added, "walks, dances, does everything."[41] Another veteran, Charles McKee, noted that for his new Navy-Fitch arm, he had selected a heavy-duty attachment with a serrated hook for improved grasp. In his testimony, he described how, just the previous week, he had gone out in his garden "to do a little digging, which I had never been able to do since I left the Army. . . . I thought my wife was in the house ironing, but she was at the window watching me, so I dug up three flower beds, each about 50 feet long." Joking that he would now be compelled to keep at the gardening work, he added, "So now I am stuck." Edith Nourse Rogers picked up the lighthearted marital complaint, responding, "You are a good husband."[42]

These testimonies helped the committee tie prosthetic limb technologies to an image of the American veteran as a man hunting, fishing, driving, dancing, and toiling in his own yard—an image made complete with a loving wife watching from the window. Instead of focusing solely on efficient manufacture and distribution of limbs, they had expanded the conversation to include quality of life. In the months after their re-view of the prosthetics research program, the committee introduced subsidies for automobiles, addressing for the first time the question of barriers in the physical environment rather than focusing on the recon-struction of individual bodies. Their eventual acceptance of this subsidy established technological access as a public concern, but one with many attendant questions about the possibilities and pitfalls of government assistance.

Adding Automobiles

Post–World War II rehabilitation included core activities set out as bench-marks of improved movement and dexterity—the kinds of activities that Harold Russell called "just the normal acts of everyday living" in *Diary of a Sergeant.* This training often incorporated one of the most ubiquitous of postwar consumer technologies: the automobile. Dr. Howard Rusk described the "Independence Hall" at the Kennedy Veterans Administra-tion hospital in Memphis, Tennessee, where disabled veterans practiced with "full-size models of house steps, street curbs and a series of different surfaces," a full-scale apartment with "low overstuffed chairs, a divan, a regular bed and standard bathroom facilities," and a "simulated garage . . . in which men may practice getting in and out of a car." Once comfortable with these spaces and activities, he continued, the patients "'graduate' to a specially equipped automobile with vacuum hand controls and receive a course in driving that ends with an examination for a license."[43] One center publicized sessions in which amputees and paralyzed veterans ably steered cars using hand controls and other specialized accessories, and boasted of driving courses "so difficult that one of three civilians who tried it failed."[44] In *Meet McGonegal* and the War Department pamphlet that featured stills from it, Charles McGonegal's demonstration of skilled prosthetic use would not have been complete without the image of him driving with his metal hands.[45]

Driving identified the veteran as both soldier and civilian—"trading Jeeps for Fords," wrote Rusk in the *New York Times*—equipped with a solid, steel symbol of American masculinity and technologized free-dom.[46] All veterans had special rights to cars in postwar America, given that they were eligible to order new vehicles during postwar shortages.[47]

Automobile makers, seeing an opportunity to address a new market and bolster their public image during a lull in new model production, began developing specialized "driving aids" for disabled drivers.[48] These devices, promoted through the Society of Automotive Engineers, included hand controls for clutch, gas, and brake; left-side pedals for those unable to use the right leg; and various assistive devices, including automatic turn signals (not standard at this period) for amputees who could not hand signal.[49] Volunteer groups donated driving equipment, as well as teaching assistance, to many hospitals, while auto companies promoted their role in teaching veterans to drive.[50] According to the Society of Automotive Engineers, the amputees who received training were "entirely normal in all respects except for wearing a prosthetic device and after training can handle themselves almost as well as whole people. . . . All these men ask is for to get back to civilian life."[51] This return, they implied, would be made possible by access to an automobile.

While auto companies and medical professionals touted the benefits of driving for disabled veterans, the U.S. government was cautious in its endorsement of cars as a key component of rehabilitation. Veterans, having learned to drive using special equipment in military hospitals, asked the Veterans Administration to supply cars, comparing them to seeing-eye dogs, wheelchairs, and prosthetic limbs. General Omar Bradley, the director of the VA, however, was unconvinced. While the plight of amputees "most certainly excites everyone's sympathy," Bradley argued, granting cars to amputees would be "a bonus for a limited group of veterans," not a need on the same level as prostheses and other medical devices.[52] Over the VA's objections, the House Committee on Veterans' Affairs drafted new legislation within months to provide a subsidy for automobiles for those who had "lost legs or the use of a leg" in World War II.[53] The committee initially defined the subsidy in terms akin to a prosthesis: the automobile would replace the function of legs, providing "mobility and locomotion" for those who had difficulty walking.[54] The automobile subsidy was limited to a onetime support, not covering maintenance and subsequent car purchases; the bill also specified that vehicles would not be provided "for pleasure purposes only."[55] These limits showed, said one senator, the intention that these were "vehicles as prosthetic appliances," to support a specific physical function and not as a compensation for service.

In her support of a broader automobile subsidy, committee chairman Edith Nourse Rogers delved into the everyday experiences of disabled veterans in postwar society, much as she did when discussing the prosthetics program. Rogers identified closely with veterans throughout her career of more than three decades in the House, both as the widow of a World War I soldier and a veteran herself of the Women's Overseas Service League.[56] In a report on the new bill, Rogers revised the stipulation that the law addressed strictly "mobility and locomotion," instead identifying the problems people with disabilities had in public spaces, whether their disabilities affected walking or not. Upper-limb amputees and the blind, she wrote, "find it very difficult to travel in crowded public transportation facilities, in maintaining their balance, making transfers, change and other necessary adjustments for their safety and welfare."[57] While Rogers referred only to the struggles of disabled veterans, her statements foreshadowed attention to the inaccessibility of public spaces and transportation in general.

The automobile subsidy was an unprecedented government benefit for disabled veterans in that it involved the world of mass-market technologies rather than specialized medical devices. It was also very popular, with reports of tens of thousands of applications within the first months, and more than fifteen thousand cars distributed by September 1947, just fourteen months after the initial passage of the subsidy.[58] The program had broader effects in the world of urban design and planning: within months of the subsidy, cities including New York extended parking passes to disabled veterans, initiating the convention of designated parking now readily associated with disability access.[59] Still, the measure remained controversial. General Bradley continued to object to the extension, warning that it "had to stop somewhere."[60] Veterans responded fiercely when presented with this kind of opposition. In response to Bradley's reserve, the "armless and deafened" veteran Edward Beamon retorted that "if General Bradley rode in a street car, he could understand the situation more fully," a comment that framed the subsidy in terms of the inaccessibility of public transportation, not an individual's impairment.[61] Likewise, when Rep. William Whittington voted against the initial bill, protesting that there needed to be fuller study of the rehabilitation benefits of the automobile, a crowd of angry veterans greeted him in the hallways of Congress, asking, "What are we going to do in

the meantime? We need cars to get back into society."[62] This statement—
that a disabled person needs a car to "get back into society"—put the
attention squarely on technology, not physical impairment, as a barrier
to inclusion.

Prosthetic Houses

When a reporter visited Staten Island's Halloran Army Hospital in
1946 to observe veterans using new, hand-driven Ford cars, one former
Army captain shifted the topic of conversation away from the wonders
of automobile use to a more long-term problem. While he was pleased
to test-drive the cars, Capt. Arthur Abramson commented, "I just wish
that I could find an apartment as easily as I can drive a car."[63] In the
years following expanded prosthetics research and the introduction of a
new subsidy for customized cars, veterans—particularly those who had
been paralyzed during their service and used wheelchairs—introduced
the new topic of accessible housing. Their demand for government
assistance in finding housing was novel for two reasons. It introduced
an ever-broader interpretation of the GI Bill provision for "fitting and
training" of prosthetic equipment; and it addressed the concerns of the
specific population of disabled veterans with quadriplegia and paraplegia due to spinal cord injury. Prior to the war, the life expectancy
for spinal cord injury consisted of a few years at most, as many died
from complications in bladder or lung function that commonly accom-
pany these conditions.[64] With advances in neurological and urological
surgery, thousands of spinal-cord-injured veterans survived injuries previously considered fatal, and began to lobby for government benefits
that would address their particular needs in everyday life.[65]

After the war, a group of veterans with spinal cord injuries began
to organize in the wards of the few military hospitals that could treat
them. Given their more severe disabilities, they felt that other veterans' groups could not represent them, and founded the Paralyzed Veterans' Association (PVA) in November 1946.[66] A primary difference
between these men and amputees or blinded veterans was that many
would expect to live in the hospital for longer periods, given ongoing
health concerns and the limited availability of accessible housing. Their
need for long-term treatment raised several issues. After the war ended,

they feared they would be shipped back to local VA hospitals, where they would be isolated from their fellow paralyzed veterans and from specialized care. Further, these veterans had difficulty taking advantage of benefits like the automobile subsidy if they could not drive or lived at VA hospitals where cars were forbidden. At the first national PVA meeting in Chicago in early 1947, New York chapter member Robert Moss convened a housing committee, declaring that "if the government is to provide us with specially adapted transportation then they should provide us with specially adapted housing."[67]

When Moss and the other members of the PVA housing committee appeared before Congress in the summer of 1947, they came prepared.[68] Through a connection with the Red Cross, the group of PVA members who lived at or near Halloran Hospital in Staten Island had collaborated with local volunteers from the New York chapter of the American Institute of Architects.[69] The architects drew up sample plans with models showing options for wheelchair-accessible design in specific rooms: bathroom, bedroom, and workroom. These plans, Moss noted, showed that only a few components needed to be altered or designed specifically for a wheelchair, with wall-mounted bars for support, wide doorways and turnaround space, and space beneath work surfaces for wheelchair passage. The "rest of the home," testified Moss, "can be like an ordinary home except for certain adjustments, like ramps instead of stairs and a little wider, considerably wider, doorways." The house design, he claimed, surpassed the hospital in allowing independence. In the hospital, he noted, "if you want to change your shirt, it would require someone to help you." But in the house, "the way the closets are constructed, the patient is able to do that himself. The wheel chair rolls up to the closet and he has ready access to it."[70] Like the veterans who testified before Congress on prosthetic limbs and automobiles, Moss drew once again on the vision of the rehabilitated veteran as living at home and able to perform daily tasks without the help of family members or medical staff.

In hearings on the proposed subsidy, the Committee on Veterans' Affairs addressed concerns that were similar to those expressed in the prosthetic limb and automobile hearings.[71] The Veterans Administration once again opposed the measure, noting that it was a "radical departure" from its existing policies. Committee co-chair Rep. John Rankin of Mississippi warned that "if you start on legislation of this kind there is no end to it."[72] Arguing her husband's cause, Mrs. Lilian Moss responded with a plea to the men's roles as husbands and providers. The subsidy, she suggested, would give the disabled veteran a place "where he is self-sufficient, where his problem is understood by his wife and children and mother and father, and when you do that you give him his manhood back again." She drove the point home with the argument that these houses were in line with existing benefits: "Artificial limbs are prosthetic devices. So are artificial teeth and eyes. It is exactly what this home is, a prosthetic home."[73]

Public Law 702 of the Servicemen's Readjustment Act, passed in 1948, granted that veterans with service-related injuries that required "regular or frequent and periodical use of a wheel chair" could receive up to 50 percent of the cost of building or renovating a house, up to a limit of $10,000 each.[74] In contrast to the parallel supports for limbs and automobiles, the housing subsidy proved difficult to implement. A "prosthetic" in the form of a large, permanent building lacked the flexibility of a wearable, portable object or automobile accessories that can be relatively easily added or removed. Some of the PVA members reported, for example, moving into houses near their local VA hospital, only to have specialized medical services move to a different location.[75] Other veterans reported that mortgage lenders were reluctant to lend to a disabled person, even with the subsidy; of course, this would also be a problem for nonwhite veterans, who could not acquire mortgages in redlined areas.[76] It would require greater measures—such as amendments to the Fair Housing Act in 1988—to improve accessible housing options for a significant swath of the disabled population.

Technology, Home, and "Social Adjustment"

The houses of Public Law 702 played a major role in World War II veteran Roger Boatwright's 1952 master's thesis for the sociology department of Southern Methodist University, entitled "The Social Adjustment of Eleven World War II Veterans to Paraplegia."[77] In his study, Boatwright honed in on the home lives of his subjects, detailing technical aspects of accessible construction as well as reporting observations of home life and relationships. Boatwright's eleven subjects were living at home, most of them having received funding from the government for accessible housing construction or renovation. The story he revealed showed veterans taking advantage of government resources to navigate the larger challenges of living as men with disabilities in a largely inaccessible society. It also showed these homes as sites for veterans to negotiate gender norms, redefining for themselves a "normal life" within the form of housing that tied them to other men of their race and class.

Boatwright's study—in which he himself was one of the subjects (though he did not identify which one he was)—documented diverse housing situations among a group of white, middle-class men, all of whom lived with family members: some with wives, others with parents. Some of their houses were purchased new, then renovated for access; some were built from scratch with assistance from the program. All aligned with the fairly typical single-family house model of the postwar era: traditionally styled, modest houses with gable roofs, carports or garages, and lawns (one of the subjects, Boatwright noted, had altered a gas-powered lawnmower so that it could attach to his wheelchair). Photographs pasted into the thesis (figure 1.4) documented accessibility measures similar to those developed in models for Halloran Hospital: ramped entrances connecting the house to lawns, garages, and backyards, and interior adaptations of bathroom fixtures, closets, and work spaces. While Boatwright gave little direct commentary on the design of the houses, his three-inch photographs show at least three houses of varying scale, with different layouts and styling. If prosthetic limbs could be like suits or shoes, selected to fit the individual tastes of amputees, these houses, too, gave veterans access to a variety of options, all of which were similar to the houses of other men of their class and race.

For Boatwright, like many of the rehabilitation and psychology specialists he cited, truly rehabilitative "adjustment" required judicious and conscientious use of the tools available. Two cases stand out in Boatwright's report: "Case 1," a man who lived with his parents, and whom Boatwright depicted as limited in his aspirations and contributions to the household, and "Case 2," a polar opposite, an active participant and planner of his household. In the first case, the man had been married and divorced twice (once before and once after his injury) and now lived with his parents. Among the subjects, he showed the least

Figure 1.4. Roger Boatwright, "Paraplegic Home," 1952. A snapshot of a modest single-story brick house is photographed from the side, with a cement ramp zigzagging up to the front façade. A suburban neighborhood of single-story houses is visible in the background. From Boatwright, "The Social Adjustment of Eleven World War II Veterans to Paraplegia" (MA thesis, Southern Methodist University, 1952).

interest in being active, in working, or in doing household chores; his mother answered "every beck and call." Echoing rehabilitation mantras of the time, Boatwright implied that Case 1's lack of participation in the household hindered his physical mobility: "It is interesting that of all the paraplegics interviewed for this study, Case 1 was the only one found in bed," he wrote.[78] In contrast, "Case 2" was an active participant in the household. Government funds had allowed for him, his wife, and children to move from a four-bedroom to a seven-bedroom house, which he "had taken great pains in planning." Boatwright detailed the work this man had done on his house, noting that his pride in the house was directed toward its functionality. The family had avoided "luxuries" of fireplace and central heating in favor of functional innovations such as "an all electric kitchen with a dishwasher, disposal, and electric stove."[79] Design emphasis was "for a purpose," whether in the kitchen, with canned fruits and vegetables lining the shelves, or hand-built furniture made in the garage workshop.

While Boatwright did not provide an explicit analysis of these different situations, his descriptions show veterans navigating expected postwar gender roles as a part of the major changes their injuries brought to household affairs. Boatwright detailed the ways the men contributed to "domestic and household chores" and found that eight of the eleven participated in at least some aspects of housework, including dishwashing, waxing floors and furniture, driving children to school, and canning and cooking. All of these forms of participation are heralded as positive ways the veterans contributed to the household and remained active. The danger to the paraplegic veteran's masculinity was not performing housework or caring for children, Boatwright implied, but allowing a wife or mother to coddle him rather than taking up the challenge of "getting his family to permit him to be as independent as his handicap will allow."[80] For "Case 1," the mother's willingness to be at his "beck and call" seemed to correlate with lack of interest in working or marrying again. In another man's case, Boatwright detailed household contributions including care for his wife, who was a quadriplegic with more severe disabilities than his. In this case, the man designed a special device to aid her in getting into the car—it was "the happiest day in our lives when I was able to swing her into the car by myself"—and noted that "she gets the pampering in the family."[81] These men's stories seem to indicate flexibility in arranging their households, but also a lingering concern about the extent to which they were able to fulfill social expectations as men, husbands, and fathers. Another of the married subjects concluded, despite his relative success in helping to run the household, "I feel so sorry for [my wife] because of the responsibility she has in me."[82]

The vision of "social adjustment" represented in Boatwright's study echoes the themes covered in films like *Meet McGonegal*, *Diary of a Sergeant*, and *The Best Years of Our Lives*, and in the hearings Congress held to discuss veterans' policy. Boatwright quoted a prominent neurosurgeon touting the medical and rehabilitative advances that allowed veterans to be "returned to states of comfortable usefulness" in lives at home.[83] But limbs, cars, and houses were just starting points in all of these stories. In Boatwright's study, these men pursued a "normal life" in the marked way Stiker suggested: a norm in which they had to over-perform household involvement in order to meet the pressure to be independent. This pressure was also evident in policy makers' objections that too much support would hinder veterans in finding their own places in postwar society. Still, patriotic support of veterans was strong enough to allow for the government to take unprecedented measures to make postwar life accessible for disabled veterans.

Limbs, cars, and houses were initial entry points for the government into creating access in postwar America. The limitations and hesitations that came with these initiatives foreshadowed the response to disability rights activism over the course of decades to follow. From the end of World War II through the 1990s, each technological move toward improving access also came with new expectations and fear of "coddling" or excessive entitlement. For the population who were able to take advantage of these measures, the limitations of small moves toward accessibility were clear. Even if equipped with high-tech prosthetic limbs, customized cars, and wheelchair-accessible houses, disabled veterans still entered into a world where everyday barriers in the environment often proved impossible to surmount. For those who lacked access to the technologies provided to veterans, the path to inclusion was even steeper. In their obstacle courses and counseling sessions, rehabilitation specialists made clear that adaptation was an individual responsibility.

The veterans' benefits and rehabilitation programs of postwar America also correspond to shifting meanings of American citizenship in this time. In *The Straight State*, Margot Canaday describes a simultaneous "expansion and contraction" of American citizenship as the government provided opportunities for some citizens, but tied these benefits to an ever more rigid definition of acceptable ways of living (in Canaday's words, "think marriage, home, and reproduction").[84] Offering generous benefits to some citizens—mainly heterosexual, nuclear families with male heads of household—while withdrawing it from others created classes of "deserving and undeserving" citizens. In the case of disabled veterans, support was not withdrawn as it was from gay servicemembers; in fact, it was expanded beyond any earlier precedent. Still, these forms of access were contained in a GI Bill that allocated benefits unequally on the basis of race and gender. Further, the piecemeal allocation of individual prosthetics (including "prosthetic" cars and houses), without attention to public aspects such as streets, sidewalks, or transportation, created a similar dynamic of "deserving and undeserving" citizenship between disabled veterans and the disabled population as a whole.

2

Disability in the Century of the Gadget

Rehabilitation and Access in Postwar America

In the spring of 2013 I visited the campus of the University of Illinois at Urbana-Champaign (UIUC). I knew from my research that the campus was the first wheelchair-accessible university campus in the United States, the site where the first set of coordinated ramps, curb cuts, and interior adjustments were made to allow its population of more than a hundred disabled students to use the campus in the 1950s.[1] In the more than fifty years that had passed since some of the first wheelchair ramps and curb cuts had been installed, the campus had changed a lot. Additions of new, glass-and-steel buildings, athletic complexes, and quads made it hard to identify the campus as an artifact of mid-twentieth-century college life. Still, I could find physical remnants of the changes the campus went through as it added wheelchair access to buildings built in the early 1900s. At the school's library, for example, a narrow, cracked cement ramp was wedged to the side of the entrance, accounting for the height of just a few steps that led into the building. On other campus buildings, wooden and brick structures of a variety of styles that house academic departments and institutes of study, I could identify wheelchair access easily in ramps attached to the sides and backs of these pre-1950s buildings. These artifacts of architectural access were probably not survivals of the first ramps that were built on the Urbana-Champaign campus, as these consisted of often-improvised, temporary installations such as wooden boards laid across low entrance steps (figure 2.1). Still, the ramps evoke a certain spirit of accessible design in the decades following World War II—design that provided the bare minimum, wheelchair-focused access with minimal disturbance to the overall architecture and landscape.

UIUC's program of access dates to the 1940s through 1960s, when professionals in the newly expanded field of rehabilitation took up the

Figure 2.1. Timothy J. Nugent, photograph, 1967. A narrow board is laid across two low stairs at the entrance of David Kinley Hall at the University of Illinois at Urbana-Champaign, a building constructed in 1924. From Nugent, *Design of Buildings to Permit Their Use by the Physically Handicapped: A National Attack on Architectural Barriers* (Washington, DC: National Academy of Sciences–National Research Council, 1967).

design of everyday places and things as a means of integrating disabled people into home lives and employment. Their work acknowledged the role of environmental barriers in marginalizing disabled people, but also reflected the primary message of midcentury rehabilitation, which put the onus on the disabled person to "overcome" their circumstances. Often improvised and nonstandard, the accessible design that came out of rehabilitation environments required training and resourcefulness on the part of the disabled user. In contrast to design that responded to a civil rights mandate in the 1970s and beyond, these earliest forms of access constructed a contingent form of inclusion for disabled people.

This chapter describes two early versions of accessible design that were developed in settings of midcentury rehabilitation practice. Dr. Howard Rusk's Institute of Physical Medicine and Rehabilitation in New York and Timothy Nugent's Division of Rehabilitation-Education Services at UIUC were both sites where the built environment was a central component of a rehabilitation program. In both cases, administrators incorporated technology and design changes into an overall vision of building "independence" for people with disabilities. However, while these efforts represent some of the very first iterations of accessible products and architecture, they did not derive from a vision of access as a right. Instead, these forms of access reflected a clear stance that navigating and negotiating the inaccessible society was the responsibility of the individual. As this rehabilitation approach drove the earliest standards and policies encouraging access, it shaped national policies on accessibility that emphasized maintaining existing modes of design.

Rehabilitation and Civilian Life

Rusk's Institute of Physical Medicine and Rehabilitation and Nugent's Division of Rehabilitation-Education Services represent the wide range of services and approaches that were grouped under the banner of "rehabilitation" in the mid-twentieth century. "Rehabilitation" had, by this time, become an umbrella term for a range of new medical specialties established in the 1910s and 1920s, including orthopedics, physiatry, and physical and occupational therapy, that attended to the stage beyond immediate injury or disease.[2] This so-called third phase of medicine following preventative and curative efforts was a medical application of Progressive-Era values of efficiency and social reform, with close links to social programs focused on poverty reduction, education, and moral uplift. Rehabilitation advocates argued that a combination of physical and social treatments would have the effect of salvaging the "human wreckage" of people who might otherwise end up on the "scrap heap" of charitable dependence.[3] Their approaches, formalized with the aid of federal funds for World War I veterans' treatment, influenced poverty support programs, including sheltered workshops such as Goodwill Industries in the 1920s, and gained official recognition as a specialization by the American Medical Association in 1947.[4]

In an era of advanced technology and science, rehabilitation specialists argued that healing the body and preparing the mind for a life beyond illness was simply a question of finding the appropriate tool or technique. Dr. Howard Rusk began his rehabilitation career as an Army Air Forces colonel at Jefferson Barracks in St. Louis, Missouri during World War II. In the hospital, he observed a large segment of patients who were neither sick nor well: too weak to return to battle, but no longer in medical crisis, they moved in "swarms . . . in their purple bathrobes and gray pajamas," idly playing cards or listening to the radio.[5] Rusk instituted new, rigorous training programs for these men, reconditioning their bodies and providing vocational training to help them find, in his words, new paths "consistent with [their] new physical condition." Rehabilitation, Rusk wrote, "did not just happen." He imagined that, without expert intervention, these soldiers "would simply lie around getting no custodial care, with nothing to do, bored to distraction, helpless, hopeless, waiting for some kind of infection or disease to carry them off."[6] Following the war, Rusk opened the Institute of Physical Medicine and Rehabilitation as a stand-alone department within New York's Bellevue Hospital. He became a prominent advocate for rehabilitation, writing a regular column in the *New York Times*, publishing a number of books, and overseeing a small army of specialists who also published actively in both medical journals and the popular press.[7]

Rusk's institute became a model for rehabilitation practice within a hospital, but his advocacy also shaped a form of rehabilitation that occurred beyond the medical setting. With government as well as private philanthropic funding, the number of rehabilitation centers in the United States tripled between 1940 and 1952, and centers that had previously offered only vocational training expanded their services to include physical and occupational therapy as well.[8] While previous programs had centered largely on injured industrial workers, with support from labor unions and private charities, federal funding opened rehabilitation to new demographics, including women and children.[9] In many of these programs, "rehabilitation" became a broader term for a variety of educational and social activities at sites including schools, camps, and athletic programs for disabled people.[10] The University of Illinois's Division of Rehabilitation-Education Services, opened in 1948 at the Galesburg campus of the university, was the largest program that aimed to integrate disabled students into the mainstream of college life.[11] Its programs of wheelchair sports and the nation's first disabled students' fraternity were far from the physical therapy equipment and device-fitting shop of the Institute of Physical Medicine and Rehabilitation, but it shared a focus on rehabilitation as a process of assessing disability in its social context—including the context of the built environment.

The previous chapter described the central goal of post–World War II veterans' rehabilitation as preparing wounded men for "productive" roles in the abundant postwar society. Disabled veterans traversed the uneven ground of government support in a system where patriotic generosity was always held in balance with pressure for veterans to prove their individual strength and willingness to surmount barriers. For civilians, the ground was even more treacherous, as disabled people faced significant barriers with fewer official measures to alleviate the logistics of mobility, housing, and work within inaccessible environments. The rehabilitation treatment they received instead echoed broader societal messages about individual self-determination, with increasing pressure exerted on those who needed assistance—the poor, the disabled, women, nonwhite people—to prove their worthiness of support.

Rehabilitation practice as it developed in the postwar era carried strong social messages that aligned with other approaches to relief and support in the twentieth century. Nineteenth-century aid programs designed to support the groups considered most deserving—single mothers and veterans—were reinterpreted in the twentieth century as instruments of social improvement.[12] Social scientists and government administrators used a language of disability as they described welfare dependence as a sign of "maladjustment" rather than need, and the goals of reform (in President Dwight Eisenhower's words) "to reduce need and increase self-help."[13] Likewise, when it came to the treatment of physical disability, arguments for expanding rehabilitation programs mixed sentiments of generosity toward disabled people with warnings about what their neglect could mean for the country. A 1947 report of the National Society for Crippled Children and Adults, for example, opined that there was a "changing philosophy" taking hold in the country toward a sense that "it is economically and socially advantageous to provide intelligent care, education, and adjustment to persons who are ill, handicapped or disabled."[14] Mary Elizabeth Switzer, the director of the federal Office of Vocational Rehabilitation, was very specific in outlining the economic side of this argument as she established the government's commitment to rehabilitation. Just six years after her office was established, Switzer reported that 58,000 people had been "rehabilitated" in 1949 at a cost of $449 per person, a number she justified as saving $500 to $1,500 per year in public aid for an unemployed person.[15]

Rehabilitation, like welfare and military service, proved to be a site of class, race, and gender training, in which "overcoming" disability also included building or rebuilding a life according to measures of normalcy that were both social and physical. Just as government allocations for disabled veterans emphasized masculine activities such as driving, smoking, and hunting, civilian rehabilitation presented highly gendered versions of mobility and independence. At the Institute of Physical Medicine and Rehabilitation, Howard Rusk and his staff guided their patients through the selection and design of specialized tools to operate in expected environments, such as industrial or corporate work for men or kitchens for women. Likewise, as Timothy Nugent and the college students under his supervision developed ramps and other installations at the University of Illinois, it was in order to allow them access to one of the hallmarks of predominantly white, middle-class American life—higher education. The college environment was one of privilege and performance, and access there meant conforming to the dominant collegiate culture. In this early site of physical access, even students who were engaged in other emerging rights movements of the 1960s did not connect those causes with the local efforts to build access. These were extensions of a university education and a rehabilitation establishment that emphasized individual achievement, not the need for dramatic social change.

Institute of Physical Medicine and Rehabilitation: Self-Help and Gadgetry

After returning from service as a doctor in the Army Air Forces during World War II, Howard Rusk began writing and speaking on the benefits of rehabilitation to aid the recovery and long-term prospects of people with disabilities. Rusk opened the Institute of Physical Medicine and Rehabilitation in 1948 with funding from financier Bernard Baruch, the Rockefeller Foundation, and the Office of Vocational Rehabilitation.[16] The institute became one of the leading centers in the United States, growing to occupy its own three-story building on the hospital grounds starting in 1951, and adding three additional floors in 1958.[17]

At Bellevue, Rusk brought the services he and others had developed in military hospitals to a civilian population. He defined his rehabilitation approach in terms of treating the "whole man"—combining physical recovery with psychological and vocational counseling to begin the process of preparing to leave the hospital. Rusk presented this approach as direct, pragmatic, and efficient. Every part of the institute was focused on the world outside. Rusk recruited William Pahlmann, a sought-after interior and department store designer who also designed Rusk's own New York apartment, to consult on these wards. The result was a space that Rusk described as "a far cry from the traditional hospital atmosphere . . . equipped with pearl-gray Venetian blinds, modernistic light fixtures, gray bed stands, individual bed lamps and radios."[18] This "real-life" interior served several purposes: it allowed patients to escape the sterile hospital feeling that otherwise surrounded them in long-term stays, while also giving them experience with typical seating, light fixtures, and other features of standard design. Intentionally or not, it also presented an aspirational model of normalcy in providing a residence styled in a way that evoked wealthy New York. Many of Rusk's patients were injured mining and industrial workers, or patients supported by government or charitable medical funds.[19]

Rusk's therapists administered a strict and demanding treatment that defined "self-help" through the everyday technologies of the period. Rusk based his treatment on his own military experience, as well as the teachings of Dr. George Deaver, who joined Rusk at the institute after nearly two decades of work at the New York Institute for the Crippled and Disabled, a site of prewar rehabilitation practice.[20] Deaver introduced a method of diagnosis and training based on a carefully compiled list of "Activities of Daily Life."[21] These were tasks that, as Rusk described them, "the average healthy person does without giving them any thought. Things like brushing your teeth, combing your hair, going to the bathroom, putting on your shirt or tying your shoes."[22] Upon intake, staff recorded each patient's ability to perform these tasks, and then designed therapy exercises around re-learning them. The institute's physical therapy program included a kind of obstacle course of inaccessible design, with stations featuring sewing machines, typewriters, telephones, and office lamps; mock-up interiors with light switches, keyholes, and doorknobs; and a variety of textured floors. Rusk recalled that the "Bellevue Bus," a full-sized, decommissioned New York City bus, was "one of the most-used pieces of equipment."[23]

Rusk and Deaver's therapy regime promised the outcome of operating in the outside physical environment, but the path to get there could be steep. In his many anecdotes of rehabilitation, Rusk, like many commentators of the period, cast the process of overcoming barriers as physically and psychologically transformative. He described, for example, the triumph of a woman named Alice, who returned to the hospital after fourteen years of using a wheelchair. Paralyzed from polio, Alice learned at the institute to walk up stairs with crutches, a skill that allowed her to travel to a secretarial job. Rusk described the method of stair climbing that she used in Grand Central Station each day:

> Her technique is to go up the steps backward balancing herself on her two crutches as she pulls up her lifeless legs. She balances herself on her two crutches, pushes down on their handles, thus lifting up the entire weight of her body. As her feet reach the step level, she wings them backward and catches her heels on the step.[24]

Rusk admitted that the "obstacle course" that Alice faced in the city was "tedious and difficult at times," but he considered it "good training." His elaborate story of stair walking showed Alice to be a tough striver, but it also seemed to suggest that these choreographed routines themselves built character. Alice was, he wrote, "resigned to bed" before visiting the institute; likewise, another woman was "a prisoner in her own house" for twenty-six years "because there was an eight-inch wall [the curb] around it."[25] In an era when a curb cut in this "eight-inch wall" was virtually unheard-of, Rusk saw surmounting it as a psychological task as much as a logistical one.

In structuring rehabilitation around the idea of "daily life," Rusk presented design as both a problem and a solution for disabled people, forecasting some of the arguments for access in later decades. Therapy routines that emphasized adaptation to existing technologies acknowledged that disability was defined in part by the built environment. At the same time, he approached the disabled body itself as a kind of technology, urging patients to assess their bodies in terms of function, not diagnosis. He reported that patients who arrived with doctors' assessments such as "prognosis: ambulation infeasible" or "prognosis: wheel chair case" could, in fact, learn to walk or move with the proper training and equipment. With expert guidance, Rusk suggested, disabled people could use available materials to navigate daily lives in an inaccessible society. Indeed, he argued that doing so was a crucial part of their psychological rehabilitation.

Rusk's anecdotes of individuals surmounting "eight-inch walls" and steep staircases presented "self-help" as an active engagement with the built environment. If the body was a form of technology run on well-practiced movements and customized devices, the patients at the institute were encouraged to become active tinkerers, curious and resourceful in the materially rich world of the postwar United States. Among the institute's offerings was the Self-Help Shop, where patients encountered a category of "self-help aids" that resided somewhere between medical devices and housewares. Along with having braces and crutches fitted, at the shop patients might learn to solder an extended handle on a spoon, wrap tape around a hairbrush, or use a bent clothes-hanger to put on a pair of nylon stockings. Muriel Zimmerman, one of the institute's occupational therapists, wrote of the shop as a place of surprise and wonder, where ordinary materials like elastic webbing, strips of leather, and soldered metal could mean the difference between dependence and autonomy. Zimmerman also highlighted the work of "disabled pioneers" who worked in the shop. These men, who had completed their own rehabilitation training and then set about working with patients themselves, represented for Zimmerman the accomplishments of people willing to "'make a deal' with physical handicap." This "deal," she suggested, had to do with "a special flexibility of mind," a resourcefulness and willingness to experiment with one's own body and with material resources available.[26] "Self-help," she suggested, was an approach to available resources, be they medical, social, or technological. Rusk, too, defined the problem of "self-help" as one of resourcefulness. Writing with another doctor on his staff, Eugene Taylor, Rusk asserted that the twentieth century was "the century of the gadget," when it seemed there was an endless array of "mechanical devices to reduce the amount of effort the human must expend."[27] In this culture eager to "tinker" and improve everyday technologies, they suggested, the eager disabled person could find helpful things given guidance and a creative spirit.

The institute's approach to "self-help aids" would seem—based on name alone—to leave the burden of adapting to an inaccessible material environment squarely with the disabled individual. And yet, at the Self-Help Shop and elsewhere at the institute, Rusk and his staff approached design as something malleable, including the possibility of designing environments to fit the disabled body, rather than only training the body to fit existing spaces. Rusk's work with women, in particular, brought him to think in terms of rooms and houses rather than individual gadgets. In his *New York Times* column, Rusk reflected on the particular situation of "handicapped housewives," a population he estimated at five million women "who [could] not fully meet their responsibilities because of disabilities incurred through accidents or disease." Rusk lamented that, while special devices could enable people with disabilities to perform office and industrial work, there had been very little research on adaptations for the home, ostensibly a woman's workplace.[28] To address the home environment, Rusk collaborated with design specialists who drew connections between standard household design and the particular issues of living with a disability.

When the Institute of Physical Medicine and Rehabilitation expanded its facilities in 1948, Rusk recruited Lillian Gilbreth, a leading expert on domestic work and kitchen design, to contribute to the new space.[29] Gilbreth was a doctor of industrial psychology who, working in collaboration with her husband, Frank, gained recognition in the 1920s for "scientific management" work in factories (and, much to her dismay, through *Cheaper by the Dozen*, a fictionalized depiction of the Gilbreth household written by two of her eleven children).[30] After her husband's death in 1924, Gilbreth shifted her focus to household management, designing kitchen and laundry spaces that minimized superfluous movement and expenditure of energy.[31] The kitchen at the Institute of Physical Medicine and Rehabilitation showcased familiar elements of Gilbreth's household design repertoire (figure 2.2).[32] She placed items within a narrow range of reach, with the dishwasher elevated on a

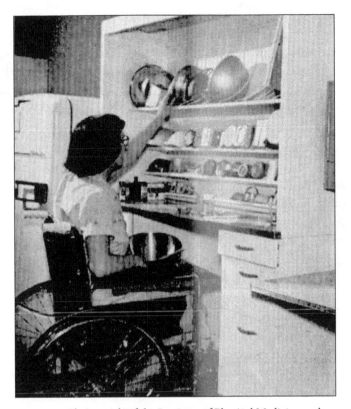

Figure 2.2. Photograph of the Institute of Physical Medicine and Rehabilitation's training kitchen, ca. 1960. A woman sits in a wheelchair in a white-painted kitchen. She reaches to retrieve a metal bowl from well-organized shelves. Lillian and Clarence de la Chapelle Medical Archives, New York University.

platform and a space below the sink to allow a wheelchair to pass. Other features in the kitchen, such as utensil racks to put tools in easy reach and fold-down work surfaces to provide flexibility in a small space, recall her earlier "scientific" kitchen work. Commenting on the project, Gilbreth emphasized the usefulness of these design approaches for many potential users. She felt that it was a "rather attractive kitchen" and that "there wasn't a single thing in it which wouldn't be equally good for a person who had nothing in the world the matter with her."[33]

Gilbreth introduced to the institute an ambitious and holistic approach to design. Throughout her career, Gilbreth had taken up projects to arrange the built environment around the variations and capabilities of different bodies, including a post–World War I project for amputee veterans. In this study, the Gilbreths discarded initial research on the possibilities of interchangeable prosthetics for industrial or office work in favor of what they called an "American" approach of producing equipment.[34] Their custom-designed one-handed typewriters remained prototypes, but this "American" principle informed Lillian's work on kitchens, including a 1945 model for the American Heart Association as well as the kitchen at Rusk's institute.[35] Rather than "elaborate prosthetic devices" to adapt the worker to the environment, she wrote, buildings and equipment could be made accessible with "simple, inexpensive changes" that would "work wonders."[36] Gilbreth's comments suggest the possibility of more widespread design change, but, like Rusk, she presented the task of producing this design change as a private and domestic one—something housewives could ask their husbands for help installing. Her American Heart Association study was published in the form of a pamphlet for households to follow at home, do-it-yourself style.[37] The kitchen at the Rusk institute, similarly, was built around readily available standard appliances with suggestions for strategies such as installing a dishwasher or oven at a higher level for wheelchair users.

Gilbreth's kitchen was prescient of accessible kitchen tools and features of the future, but remained a "self-help" project within the context of Rusk's rehabilitation practice. In other projects, however, Rusk worked with designers to develop entire environments that would be readily usable by people with disabilities. In 1959 a Florida developer, James Rosati, donated a complete model of his "Horizon House" that incorporated features for "the physically disabled, the elderly and the cardiac," for the grounds of the institute, by this point a stand-alone building within Bellevue Hospital.[38] Rosati had consulted with the staff of the institute on the design of the house, which included such features as wide doorways, flat thresholds, lowered counters and work spaces, and a special carport with space for wheelchair transfer. Rusk had William Pahlmann select chic, modern furniture and uncluttered layouts to make the house an attractive public face for the institute (figures 2.3 and 2.4).[39] Rusk presented the Rosati house, which he dubbed a "Functional

Figures 2.3 and 2.4. Institute of Physical Medicine and Rehabilitation's "Functional Home," drawings, 1959. *Top*, a flat-roofed house with angled glass windows in a manicured landscape. *Bottom*, a modern house interior with metal-framed furniture and abstract artworks. Lillian and Clarence de la Chapelle Medical Archives, New York University.

Home for Easier Living," as a public information project within the hospital. He used it for tours with visiting dignitaries and allowed celebrity patients to stay there, including Joseph Kennedy Sr., who underwent rehabilitation after a stroke in 1961.[40]

Were the institute's kitchen and the Functional Home early models of accessible design? Rusk was aware of other developments that suggested an architectural approach to inclusion for people with disabilities. The institute's booklet on the Functional Home related it to other new building projects, including a wheelchair ramp to the New York Public Library, accessible public housing projects, and the "wheelchair homes" funded by federal grants to disabled veterans (see chapter 1).[41] Further, the brochure emphasized the same conclusion that Gilbreth had offered a decade earlier: that this approach to design "makes living more functional and efficient for everyone." The house, Rusk and his staff noted, provided "easier living" by eliminating "steps, narrow doors, hallways and closets, inaccessible fixtures and shelves, slippery floors, and unfunctional furniture."[42] In contrast to the functional curiosities in *Living with a Disability*, these architectural projects proposed design changes to the permanent, domestic environment, and to collective space rather than individual devices.

These forays into accessible domestic design marked a departure from the tough and practical training that emphasized the disabled person's responsibility to surmount and adapt to existing barriers. The Functional Home, based on a retirement residence in Florida and built within the institute's first-floor courtyard, seemed to evoke a warm-weather vacation. The courtyard also included a greenhouse garden, adding to the house's otherworldly feeling, far from the busy streets and hospital complex outside the institute's doors. The photographs and drawings of the Functional Home were of a place far from New York City as well: the modern, undecorated furniture and open spaces that flowed into one another were in keeping with contemporary suburban styles of one-story structures with drive-up carport access.[43] In the world of this house, we seem far from the streetcar landings or subway stairs that Rusk introduced within the physical therapy routines of rehabilitation. Even the separation of the house—downstairs in the protected courtyard, rather than in the wards of the institute—seems to suggest its distance from the active process of rehabilitation.

The elegant interiors of the Functional Home set up an ideal of access that went beyond the daily exercises of rehabilitation. Within the institute, Rusk maintained the message that finding access was an individual project, and that technologies were tools to be activated by the curious and resourceful user. His descriptions of technological activity—of people eagerly constructing and reconstructing equipment, of complex stair climbing and eager adventuring in the city—contrast with the quiet, empty rooms of the Functional Home as pictured in its brochures. As other projects emerged to focus on the built environment, they once again emphasized the responsibility of the disabled person to navigate and surmount barriers. The features of improved access were hard-won, and did not appear in the form of elegant interiors and manicured landscapes. Instead, they arrived piecemeal, through regulations that required specific measures such as ramps, widened doorways, and designated parking spaces. These developments, beginning with work at the campus of the University of Illinois in Urbana-Champaign in the 1950s, reflected the rehabilitation approach that placed the primary onus for access on the disabled person, not the built environment.

University of Illinois: Ramps to Independence

If Howard Rusk's Institute of Physical Medicine and Rehabilitation used technology to expand medical rehabilitation in the United States, another program, outside the medical context, established practices that would influence architecture for decades to come. The University of Illinois at Urbana-Champaign's college program for students with disabilities provided the context for new experiments in physical accessibility. Timothy Nugent, the director of the program that came to be called the Division of Rehabilitation-Education Services (DRES) from its start in 1948 until 1985, intervened in Urbana-Champaign's local infrastructure to create wheelchair access on campus and in the local town to accommodate hundreds of wheelchair-using students who enrolled at the university. His work at UIUC gave him expertise in the virtually uncharted territory of accessible architecture, and led to his involvement with the first building standard that addressed disability. This standard, published by the American National Standards Institute in 1961 and titled *ANSI 117.1*, became the basis for accessibility regulations in communities across the country, and informed the first federal regulations passed in 1968. A revised version of this standard still provides the technical basis for accessible building codes and laws.[44]

The UIUC program demonstrates the deep connections between the project of building access and American values of individual achievement tied to gender, class, and race. The program was groundbreaking in many ways—providing a space for disabled students within a large, public university, and establishing a level of physical access unmatched in any city or town in the United States in the 1950s. It also reinforced the messages that Rusk and other rehabilitation leaders presented—namely, that success in rehabilitation could be measured through a person's ability to perform, seemingly at any cost, the familiar activities of middle-class, white, and gender-appropriate life. By the mid-twentieth century, college was increasingly one of those activities: an aspirational move that affirmed a person's entry into productive citizenship. The GI Bill did much to democratize college campuses, including changing the very image of higher education as something accessible to "average" rather than solely elite Americans.[45] At UIUC, rehabilitation came in the form of advocacy for the students' inclusion in the university system, as well as firm pressure on them to perform academically, athletically, and socially.[46] Like Rusk's institute, Nugent's DRES framed access as a tool for the resourceful person with a disability.

The University of Illinois's program began, as many services for people with disabilities of the 1940s and 1950s did, as a program for veterans of World War II. In the years following the war, the university opened a new campus at a former hospital in Galesburg, Illinois, to handle the overflow of students, including new enrollments under the GI Bill.[47] Nugent had been a recreation officer in the U.S. Army, but had no formal rehabilitation training. He drew on his experience as an athlete and coach as he took up the director's role; later, he pioneered wheelchair sports at the university, establishing the first collegiate wheelchair basketball league and cheerleading squad.[48]

Physical access became an issue for the division in 1950, when the Galesburg campus closed and Nugent proposed moving the program to the Urbana-Champaign campus. At Galesburg, the former hospital provided an easy site for physically disabled students to navigate:

Nugent installed only a few ramps, added "a rail here and there," and modified a small number of restrooms.[49] The more established campus in Urbana-Champaign, however, had more conventional, multistory classroom buildings with stairs in front of most buildings and steep curbs throughout the town and campus.[50] Although Nugent encountered initial resistance from university officials, he and his students endeavored to show the university that ramps could be easily and cheaply added to existing buildings and new plans.[51] Off campus, he convinced the towns of Urbana and Champaign to install curb cuts by building on personal relationships with city workers who could construct makeshift ramps by layering cement to the street level.[52] By 1959, he reported, the program had built more than a hundred ramps, and he had overseen the construction of fourteen new buildings that incorporated wheelchair access.[53] Through his on-the-ground work, Nugent created unprecedented levels of access for this time. Although other towns and college campuses installed isolated ramps and sidewalk curb cuts in the postwar years, these examples were rare, often related to medical sites, and did not form cohesive, accessible environments.[54] Yet by 1953 the university had adopted a policy for all new construction to be wheelchair-accessible—a policy without equal in American higher education.[55]

Despite the pioneering qualities of the Illinois program, the forms of access that Nugent designed and installed fit within the postwar paradigm of rehabilitation that defined adaptation as an individual responsibility. Nugent's alterations for accessibility were rugged and improvisational.[56] A basic ramp might consist of a narrow installation of off-the shelf lumber, with a handrail on one side—just barely wide enough for the chrome wheelchairs of the period (figure 2.5). In other cases, the solutions were more dramatic, introducing new pathways into and through a building. In one building, Nugent later recalled, there was no clear way to ramp the entrances, so he altered a basement window to allow a ramp to pass through a low entrance. Within two weeks, he remarked, the majority of faculty, staff, and students who used this building used the new basement entrance.[57]

Like Howard Rusk, Nugent approached accessible design as a component of an individually oriented rehabilitation program that delivered tough lessons in "self-help." He required students to achieve what he

Figure 2.5. Four students at the University of Illinois, 1950. Four young men sit in metal wheelchairs on a narrow wood-slatted wheelchair ramp with a single handrail. Timothy Nugent Papers, University Archives, University of Illinois at Urbana-Champaign.

called "personal independence," defined as complete autonomy from assistance, in order to enter the DRES program.[58] He would not allow the use of attendants, preferring to pair roommates who could help each other with daily tasks such as dressing or getting into bed.[59] In a program initially dominated by veterans, Nugent applied a tough, military style. In an oral history interview, he told a story of sending one paraplegic student to counsel another who was hesitant to perform some of these daily activities alone. By Nugent's account, the more senior student yelled at the new recruit, "Listen, you lazy son of a bitch. You get out of that bed by yourself and you get dressed by yourself or go home. We don't want you here."[60] Framing his stern approach as realism, he imposed restrictions on behaviors he considered to be signs of dependence. In addition to his bar on personal attendants, he discouraged the use of power wheelchairs, as well as "pushing"—that is, allowing a non-wheelchair user to give help as students wheeled across campus or up steep ramps, even in Illinois winter conditions.[61] Nugent asserted that the students in his program could, and would, compete with their nondisabled peers socially, academically, and athletically.

Nugent's students, interviewed decades later, recalled an atmosphere of pressure and discipline. Mary Lou Breslin, who attended the program from 1962 to 1966, remembered her initial interview with Nugent as "terrible," and that he "scared the bejeezus out of me."[62] Breslin remembered him telling her, "You have to be able to function independently. You have to be able to push your wheelchair long distances and through cold and snow."[63] Breslin felt that Nugent influenced a feeling of peer pressure and competitiveness among students, as each strove to prove his or her ability to muscle across campus and up "incredibly steep ramps."[64] On campus buses that had been outfitted with hydraulic ramps, Breslin noted that "of course it became a game to see how cool you could be on the lift" by not holding on to the bars or putting on the wheelchair's brakes.[65] Another UIUC student, Fred Fay, who attended in the late 1950s, remembered Nugent more fondly, but also described the program as "a very spartan, high expectations place."[66]

The memories of Nugent's former students, recorded in recent interviews under the auspices of a disability rights–focused oral history project at the University of California at Berkeley, make clear the distinction between the kinds of access students encountered at UIUC and the legal forms that developed during the disability rights era of the 1960s to 1990s. For many of these students—particularly civilians, who had not undergone the structured rehabilitation practiced in veterans' hospitals—this was the first time living without parents or in a non-hospital setting. For them, the steep ramps and rugged terrain of the campus fit into a larger experience that often involved arduous work to qualify as "independent." Fred Fay spoke of the "refreshing" nature of Nugent's "can-do philosophy" and "tremendous emphasis" on independence after feeling himself the object of pity during his childhood: for example, when he was at the bottom of a ramp, "I could let some student push me up the ramp, but that wouldn't help me in the long run. If I forced myself to push myself up the ramp, I developed the strength later on to be able to do it myself."[67]

For others who attended the program, the memory of Nugent's approach was more troubled. Kitty Cone, who attended UIUC in the early 1960s, spoke of this "can-do" approach in different terms, describing the seeming conflict between physical access and the constant reminder of the barriers beyond the world of the university:

> It was kind of ironic because everything was accessible at U of I: there were ramps; they would get you a class anywhere you wanted; they had buses, the dorms, everything. But the prevailing ethic was that the world is the way it is; you need to be prepared to deal with whatever you encounter, and you just go out there and deal with it.[68]

The idea of "just deal[ing] with it" reflected the rehabilitation philosophy Nugent espoused. It also related to the relative conservatism of the large, midwestern university in the early 1960s,when campus activism had only just begun among the more progressive campuses in the United States, such as Columbia University or the University of California at Berkeley. Breslin likewise saw the activities of the program as a part of a conservative campus where everyone, she felt, "had their pocket protectors on and their circle pins and matching pant suits," and where the social scene revolved around fraternity and sorority life.[69] For these women, ramps and access were a part of the establishment at their university, not a statement of distinctive rights or protections.

Fay, Cone, and Breslin were three UIUC graduates who went on to political roles; however, none recalled their college years as the starting point of their disability rights activism. Fay categorized the university along with his rehabilitation facility, Warm Springs, as places sheltered from inaccessible reality: "the real world," he felt, "was just so totally different from these islands or oases of accessibility."[70] Breslin and Cone became involved in activist scenes on campus and beyond. Cone was a member of the on-campus branches of the NAACP and Students for a Democratic Society (SDS), participating in activism around civil rights and workers' concerns. Cone ultimately took leave from UIUC to join in socialist causes in Chicago; Breslin remained connected to civil rights and anti-war activism circles after her graduation. Both women struggled to find work and housing with their disabilities, but neither connected her disabilities to civil rights issues until they moved (separately) to Berkeley—a hotbed of disability activism by the late 1960s.

UIUC's unprecedented level of wheelchair ramping, like Howard Rusk's technological experiments at the Institute of Physical Medicine and Rehabilitation, present examples of early access that was linked not to civil rights, but instead to a vision of independence as the hard-won struggle of a determined individual. The rhetoric of the "whole man" and of the tough, independent student-athlete reflected the ideal of a self-directed citizen who makes the most of available resources rather than depending on others for help. The accessible design that these programs produced was a limited resource, a part of a rehabilitation process that a determined disabled person must follow closely to be considered successful. Rusk's institute's "gadgets" for everyday life show a kind of technological stubbornness, as specialists and their patients welded and glued together solutions from available materials. Only rarely did they imagine the possibility of a world designed to be accessible from its origins—and this remained an ideal, embodied by the model Functional Home within the institute, rather than a lived reality. Likewise, the ramps that Nugent forced into the doorways and windows of UIUC buildings, by necessity, worked around and through the layouts of existing structures. The legacies of both of these programs materialized in the first national standards and laws requiring access, which presented a bare-minimum approach designed to adapt to existing built environments.

Inching toward Access: The American National Standard

When Tim Nugent warned his students about the general inaccessibility of the world beyond Urbana-Champaign, he knew the subject well. In the late 1950s, Nugent began discussions with the Veterans Administration and the American National Standards Institute (ANSI) on the idea of a new standard related to physical accessibility for people with disabilities.[71] Nugent became the director of the research project, codifying for the first time measurements, features, and graphic elements of accessible architecture and planning. The project culminated in the 1961 publication *ANSI 117.1–1961: American National Standard Specifications for Making Buildings and Facilities Accessible to, and Usable by, the Physically Handicapped.*[72] This first guideline provided the technical basis for decades of local and national regulations, including the 1968 Architectural Barriers Act. It also established certain principles of publicly governed design: it defined access in terms of minimum quantities; it emphasized non-intrusiveness in the designed environment overall; and it maintained that it was the responsibility of disabled people to find and navigate existing accommodations.

Nugent described the ANSI project as a translation of the ad hoc design work he had produced over the years, remembering that "a lot of times I did research today to prove that what I did yesterday was right."[73] With disabled students as both test subjects and researchers, the program compiled comprehensive measurements of wheelchairs, wheelchair turning space, and range of movement and reach. They tested ramps from thirty-two different positions, of varying lengths, with and without handrails, and with various ground surfaces. They surveyed available commercial floor coverings, finishes, door hardware, and built-in features such as telephone booths and water fountains.[74] With no other published guideline for architectural access, these studies reinforced Nugent's "ad hoc" work while also integrating disabled students' own lived experiences.

The research Nugent and his students conducted provided much of the basis for the 1961 standard.[75] *ANSI 117.1* consisted of a slim volume with six pages of text defining common physical impairments and detailing parameters for access in landscapes and buildings. The guide's specifications informed local and federal accessibility requirements published in the 1960s and 1970s, including a minimum 1:12 gradient (one foot rise per twelve feet of length) for a wheelchair ramp and the recommended height of thirty inches for tables, water fountains, and other features to be reachable by wheelchair users.[76] Additional specifications reflected the contributions of other organizations, particularly with reference to vision and hearing impairment, issues with which Nugent had limited experience. The specifications for these groups were brief, with requirements that "audible warning signals shall be accompanied by simultaneous visual signals" and "visual signals shall be accompanied by simultaneous audible signals."[77] It was not until 1980 that *ANSI 117.1* was revised to include such details as the size and placement of Braille lettering and flashing frequency for visual alerts, along with variations on wheelchair ramp grades and other design features.[78]

ANSI 117.1 codified Nugent's view of physical access as a component of rehabilitation. The regulations presented technological elements to fit into an existing system, not a holistic design approach. Nugent described his fellow authors and researchers on the project as "professional people dedicated to rehabilitation."[79] In the writing of the standard, Nugent and his colleagues assumed a certain level of physical conditioning and training familiar from rehabilitation practices such as those developed by Howard Rusk. The 1:12 rise specified for wheelchair ramps was more gradual than some of the ramps students used at UIUC, but it was still steep, and required a certain wheelchair skill to climb. A study conducted in 1979, in preparation for a major revision of the standard, found that almost half of wheelchair users were unable to use such a ramp, and many climbed it with great difficulty.[80] Other sections of the standard also referred to conventions of rehabilitation training. One of the two illustrations in the guide was of "knurled," or textured, surfaces on door handles to indicate dangerous paths for visually impaired people, such as fire escapes or equipment rooms (figure 2.6). This practice was part of a system that assumed a certain level of shared knowledge gained in formal rehabilitation training. We might contrast this kind of approach to tactile or audible alerts that can be understood by any users, whether they have been trained or not. Bumpy or otherwise textured surfaces at the edges of train platforms or on curb cuts, for example, demarcate changes in terrain even for those who might not be aware of this purpose.

With its requirements keyed to familiar aspects of midcentury rehabilitation, *ANSI 117.1* addressed the issue of physical access while maintaining that barriers were largely a personal problem. Nugent described one of the core principles of the project as the idea that "the severely, permanently, physically disabled can be accommodated in all buildings and facilities used by the public . . . independently and without distinction" and "with minimal cost."[81] In setting this goal, Nugent defined "independence" the same way he did at the University of Illinois: operating without the help of friends or assistants, and meeting challenging physical barriers with strength and will. His emphasis on making access without significant expense or dramatic design change had a

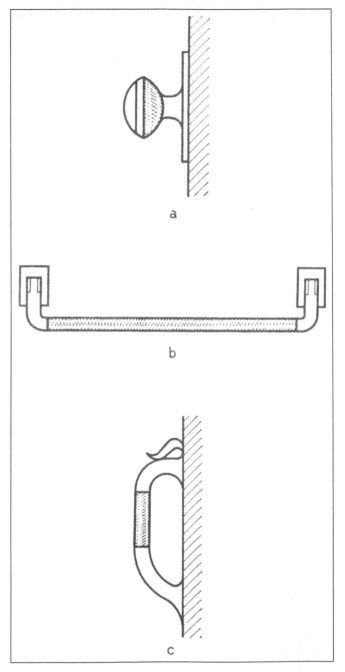

Figure 2.6. Knurled handles, drawing, ca. 1961. Line drawings of a bar handle, circular handle, and doorknob with cross-hatch markings to indicate specialized textures to be recognized by blind users. American National Standards Institute.

tactical purpose of placating possibly resistant architects or planners. It also echoed Howard Rusk's description of tools for daily life as "gadgets" or oddities rather than proposals for a new norm.

ANSI 117.1 had limited impact at first. Because it was most often adopted as a part of local codes, it applied only to new construction and major renovation, meaning it could take years or decades to implement access on a broad scale. Four years after the passage of the federal Architectural Barriers Act of 1968, which used the standard as a measure of access, a General Accounting Office report found that only 10 percent of buildings covered under the law followed it. In many local regulations that followed the standard, its measures were required only in new construction or significant renovation, meaning that inaccessible sites could remain undisturbed. It was only after national protests in 1977, and subsequent government regulations specifying the requirements of accommodation, that legal standards started to change the physical environment on a national scale.

These early rehabilitation programs that acknowledged barriers in the broader environment made clear steps toward defining the environmental factors that shaped the meaning of disability in the United States. Still, these programs and their administrators maintained an individualist view of disability as they affirmed the responsibility of disabled people to adapt and adjust to these barriers. In accounts of Rusk's Self-Help Shop or his publication *Living with a Disability*, rehabilitation specialists seemed simultaneously to revel in the wonder of these constructed things and dismiss their significance. In *Living with a Disability* Rusk and Taylor gave detailed advice about how to find the materials for these devices: "try the hardware, department, and other stores," they wrote; *Popular Mechanics* is "full of suggestions." And yet, they cautioned the do-it-yourselfer not to get too ambitious. "While there is a great need for this type of equipment," they wrote, few of these devices would be viable in mass production: "the problems are so individual that often a universal type of device is not suitable for everyone." When it came to building access, likewise, Rusk, Nugent, and other rehabilitation specialists understood access in terms of highly specific needs and individual efforts.

The "gadget era" yielded initial moves toward forms of access in specific objects and structures, but fell short of a vision of design based on inclusion rather than individual accomplishment. Both Rusk and Nugent contributed knowledge and advocacy for changes in design that would inform coming generations' more activist work. Both also defined design in terms of limited resources, reminding disabled people at every turn that they faced an uphill path to inclusion, and shying away from any kind of design that might be seen as excessively accommodating. As the next chapter shows, many disabled people found their own forms of access in the technological world of the postwar United States. Some of their work resembles that of Rusk and Nugent's rehabilitation sites in that it was improvised, constructed from available materials, and local in its reach. But documents of homemade access also reveal a less constrained style as disabled people and their families embraced the personality and expressiveness of postwar consumer culture.

Electric Moms and Quad Drivers

Do-It-Yourself Access at Home in Postwar America

In 1958 a young mother named Ida Brinkman reflected on her life after contracting polio. Five years had passed since she had become paralyzed, she told the readers of the *Toomeyville Junior Gazette,* a newsletter for polio survivors. After two years in rehabilitation at the Toomey Pavilion in Ohio, she had been eager to return to her husband and three children, though "secretly frightened" about her home life now that she used an iron lung at night, a "chest shell" respirator during the day, and a wheelchair to get around.[1] But the news she delivered to her readers was overall good: "This is beginning to sound pretty grim," she wrote, "when really it hasn't been at all." At home, she reported, her husband, Johnny, had taken up shopping duties, while her three children helped keep house and prepared their own breakfasts. A cartoon accompanying the article showed Ida in a wheelchair, a tube at the center of her chest connecting her to an electric respirator, as her small daughter gazed at her quizzically: "Bonnie gets acquainted with her Electric Mom," read the caption. "To my glee," Ida reported, "she accepted me."[2]

Ida Brinkman's life as an "Electric Mom" extended beyond the plug-in respirator that drew her chest muscles up and down. She listed a number of tools she and her husband had selected and, in many cases, customized to support a busy and active life at home. Johnny had constructed a new, flat aluminum connector for the hose of her respirator, making the breathing apparatus less bulky. The electric Hoyer lift that Ida used to get into and out of bed included "a new wrinkle added to it ala hubby [*sic*]": he had fashioned a shorter hook that could be used to help her into the car, effectively making two lifts out of one. Ida's father had built a wooden ramp that was "especially practical for steep declines." She had purchased an extended cord and headset for the telephone, and, in case of "urgent s.o.s." while alone with her children, she had set up an

Figure 3.1. "Horizontal Editor" Ida Brinkman, photograph, from "Happy Birthday," *Toomey J Gazette*,
Fall–Winter 1959.

"alarm box which can be set off by a flick of a foot."[3] In a later issue of the
Toomey J Gazette, as the magazine came to be known, Ida appeared in
a photograph (figure 3.1) propped up in bed, reaching past the customized respirator tube to type with a specially made mouthstick—probably
a simple dowel with a sharpened tip—clenched between her teeth.[4] The
photo caught Ida in action, not passively lying in bed or merely dis-
playing her disability for the camera, as was the convention of many
popularly circulated images of disabled people in this time. Surrounded
by her collection of medical, homemade, and standard consumer technologies, Ida was poised to write for herself and connect to others as a
contributor and editor for the *Gazette*.

Ida Brinkman was among a growing number of people with significant physical impairments, such as those resulting from spinal cord
injury, cerebral palsy, or the polio virus, who created new forms of access in the spaces and communities of postwar America.[5] The elaborate
training routines and assistive devices that specialists like Dr. Howard
Rusk introduced in the 1940s and 1950s were not sufficient to allow a
person to operate easily in the world of mass-produced technologies and
standardized spaces. While many local governments adopted *ANSI 117.1*,
the accessible building standard developed by the American National
Standards Institute in 1961, systematic change to the physical environ-

ment was very slow. Ramps and curb cuts remained the exception, not the rule, well into the 1970s.[6] In their homes, disabled people created forms of access that were more elaborate and idiosyncratic than the architectural standards that eventually governed public places. These were highly personalized interventions, reflecting the individual needs and ambitions of disabled people and their families, rather than the prescriptive intentions of "self-help aids" and standardized building ramps.

People who customized technologies to improve their and their family members' living environments approached the problem of access as tinkerers rather than specialists seeking standards and formulas. Their accounts highlighted three main arenas of technological work. First, many adapted specialized medical equipment. Finding devices that were comfortable and functional often proved difficult, and as a result people would learn to repair and reconfigure equipment at home. Second, they altered their own houses in projects ranging from altering floor plans to choosing drawer pulls. Their self-made devices and home modifications were often cobbled together from store-bought elements and adapted to accommodate individual bodies and tastes. Finally, they found ways to enter inaccessible public places, whether by forcing their way past street-level barriers or avoiding these barriers in an automobile.

To make headway into the inaccessible environments of postwar America, disabled people took a "do-it-yourself" approach to physical access not unlike other creative work performed in American households of the time, but their alterations hold different, and varying, cultural meaning when compared to those carried out by nondisabled peers. The projects document a particular relationship between disabled people and consumer culture: one in which mass-produced, standard designs were both barriers and solutions. The stairs, passageways, appliances, and fittings of typical American houses were constant reminders of a world built without consideration of disability, but altering these spaces and products to work provided a means of access to material experiences of mainstream American culture. These disabled tinkerers and inventors are part of a long history of consumers who have reconfigured modern technologies for their own needs, from rural farmers who used early automobile motors to power appliances in their houses to indigenous groups who appropriated tourists' video cameras to tell their own stories of cultural endangerment.[7] To an extent, these disabled do-it-yourselfers created a resistant form of consumer culture when they made everyday products work for themselves. And yet, narratives such as Ida Brinkman's convey delight and adventurousness that link her with other middle-class consumers in postwar America. Their work affirmed the significance of consuming things in the making of American identity in the late twentieth century, and presaged the disability rights movement's arguments for material change as a priority.

In her writing on the "Consumers' Republic" of postwar America, Lizabeth Cohen describes consuming as a primary activity of American citizenship in the mid- to late-twentieth century. With unprecedented government investment in the consumer economy, the single-family, suburban house and its close proximity to shopping, in particular, came to represent the success of American democracy.[8] Even as politics shifted in the 1960s, Americans held on to the idea that consumer choices could be forms of self-expression, and that the variety and availability of consumer goods represented a distinctly American privilege. Civil rights and consumer advocacy movements, Cohen argues, also operated on the assumption that consumer goods and services could and should play a part in realizing their social agendas.[9]

In their engagement with consumer culture as a means to creating access, do-it-yourselfers provide a precedent for the later political movement and its emphasis on design change in public spaces. They mark a subculture that valued what Aimi Hamraie calls "crip technoscience," or disabled people's access-knowledge that often revealed dimensions of design not addressed in official research contexts such as rehabilitation.[10] These efforts also highlight contradictions in the task of assigning political meaning to consumerism. These technological interventions, particularly as they pertained to kitchens and cars, often perpetuated the idea of the "typical" American nuclear family with husband, wife, children, and a sense of economic mobility. In this sense they also embedded their access-knowledge into the normative social prescriptions of postwar America.

Constructing White, Middle-Class Disability

The community publications that documented home technologies used and created by disabled people reflect the demographics of those who were able to live at home in midcentury America, create their own forms of access, and share them through photography and correspondence. The contributors to these magazines tended to be white and relatively middle-class, and the majority of articles were written by and about people living in single-family houses, in suburban or small-town settings, with some form of support in daily life from family members or, more rarely, hired attendants. The publications also tended to focus on members of two specific groups within the entire population of people with disabilities: veterans and people who had become disabled by polio. These two groups also dominated mainstream media- and government-issued accounts of disability in the postwar era. As the previous chapters describe, the U.S. government funneled significant resources into helping disabled veterans transition into civilian life, promising that they, like nondisabled servicemembers, would share in the prosperity of postwar life.[11] Likewise, during and after the peak polio epidemic of 1937–1955—a period when more than 415,000 cases of the virus were reported, declining only after Jonas Salk's discovery of a vaccine—polio became central to a new public discourse on charity and public health.[12]

The midcentury polio epidemic dramatically altered perceptions of disability in the United States by providing an image of innocence associated with white middle-class childhood. "Polios," as those who had contracted the virus were often called, were primarily depicted as young children who had become the "victims" of an illness widely known as "infantile paralysis" despite being most severe for people who were exposed in their teenaged or adult years.[13] The disease was believed to disproportionately affect white, Western and Northern communities of the United States, where modern sanitation reduced the chances that children would develop immunities through exposure in infancy, and where geographic mobility increased the spread of the virus. This assessment, which goes unquestioned in many medical histories of the virus, is difficult to prove given that polio diagnosis and treatment occurred in a segregated society.[14] As early as the 1930s, African American physicians began to challenge perceptions of the disease as one only affecting white and relatively affluent children.[15] Still, this perception remained, and resulted in a cultural response to the disease that highlighted the potential effects of disability on young, promising middle-class lives. Those who had disabilities due to polio were, like disabled veterans, portrayed as most deserving of rehabilitation and, ultimately, reintegration into society.[16]

Polio, like other diseases, is an individual medical experience that takes on social meaning through media depictions and institutional approaches: in the postwar United States, polio was depicted as a white children's disease, and responses often centered on class- and race-associated contexts such as suburbia. In media coverage and publicity campaigns by the National Foundation for Infantile Paralysis (also known as the March of Dimes), polio survivors were almost invariably white, well-cared-for children, smiling as they posed with crutches and braces or out from the top of a full-body "iron lung" respirator.[17] In a typical image, a 1950 March of Dimes poster shows a group of children playing on a pickup truck with the slogan "Back with the Gang" (figure 3.2). The image of the children in action visually minimizes the presence of disability, as one has to look closely even to see that one boy wears leg braces, and nothing in his actions suggests he is in pain or paralyzed. While the children play outdoors, they are not in a public park, but on what appears to be private property rather than the parks or swimming pools where parents were discouraged from taking children for fear of contagion. The truck evokes rural life and a separation from the unhealthy, contagious spaces of the city and intermingled classes and races. The innocence of these children is also a contrast to families who might not have access to such private spaces, and whose protection was not guaranteed in polio care and recovery.

The race and class associations of polio are also a subtext in the domestic work that disabled people documented in community periodicals. The *Toomey J Gazette*, a sometimes-annual, sometimes-quarterly magazine that began with 125 mimeographed copies in 1958, grew to a circulation of 2,000 after its first year, and more than 10,000 within a decade.[18] The *Gazette* was a work of feminized community service, boasting an all-female editorial board of "three horizontal respos"—women paralyzed by polio—and two nondisabled "vertical volunteers" whom these women had met at the Toomey Pavilion rehabilitation center. All were "volunteers" in that the publication was an unpaid project that was produced in the women's homes. Even as the readership expanded beyond the hospital's alumni, the editors continued to assume a common experience of rehabilitation treatment among their readers. They used a

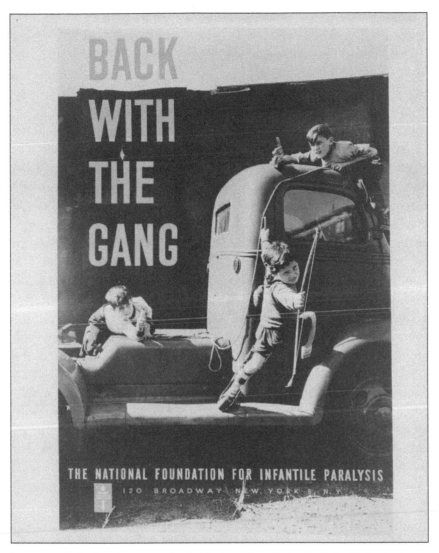

Figure 3.2. Helen Leavitt, poster for the National Foundation for Infantile Paralysis, 1950. The large block text "Back with the Gang" is printed over an image of three young children playing on a 1930s-style pickup truck. The boy in the foreground of the picture, hanging off the side of the truck, wears braces on one leg. March of Dimes.

form of shorthand borrowed from the hospital to address their readers: "respos," referring to those whose polio had affected their respiratory system, "quads" (quadriplegics), and "paras" (paraplegics) were all terms that frequently appeared in articles. This conversational tone implied a set of shared experiences among editors and readers, and drew upon the language of caretaking at the rehabilitation center. In the third issue, editor Sue Williams wrote that the board was "particularly interested in having this reach respiratory polios who have had little contact with others like themselves. We have all met such individuals who have been tucked away in their homes for years, thinking that they are one of a kind, and that no one has lived a fate quite like theirs."[19] This concern over isolated people "tucked away in their homes" suggests the simultaneous role of disabled peer and caregiver that Williams took on within the periodical.

As many as three-quarters of the articles in a given issue of the *Gazette* addressed technological issues, from user reports on assistive devices in the regular "Equipment" column, to an eclectic mix of do-it-yourself and imagined products under the headings of "Oddments and Endments" and "Brainstorms." Although this publication provides the most extensive store of amateur technological reports, other periodicals targeted toward physically disabled readers also addressed these activities. In the Paralyzed Veterans of America's *Paraplegia News,* first published in 1951, a different population shared suggestions on such things as new automatic and remote-control appliances, preferred commercial and homemade solutions for wheelchair ramps, and customized, hand-controlled cars.[20] Additional personal documents, memoirs, and oral histories of the generation that survived the peak epidemic of polio fill out the picture of a population that managed daily activities through technological adaptation.[21]

These periodicals and their coverage of technological work indicate the complex intertwining of race and gender in shaping disability experience. Contributors described their aspirations to a certain model of midcentury American life: living in single-family homes, driving automobiles, and using the appliances and conveniences of middle-class comfort. These activities were linked not only to the recovery of individual physical function, but to social identity in a highly gendered, racially segregated society. If markers of a "normal" middle-class American life were hard-won for those whose families could provide personal care and economic support, they were entirely out of reach for those who lacked these resources. Class, race, age, and gender all affected the chances one would be seen as worthy or capable of rehabilitation. In the eleven-year run of the *Gazette*, there were only three photographs of identifiably nonwhite people. All were men who appear to be African American, and all were described as living in residential institutions, reflecting the disproportionate number of poor and nonwhite persons among the institutionalized population.[22]

As Henri-Jacques Stiker observed, modern rehabilitation approaches tended to reinforce existing categories of respectability and acceptance.[23] For each group considered viable for rehabilitation, there remained those considered incapable or unworthy of "return" to mainstream society. To be a white, middle-class veteran or polio survivor in the 1950s was to be in a place of privilege, but also of pressure. As patients, these individuals were encouraged to learn to operate in the mainstream world. At sites like Rusk's institute or the many polio-specific treatment centers funded by the March of Dimes, rehabilitation entailed learning to drive, walking with canes and crutches, and preparing for mainstream employment and education. As they used technologies to improve their access and mobility within the postwar household and to participate in consumer culture, disabled people also received clear messages from rehabilitation authorities about the need for independence, conventional gender roles, and other marks of "normal" life. For a population often physically and socially excluded from mainstream society, enactments of familiar activities such as shopping, housework, and cultivation of hobbies took on new meaning as a way of attaining this ideal life.

While the work documented in the *Gazette* foreshadowed political activism for access, claiming a place in postwar homelife was depicted as a private act. Even if these hands-on projects fostered an emergent sense of belonging in the public world of midcentury consumer culture, the writers did not explicitly connect this technical activity with notions of identity or solidarity beyond their individual households. Many of the leaders of the disability rights movement that emerged in the 1960s and 1970s had grown up in middle-class households like those depicted in the *Toomey J Gazette*. Some even appeared in its pages. When they began to organize in the 1960s, disability rights activists drew on their own experiences of personal effort and techno- logical adaptation in formulating an agenda of access on a larger scale. They, too, often framed access in terms of individual concerns in hous- ing and home life, but they also combined these personal concerns with a sharp attention to the structural power dynamics embedded in social and medical services.

Technology from Hospital to Home

For many people who became disabled in the 1940s to the 1960s, the trials of finding useful and usable technologies began in the hospi- tal. Doctors, insurance companies, and medical administrators had enormous power in choosing the medical equipment patients would use throughout their lives. Members of the medical establishment often ignored or dismissed patient input, assuming that whatever medical supply companies or research programs had produced was good enough. The difficulties disabled people encountered in acquir- ing, fitting, and using assistive technologies introduced them to life on the margins of consumer culture. For many, experiences negotiat- ing with and circumventing the medical equipment system instilled a sense that available products and technologies were just a starting point, and that suitable, comfortable, appealing tools might require intervention.

In rehabilitation, people recovering from disease or injury learned to use adaptive and assistive technologies that many of them would keep for the rest of their lives. Patients with partial or even complete lower- body paralysis wore steel braces to support and straighten their legs, and were strapped into corsets to force their spines straight.[24] When acute cases of polio caused paralysis in the chest cavity (or "respiratory" polio), patients battled the peak of symptoms in an "iron lung" respira- tor, a full-body-sized tube with bellows-like air pressure mechanisms that forced the lungs to expand and contract. Rehabilitation doctors and therapists encouraged "weaning" from it, but many people con- tinued to use the iron lung either full-time or for limited periods each day, particularly while sleeping. Respiratory polio came with a variety of other accessories, including the "chest shell" respirator that Ida Brinkman used, which was less powerful than an iron lung but wearable in a sitting position; rocking beds, which used a seesaw motion to force air in and out of the lungs through gravity; and standing beds, to which patients were strapped in order to stretch their legs into a vertical position.[25]

Polio rehabilitation was a site of technological research in itself, given a steady flow of funding from the March of Dimes and cultural pressure to return patients to "normal" and "independent" lives. Specialists pursued aggressive technological approaches to push even those with significant impairments to walk, stand, eat, and dress without assistance.[26] Rancho Los Amigos Hospital, Los Angeles County's longterm care facility, gradually changed from a county "poor farm" to a respected research facility and rehabilitation center over the course of the 1930s and 1940s, due in part to the increased demand for polio care. In the 1950s, Rancho Los Amigos opened a dedicated polio ward, staffed with specialists recruited from other leading polio hospitals, and a facility to house more than two hundred patients.[27] The hospital's orthotics department developed devices such as the "Rancho feeder," a series of metal struts and braces that propped up a paralyzed or weakened arm at face level, allowing a person to swivel the hand back and forth to feed themselves.[28] The department also developed a version of this arm support that used an "artificial muscle" or "CO_2 muscle," an air-pressure-operated electrical system that allowed the patient to maneuver the swivel-arm through outside power, including switches operated by the toes or teeth.[29] Patients were often fitted with multiple devices, with functional braces pinned to their sides or attached to armatures on their wheelchairs and used in combination to support, straighten, and guide their bodies. These devices were part of a vision of "total rehabilitation," in which hospital administrators insisted that even the most severely impaired patients could gain independence in daily tasks such as walking, eating, and dressing.

The elaborate technical fittings prescribed at centers like Rancho Los Amigos proved difficult to use in the long term. The "trough and swivel" mechanism of the "feeder" arm required, according to one technical review, "care in both initial setup and regular maintenance by clinicians and caregivers," and could easily become disconnected with a bump against a chair or doorframe.[30] Patients too affirmed that the rigid instructions of specialists did not always work for them. Richard Daggett, a patient at Rancho in the early 1950s, recalled that the hospital had "set ideas" for how patients could feed themselves, but that he learned a different technique on his own.[31] Likewise, Paul Longmore, a disability historian who stayed at Rancho for a period of fourteen months starting when he was eight years old, remembered resisting the use of the "swivel feeder" on his left arm, where he lacked muscle movement in his shoulder. As Longmore recalled,

> I said, "My left arm's completely paralyzed, my hand's paralyzed." "We'll put a prosthetic hook under that hand" [they said], and they ran a wire up my arm and down my side so that I could open and close the hook with my left foot. And I said, "Well, I don't have any shoulder muscles that work in my left shoulder. I won't be able to control it at all." So sure enough, when I had that thing on, I couldn't control it so it would swing that hook right in front of me and block my right hand, so I couldn't use my right hand either. So, you know, I tried it for a few times, and then my mother and I agreed that this was useless. Well, that got us labeled as uncooperative and resistant.[32]

Longmore's statement describes the tension inherent in the rehabilitation process. These resources and technological devices were intended to help children with polio go "back with the gang" by rejoining society with bodies and motions that resembled a nondisabled state. These rigid rules and standards of "independence," however, constrained disabled people from making their own choices—including the choice to use personal attendants or family help in these daily tasks.

If rehabilitation specialists were at times unresponsive to patient preferences, manufacturers of medical equipment all but ignored them. Though the number of Americans using assistive technologies was significant—one survey conducted in the late 1950s counted just under a million Americans who used wheelchairs, arm or leg braces, or artificial limbs[33]—producers made few direct appeals to users.[34] In a time when American consumers had access to an ever-widening array of choices in hardware, grocery, and department stores, medical equipment remained firmly separate from the mass market. Not surprisingly, medical professionals and equipment suppliers were quick to assert that patients needed their help and guidance in selecting these devices. In a survey conducted in New York in the mid-1970s, doctors, prosthetists, and orthotists all agreed that "consumers [should] avoid the risks of shopping on their own in all instances."[35] Even as they consulted with professionals, patients found that communicating their own needs could be difficult. In her memoir of a childhood after polio, Mary Grimley Mason remembered that a tight new brace "felt as if a hundred little fingers were pinching me up and down my legs," and that the brace maker adjusted it only reluctantly, mumbling that she "was probably just not used to them."[36]

Even if patients did order their own equipment, the limited range of products offered did not serve the variety of users' bodies. Wheelchairs came in three sizes (adult, junior, and child, with the occasional addition of "adult narrow"), and braces in only small and large versions that needed to be adjusted by specialists.[37] Wheelchair companies produced many types of metal goods, of which hospital supplies were just one category: for example, the Colson Corporation, one of the largest wheelchair makers of the 1940s and 1950s, manufactured carts and casters, and, as an offshoot, wheeled chairs. Its catalogs included tens of pages of industrial wheels and carts before one or two with wheelchairs. Descriptions were brief, with listings simply declaring "sturdy construction" or touting easily replaceable, smooth-running "ball-bearing wheels."[38] The images in Colson's catalog showed wheelchairs in hospital settings, not in homes or in public. These trade materials communicated the message that these were medical, not consumer, products, and that people who used wheelchairs did not fit easily into the home or public environment.

Among the four largest wheelchair companies of the postwar decades, only one—Everest & Jennings—took a consumer-focused approach.[39] The company, founded in 1932, was a partnership between an engineer (Jennings) and a businessman (Everest), whose legs had been paralyzed in a mining accident.[40] The pair found success after patenting a wheelchair that could fold into the trunk of a car—itself a statement of a disabled user's ambitions to use the everyday American technology of the automobile.[41] Everest & Jennings advertised in disability-community publications in the 1950s, showing its chairs as equipment for people who lived active lives at home and in public. The headline of one advertisement promised that the folding model would "bring independence to the handicapped," a phrasing that highlights the benefits to the user.[42] The advertisement showed a woman talking on the telephone, in a home setting, not a hospital; another advertised the chair as flexible for varied terrain, as it "rolls over carpet edges and small obstructions inside or outdoors."[43] By the 1970s, Everest & Jennings came under criticism for abusing its hold on the wheelchair market, producing few innovations and neglecting customer service.[44] This dominance may have been the result of its successful marketing strategies in the postwar years. As the only wheelchair company to advertise in the pages of *Valor* and *Paraplegia News* in the 1950s, Everest & Jennings was able to claim a large segment of wheelchair users as its customers.

While doctors and other medical professionals mediated access to wheelchair and hospital equipment producers, a small number of retailers offered specialized products directly to disabled consumers. The New York–based retailer Fascole advertised in a number of disability-community publications, touting its "shopping center for the Physically Disabled" with a "treasury of intimate personal items and self-help devices."[45] Entrepreneurs operating on an even smaller scale sent announcements to the classified "Market Place" page of the *Toomey J Gazette*, available only to disabled advertisers. One contributor, who identified himself as "post-polio," set up business as a third-party dealer for wheelchairs, cushions, and intercoms, and offered a machine shop for custom work as well.[46] The work of mail-order and custom production was a difficult one, given competition from large manufacturers and suppliers. One entrepreneur reported in the *Gazette* on the mail-order business he and his physical therapist had started for "rehabilitation equipment—grab bars and all sorts of other helpful gadgets." Unfortunately, the writer noted, the competition with "large-well-financed outfits that published catalogs and were able to engage in real publicity jobs" had proved too stiff for the independent dealers, and, he lamented, "the returns were quite disappointing . . . well, our dream of a personal yacht for each of us has faded!"[47] These small, community-based efforts stood out as exceptions to a commercial culture that rarely addressed individual users directly.

Constructing a Life at Home

Much of the technology use described in the *Gazette* resembled familiar activities for middle-class consumers of this period. Whether sewing their own slipcovers and curtains, installing cabinets in their kitchens, or soldering and welding in their garages, American homeowners performed a variety of creative and skilled work to maintain and improve their houses, furnishings, and automobiles; supplying this market was itself an emerging consumer sector.[48] Do-it-yourself activities allowed men and women of the 1950s and 1960s to express individual taste and style within the mass-produced consumer culture of postwar America.[49] Despite a shared sense of excitement over clever and useful adaptations, however, for disabled people, these projects carried high stakes. Eating, dressing, bathing, and getting around the house provided a sense of personal independence, particularly for those who, like Ida Brinkman and her fellow "respos," required family or attendant help in many basic activities. Further, performing these activities with as little help as possible meant avoiding being perceived as "homebound," "invalids," or "shut-ins," or having to live in an institution. If suburbanites who built on to their subdivision houses and accessorized their cars did so to distinguish themselves as tasteful or creative, disabled people did the same work to fit in, to prove their worthiness of inclusion in a society where many considered incapable or unworthy of rehabilitation were shut out.

For households with a physically disabled family member, the house itself often presented a technical challenge. Small, single-family houses were common in many American communities, from urban neighborhoods built in the 1920s and 1930s for a new industrial working class to rapidly expanding suburban Levittowns and other planned neighborhoods of quickly constructed single-family houses constructed on America's former rural landscape.[50] The efficient, modestly scaled Levittown Cape Cod house, first built on Long Island in 1947, included doorways of 28 to 29 inches and hallways not much wider.[51] Standard-sized wheelchairs, which typically measured 25 to 29 inches in width, not to mention iron lungs and rocking beds, fit awkwardly into these spaces.[52] Contributors to the *Toomey J Gazette* reported experiments working with narrow hallways and door frames, such as cutting a hidden swinging door into a wall with wallpaper to camouflage.[53] Readers wrote in with descriptions of improvised "wheelchair narrowers"— contraptions that consisted of wire hangers or a belt looped around the handles to draw a chair inward by an inch or two to fit through these passageways.[54]

As they renovated their houses, families sought to balance practical concerns of disabled and nondisabled inhabitants. One couple sent the *Toomey J Gazette* photographs of a clever ramp built by the husband for his wife (figure 3.3).[55] The long ramp hugged one side of the house, leading to a side door, with a trapdoor in the middle to allow ambulatory members of the household to use an existing flight of stairs. Inside houses, barriers built into the layout were even more difficult to remedy. In some cases, families had to move or conduct extensive renovations to accommodate a disabled relative. Ed Roberts, later a prominent figure in the disability rights movement, was almost completely paralyzed from the neck down after his teenage case of polio. His family moved to a new house after he returned from the hospital to accommodate his hospital-sized bed; still, the only room large enough was the dining room.[56] Given the extent of Roberts's disabilities, it was easier to gather family around the bed than to move Ed to a wheelchair, a process that involved strapping him into a corset and then to the back of the chair—especially considering that the wheelchair could not be easily used beyond the threshold of the house in an era with few curb cuts or wheelchair ramps in public.[57]

Over the weeks and years following rehabilitation, disabled people continued making adjustments to their everyday environments. Women who took on homemaking roles after polio or other paralyzing conditions became consumer product testers, vetting new gadgets and materials from the standpoint of their own physical needs. The 1968 issue of the *Gazette* featured an eleven-page section entitled "Homemaking" with forty readers' suggestions on arranging kitchens, doing laundry and cleaning, and cooking from wheelchairs or with limited manual strength or dexterity.[58] Their notes describe everyday life in households where floor plans, furniture, and appliances posed obstacles. Readers wrote of practices such as filling a pot on a stove one cup at a time, as the height of the standard stove made it difficult for a wheelchair user to carry a full pot from sink to stovetop. With outlets at the back of countertops, hard to reach from a wheelchair or with limited arm strength,

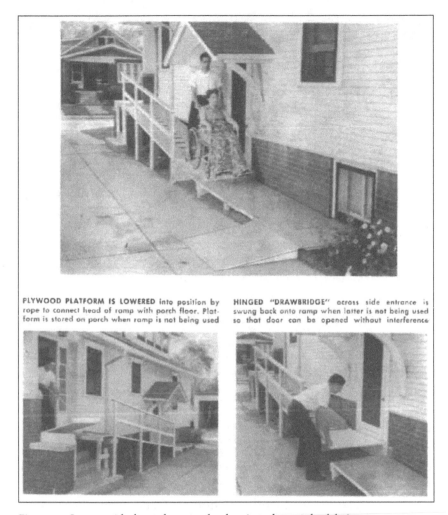

PLYWOOD PLATFORM IS LOWERED into position by rope to connect head of ramp with porch floor. Platform is stored on porch when ramp is not being used

HINGED "DRAWBRIDGE" across side entrance is swung back onto ramp when latter is not being used so that door can be opened without interference

Figure 3.3. Layout with three photographs showing a home wheelchair ramp; a man demonstrates the ramp's trapdoor opening and closing. From "Equipment," *Toomey J Gazette*, Spring 1961, 11. Post-Polio Health International.

they connected extension cords to bring appliances closer. Other contributors described the challenge of using small drawer handles and stiff faucet heads with shaky or paralyzed hands. "I walk my fingers around the sink to the water faucet," wrote one; another used "a long wooden spoon with four nails in the bowl section" to twist the small handles (figure 3.4).[59] Some wrapped rubber bands around "small slick knobs"

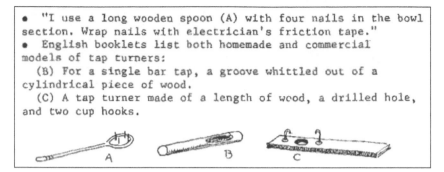

● "I use a long wooden spoon (A) with four nails in the bowl section. Wrap nails with electrician's friction tape."
● English booklets list both homemade and commercial models of tap turners:
  (B) For a single bar tap, a groove whittled out of a cylindrical piece of wood.
  (C) A tap turner made of a length of wood, a drilled hole, and two cup hooks.

Figure 3.4. Drawings of three faucet turners with descriptions of how they are made from wooden spoons, a cylindrical piece of wood, and a length of wood with a drilled hole and cup hooks. From "Homemaking," *Toomey J Gazette*, 1968, 18. Post-Polio Health International.

for better grip, while one contributor, perhaps frustrated with various experiments, suggested that "if you are unable to use the hardware on drawers and cabinets, just skip it and fasten on inexpensive towel racks for easy pulling."[60]

In the pages of the *Toomey J Gazette*, contributors balanced frustration with the constraints of mass-market products and furnishings with delight in finding the right tools for a given job. Contributors advised careful selection, suggesting that fellow readers "think about weight as opposed to ease of handling. . . . Handles are quite different on knives. Very individual decision is needed here."[61] This individual decision making, based on one's relative strength and coordination, as well as personal taste, engaged disabled people in an intensive form of shopping. The *Gazette*'s self-identified "homemakers," who were mostly women but also included some single men and husbands, took careful note of brand names, noting specific models of automatic can openers, electric knives, and mixers they found most promising for persons with limited hand strength. For those who fumbled with glass and ceramic dishware, new plastics offered more than just colorful or airtight storage: "Bless Tupper Ware [*sic*]," wrote one contributor. "You can drop it and it doesn't fly open and spill contents."[62]

The *Gazette*'s special "Homemaking" section had much in common with mainstream domestic literature. The section featured a two-page drawing of ways of arranging kitchen equipment, with crisp outlines of pegboard storage, lazy Susans, and pull-out shelves to hold efficient, organized rows of pots and pans, dishes, jars, and bottles. The outlines of dishware and familiar appliances recall the graphics of midcentury consumer magazines, which often showed products floating in space or tidily arranged in ideal kitchens.[63] The "Homemaking" spread and other reader-contributed household tips were reminiscent, for example, of "Hints from Heloise." Nationally syndicated after 1961, Heloise Cruse's domestic advice column published submissions by readers, with tips and shortcuts for using everyday items, such as looping a soda-can tab over a hanger to store a belt with its matching outfit; keeping out-of-season clothes in empty suitcases to maximize storage space; and setting plywood atop rubber bands to provide a "rolling platform" for a stand mixer that would eliminate "lifting or tugging."[64] Heloise rewarded her readers with occasional comments like "What a smart cooky [sic] you are!" and "That's a really sneaky one. And it works like a charm." Heloise even included a few hints from women with disabilities, such as an eighty-eight-year-old reader whose daughter altered a hanging shoe bag to make pockets for her walker, and a female amputee who shared a hint for attaching a cleaning brush to a cutting board for one-handed vegetable scrubbing.[65]

Although their needs were more specific than those of homemakers concerned about storage space or matching belts, contributors to the *Toomey J Gazette* showed similar excitement over the world of consumer products. A page from the 1960 *Toomey J Gazette* (figure 3.5) featured sixteen different designs for homemade mouthsticks in a cheery, sunburst layout.[66] People with limited use of their arms and hands used these sticks, assembled from various available materials, to type, write, dial the telephone, and do other small tasks using their mouths for leverage. The mouthsticks incorporated synthetic materials and novelties newly available for affordable consumption in postwar America.[67] Most were made of simple dowels or pens, with rubber erasers or eye-dropper tips to provide a soft surface to be gripped between the teeth. Some incorporated more novel materials, such as the rubber heel of a doll's shoe, a cigarette holder, and a spring-loaded clamp that could be operated with the tongue. In the illustration, these simple implements radiated from a sweetly outlined mouth. One stick with a paintbrush attachment

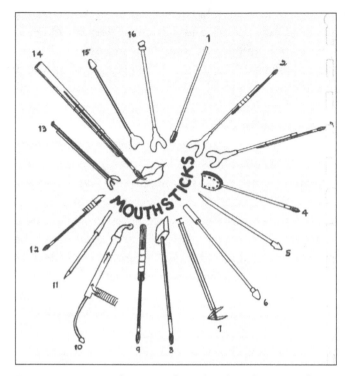

Figure 3.5. Drawing of an array of mouthsticks radiating out from
a drawing of lips. "Mouthsticks," *Toomey J Gazette*, Spring 1960, 8.
Post-Polio Health International.

pointed inward, completing the illustration and suggesting the action of
mouthstick painting, a common hobby taught in rehabilitation centers
and often celebrated in the *Gazette*.[68] The illustration of these different
options and the cheery mouth at the center took a cue from the visual
culture of the 1950s: we can imagine a similar layout in an advertisement
or magazine editorial showing kitchen utensils or lipsticks. In these collections of readers' inventions, the *Gazette* translated some of the light,
joyous appeal of midcentury consumer culture into the world of highly
specific and personal assistive equipment.

Disabled people's interactions with the world of products and spaces
reinforced their difference from the mainstream—and yet, in these intra-
community documents, they presented technical adaptation as part of

familiar, expected activities of household life, akin to the housework or home decoration discussed in women's home magazines of the time. Articles such as the "Homemaking" feature depicted the tasks of finding and customizing consumer goods as components of conventional postwar home life, including style-conscious shopping and clever use of available tools.

Access on the Road

In a final category of adaptation, automobiles provided another area of creative technological work through which disabled people participated in the public life of postwar America as individual consumers. Although disabled people living at home could create a modicum of access within their own houses, they could do little to change the abundance of street-level barriers in American cities and towns. According to one polio survivor who recalled returning from rehabilitation in the 1950s, home alterations to facilitate wheelchair use were "enough to help, but not enough to get me accustomed to living in any sort of specially constructed world" given pervasive barriers beyond the household.[69] Nonetheless, in this era before ramps and curb cuts, wheelchair users did find ways to get around in their communities, albeit with great difficulty and unpredictability. Some told of wheeling down driveways to avoid curbs, entering traffic until they reached the next block and then the next driveway.[70] Others relied on friends, family, or passing strangers to help them get over curbs and up front steps, which could be an uncomfortable or even frightening experience.[71] Portable ramps—both commercially manufactured and homemade—were used to traverse a small number of steps, although most required the help of a companion or helpful stranger.[72] Some industrious inventors devised more complicated devices, such as the "outdoor elevator" that Vince La Michle described in a 1959 article in the *Toomey J Gazette*. Powered by a 1/6 horsepower motor, the elevator raised or lowered at one inch per second and, according to La Michle, was "certainly easier than a ramp."[73] Whether rudimentary or complex, these devices provided ways to enter the inaccessible public environments of postwar America.

In the *Toomey J Gazette* and the *Paraplegia News,* one of the most-discussed tools for accessing the public world was not a piece of medical equipment, but one of the iconic technologies of the twentieth century: the automobile. Historians of American car culture have described "automobility" as the way the personally driven motor vehicle became linked with a sense of freedom and independence.[74] For disabled drivers and passengers, automobility had an extra layer of meaning, as it offered a chance to move freely past barriers such as steps and curbs. In pursuit of what the *Toomey J Gazette* called "quad driving," disabled people became auto enthusiasts and used available accessories and technological options to achieve their own form of automobility.[75]

The first devices that allowed people to drive with limited or no use of their legs were developed in the 1930s to target an elite audience. De Soto developed a custom car for President Franklin Delano Roosevelt in 1933, in which not only steering but also acceleration and braking were controlled by hand.[76] In the following year, the *Polio Chronicle,* the in-house magazine of Warm Springs, the polio rehabilitation center that Roosevelt bought in 1926, extolled the promise of several new, patented hand controls to let "the President and other polios become their own chauffeurs."[77] Despite the enthusiasm at Warm Springs, the hand controls of the 1930s and 1940s were difficult and dangerous to operate. Driving a manual-transmission car entirely by hand meant juggling the levers for brake, clutch, and accelerator, not to mention the steering wheel. Inventors devised several approaches to dual clutch-brake hand control, including buttons and switches allowing the driver to use the same handle to depress the clutch alone, or the clutch and brake at the same time.

The greatest technological improvement for disabled drivers was not a new hand control, but the automatic transmission. Automakers introduced a few models with automatic transmissions in the early 1930s; they became widely available in the 1940s.[78] This new technology coincided with a new demand for cars for disabled people, particularly disabled veterans who could request a subsidy for hand-operated and other customized cars (see chapter 1). This subsidy made cars and driving a distinct component of veterans' culture, with models and accessories discussed in a special "Hand Controlled" column in the *Paraplegia News.* The column's author, Joe Jordan, wrote of the special connection veterans had to cars, noting that "there is very little controversy and possibly near unanimous agreement that 'mobility,' our effort to get around once again, rates a high and very special place among [veterans'] problems."[79] As Jordan noted, however, not all available vehicles worked well for the needs of disabled drivers. Even with an automatic transmission, drivers had to vet the specific configurations available, since many name-brand "drives" still required some clutch-shifting by foot.[80] Jordan noted, for example, that the Oldsmobile Hydramatic, which had a clutchless shift mounted on the steering column, was widely used among veterans more than a decade after its introduction.[81]

In the pages of the *Toomey J Gazette*, disabled people and their families showed off a broad variety of customized cars that went far beyond commercially available models with hand controls and automatic transmissions. Fred Taberlet's "Para-car" (figure 3.6), described in a 1968 *Gazette* article, was a Citroen 2 with the top and back completely cut off to make room for an elevating floor. Accompanying photos featured Taberlet lifting himself, wheelchair and all, into the driver's position, eliminating the need to climb into the driver's seat and stow a wheelchair, as required in a standard car equipped with hand controls.[82] The customized vehicle had not one but two sets of hand controls, so that he could rotate completely and drive the car forward or backwards, keeping him from having to crane his neck to see while driving in reverse. Fellow *Gazette* contributors showed off other creative approaches to driving.

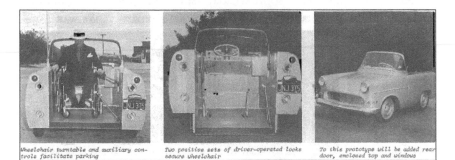

Figure 3.6. Three photographs showing Fred Taberlet's "Para-car," a Citroen 2 with the top and back removed for wheelchair access. In the first photograph, Taberlet, dressed in a dark-colored suit and white hat, demonstrates the car's usability from his wheelchair. "Equipment," *Toomey J Gazette*, 1968, 54. Post-Polio Health International.

One British reader displayed a pair of leather gloves that helped him grip the hand controls. For those with more coordination in their legs and feet than upper extremities, an American entrepreneur developed "a kind of ski boot attachment" that could be used to operate a steering wheel by foot.[83]

"Quad driving" was for passengers as well. For people whose impairments meant that they would never drive themselves, riding in a car was a way to move about within and beyond their communities without being strapped into a wheelchair, let alone contending with steps, curbs, and the stares of other people. "Electric Mom" Ida Brinkman named drive-in movies as a favorite activity of her family, and showed off a special headrest she used in the family car.[84] Other families went to dramatic lengths to include their disabled relatives in car travel. More modest—and more legal—than Fred Taberlet's Citroen convertible, but no less inventive, were the alterations the Ray family made to their family car so they could travel with their daughter Susan and her reclining wheelchair and respirator. Susan's father, Cecil, a Baptist minister (and "mechanical whiz," according to his wife), removed both front and back seats on the passenger side of their 1955 Ford station wagon and installed a smooth platform for her recliner. He moved the post between doors and re-hinged the rear door, making a double-wide entrance for Susan in her chair. The Rays traveled with a small homemade trailer with compartments for extra respiratory equipment and doors on both sides for easy access. The family reported traveling in this car from their home in San Antonio, Texas, to the Southern Baptist Convention in Miami, Florida, and national parks including the Smoky Mountains, Yellowstone, Mesa Verde, Arches National Monument, and the Grand Tetons.[85]

The accessories disabled drivers used linked them to other drivers' groups and specialty auto workers. Local mechanics who installed specialty equipment for disabled drivers had experience customizing cars for other uses, such as hot-rodding or camping. In some cases, modifications made for other purposes proved to be useful for disabled drivers as well. For example, many catalogs and articles suggested installing a knob for the steering wheel to aid driving with a prosthetic or a single hand.[86] These knobs were not exclusive to the community of disabled drivers, but were available as options from major car manufacturers throughout the 1940s and 1950s. Though they ostensibly offered a more secure grip for any driver, they were known colloquially as "necker's knobs" for one-handed drivers who kept one arm around their dates.[87] Modifications made for disabled drivers also relate to those made by fellow tinkerers who altered sedans, station wagons, and buses for long travel. As Roger White has explored, in the days before the commercial introduction of "recreational vehicles," car owners made motor homes by removing back seats to make room for beds, hanging curtains for privacy, and installing shelves to hold amenities like camp stoves and washtubs.[88]

People who altered familiar technologies to work for their own disabled bodies shared much with their nondisabled counterparts. As with household technologies, customized cars took on different meaning for a population for whom everyday mobility could be difficult or impossible. "Quad driving" provided access to a kind of mobility that disabled people could not experience on the sidewalks of their hometowns. It also allowed disabled drivers to participate in the American hobbies of picking out, tinkering with, and finding adventure in automobiles. In the pages of *Paraplegia News*, veterans shared insights on how to make the best of their special access to subsidized cars, while the tinkerers of the *Toomey J Gazette* seemed to revel in the design variations of home-adapted cars. This creative work was both normative and extraordinary.

Technology and Rights

The technological efforts that disabled people made to "fit in" to the spaces of postwar life were a form of self-preservation in a society that presented few options for disabled people to live independently. When Ida Brinkman confessed to *Toomey J Gazette* readers that she had been "secretly frightened" about her return home, she voiced a feeling many readers and writers of the *Gazette* surely felt. The insecurity with which disabled people lived—particularly those whose injuries or impairments meant they needed daily assistance—should not be underestimated. The specter of being sent to—perhaps forced into—an institution hovered over many, especially those who were poor or whose disabilities resulted from injuries or diseases not supported by charities such as the March of Dimes. People who returned home from rehabilitation were hardly exempt from these worries. In less optimistic narratives than those of the *Toomey J Gazette*, some polio memoirists reported isolation and mistreatment in their home lives, with parents or spouses leaving them in bed for days, withholding help in bathing or eating, or subjecting them to emotional and physical abuse.[89] Even those who, like Brinkman, had families willing and able to support them had to wonder what would happen if family members died or could no longer assist them. Starting with the "daily life" training they received in hospitals, people with disabilities were given strong messages that they needed to show continual progress and a good attitude, lest they be labeled "bitter" or "uncooperative."[90] While they expressed excitement about creative work on their kitchens, cars, and houses, these technical tasks were also a constant reminder that if they wanted to fit in to the world of their nondisabled peers and family, the burden was on them to figure out how to do it. Whether they performed this technological work themselves or with the help of family members, adapting to the inaccessible built environment remained a private affair.

In the eleven-year run of the *Toomey J Gazette*, there were only small hints at a sense of political identity or consciousness in this community publication. In a 1959 editorial, Sue Williams warned readers of the *Gazette* of the need to turn public attention to polio cases into long-term, sustained support. "The 'iron lung story' that has been told about each of us was a heart-wringer and a purse-opener," she wrote, suggesting experience with charitable campaigns and the mainstream media.[91] "Now that we cease to be a sensation in this way, there is quiet un-newsworthy work for us to do," she continued. Four years after the discovery of a vaccine, these "polios" were aware that their time in the spotlight was coming to an end. The *Gazette* documented a practical means of survival in an inaccessible society, but Williams seemed to suggest that it might also provide a way of building political agency.

Disabled people's engagement with technology and consumer culture in the 1950s and 1960s suggests an alternate origin for accessible design than the expert-driven work of rehabilitation specialists. Unlike the earliest accessibility regulations and guidelines developed in the same period, the adaptive work of these consumer-tinkerers informed a personalized and imaginative form of design. In the rights movement that emerged in the decades following this period, advocates for access drew on experiential disability knowledge and a sharp rebuke of medical authority in defining the lives of disabled people. While their political orientation was much different from the largely domestic focus of the *Gazette* and other disability media of the 1950s and 1960s, they produced a form of access that also retained the spirit of local knowledge and do-it-yourself technical work.

4

Berkeley, California

An Independent Style of Access

In 1977 the magazine *Progressive Architecture* published a "Report from Berkeley" for its readers, noting new installations of wheelchair access in the city. The two reporters, Barbara Winslow and John Parman—both students in the architecture department at the University of California— noted new changes happening on the campus and surrounding city, brought about by disabled residents and their allies. On campus, student teams "consisting of one able-bodied and one disabled student" had surveyed sixty-six buildings at the university to evaluate access "not only in terms of codes and regulations but also in terms of the direct evidence of barriers and inconveniences."[1] New sidewalk curb cuts and building ramps were a product of a distinctive community with a large and politically active disabled population, they wrote, but they were also a harbinger of things to come in the rest of the country. A new federal code for access had been published earlier that year, and raised "a number of questions for the institutions and their architects who must comply with it: What is a barrier-free environment? What is accessibility? At what point are the disabled served and the law upheld?" they asked. More to the point for their own profession, they noted, was the question of how to address these issues well—a task requiring more than attention to "dimensions and performance." For the architects who would have to comply with new laws, "the challenge is to design so that the environment grows more accessible without becoming boring."

As the *Progressive Architecture* report suggested, Berkeley's history of access was distinctive for raising bigger questions around the meaning of physical landscapes and the place of people within them. Berkeley was an important early site for the U.S. disability rights movement that gained a national scope by the mid-1970s. The local iteration of the movement, often called the Independent Living movement, lobbied for street-level access as a component of a fiercely independent, anti-institutional vision of individual rights. Instead of addressing access through codes and guidelines, as the government had started to do by the 1970s, this local community developed a process for creating access that was generated by disabled people and considered issues not addressed in codes, such as existing uses of city space and social and psychological contexts that might exacerbate physical barriers.

This chapter describes the kind of accessible design that emerged in Berkeley out of the Independent Living movement. This movement had its origins in student action at the University of California in Berkeley, but came to merge with and include a broader range of community members through the founding, in 1972, of the Center for Independent Living (CIL), a grassroots organization that became a model for community-run service agencies of and for disabled people.[2] This organization and its related community redefined the goal of "independence" from the rehabilitation profession's definition of an ability to perform daily routines without assistance.[3] Instead, they embraced a notion of independence in terms of being free to make life decisions for themselves, particularly in reference to living on their own rather than in institutions.[4] Sometimes the means of attaining independence involved aspects of the built environment, such as housing, transportation, and urban streetscapes, and sometimes it did not. When it did, members of this community developed a design approach that prioritized disabled people's experiences and input rather than working toward a widely applicable set of technical guidelines, as Timothy Nugent did in his work for *ANSI 117.1*, the American National Standards Institute's 1961 guidelines for access.[5] A "Berkeley style" of access would be something of a misnomer, as the forms that emerged were far from uniform or standardized. Instead, the people who built access in Berkeley challenged the very idea of a standard that could be imposed from outside.

The approach that Berkeley's disabled community took to access broke from previous efforts by governmental and medical institutions in both form and method. By the end of the 1960s, when an activist scene organized in Berkeley, existing codes and standards governing access still left much of the work of navigating barriers to disabled people. Individual buildings that included wheelchair ramps and interior modifications were isolated exceptions to a public landscape of inaccessibility, as transportation and sidewalks remained unaltered. Building codes that required accessible design based on *ANSI 117.1* applied only to new construction or significant renovation, meaning that it could take years or decades for consistent access to be established. Even more ambitious laws such as the federal Architectural Barriers Act of 1968 contained few means of enforcement, and went unheeded for years.[6] By contrast, in Berkeley, the disability community advocated for cohesive access that would function immediately, even if this meant design compromise. Further, accessibility advocates did not treat design as an isolated factor, but instead framed material change as embedded within human networks of advice, activism, and labor. In acknowledging the ways design operated as a part of human networks—particularly involving maintenance and coordination performed by hired attendants—Berkeley's advocates proposed a form of design that could never be summarized in a technical manual.

This history begins in the 1960s, as a small group of disabled students took up residence on the campus of the University of California. Initially, they addressed access issues in their immediate surroundings, focusing on barriers to students' and graduates' independence. The Independent Living movement grew to make more systemic and planned change in the city over the 1970s, pressuring the city of Berkeley to create consistent routes of wheelchair access and establish requirements to include disabled people in ongoing planning processes. Berkeley's local moves toward access, coordinated with regional efforts such as the accessible Bay Area Rapid Transit (BART) regional rail, predated national regulations that were published in 1977. But even as members of Berkeley's Independent Living movement became important figures in the national movement for disability rights, the local community maintained its own culture of access in which physical design was always related to a larger vision of independence for disabled people. This chapter explores several dimensions of that local culture, from the university campus, to the growing streetscape of wheelchair access, to a creative and flexible approach to accessible housing. These approaches were not all adopted in the national movement, but remained instead artifacts of a community of disabled people that linked personal needs for independence with disability rights activism.

Origins: Finding Independence in Berkeley

In the early 1960s, several physically disabled students moved into a makeshift dormitory on the top floor of the University of California at Berkeley's on-campus Cowell Hospital, creating the beginnings of a community that was central to the U.S. disability rights movement in the 1970s and 1980s.[7] These students were not the first disabled students to attend an American university, nor even the first to attend Berkeley.[8] The extent of their disabilities and the accommodations they obtained, however, distinguished them from others who either lived off-campus or were able to use standard dormitories: at the University of Illinois at Urbana-Champaign, for example, the Disability Rehabilitation-Education Services program did not allow students to live on campus if they needed assistance getting into and out of bed.[9] Most significantly, the Berkeley students made direct connections between their own individual experiences and an ideological argument for civil rights.

The participants in disability organizing in Berkeley in the 1960s to 1970s were predominantly of white, middle-class, educated backgrounds, including many students or graduates of the University of California. A number of them had directly experienced the postwar polio epidemic that reshaped the image of disability in the United States in the 1950s; most had received rehabilitation and social services that pushed strongly an idea of "overcoming" disability.[10] The first of the students who moved into the university's on-campus Cowell Hospital was Ed Roberts, who at the time of his college entrance was a twenty-three-year-old polio survivor paralyzed in most of his body, with movement in one hand and one foot. Like many families of disabled people in the 1950s, Roberts and his parents had battled to gain access to mainstream education. After his case of polio at fourteen, Roberts completed high school from home using a telephone connection to his classrooms that he operated with one foot; he and his mother, Zona, had to petition the school board for his graduation without completing the drivers' education requirement.[11] The first student to join Roberts on the top floor of Cowell was John Hessler, a twenty-five-year-old quadriplegic who had lived in a public nursing home for five years before entering Berkeley. There were a dozen students living in Cowell by 1969.[12]

The dormitory that was created over time on the top floor of the six-story Cowell Hospital provided a medically supervised space for students, but also a space of freedom and peer support. As Herb Willsmore, who moved in to Cowell in 1969, remembered, "Once a bunch of us got up there," friendship and socializing mixed with practical conversations about living with a disability:

> We started talking about our rehab experiences, and the fact that they didn't teach us how to transfer in and out of a car, or how we were going to manage once we got home, and how to set up a room or a house to where it's workable for someone with a disability like ours, or how we were to empty our leg bags, or what it's all about, hiring attendants, how you interview, and all those kinds of things.[13]

All of the Cowell residents were wheelchair users, and many required daily attendant assistance in getting in and out of bed, bathing, and dressing. For those who had relied on family help or lived in state institutions, hiring and managing their own attendants gave them a new sense of control. By 1969, John Hessler wrote, he had "been an employer for six years of orderlies, attendants, cooks, maids, secretaries, and research assistants." These experiences, he asserted, helped him feel "less dependent on any single human being, or any way of life."[14] Hessler, who had pursued a master's degree in French, traveled to Paris for ten months with two attendants.[15] As one of his attendants, Eric Dibner—who would remain involved with the community as a specialist in accessibility—noted, for people like Hessler who had lived in institutions, "there was a feeling of not wanting to go back. People wanted to go forward."[16]

The students' individual feeling of freedom at Cowell also related to a campus where, as one attendant recalled, "there wasn't one square inch . . . that was not seething with the potential of being political."[17] By the late 1960s, tensions arose as a new rehabilitation counselor began to tighten rules on behavior and academic performance. Students fought back, including going to the press.[18] Fortified by the conflict, members of the group began calling themselves the Rolling Quads, giving them an identity distinct from their campus residence.[19] Their name gave a certain rock band or street gang image, subverting the term "quads" from the medical shorthand for quadriplegic and applying it to an image of speed and motion. They sought to make their status on campus official and under their own control, applying for a $50,000 federal grant to start a Physically Disabled Students Program (PDSP) to provide housing and attendant referral, research wheelchair accessibility, and establish on-campus wheelchair repair services.[20] To fund this program permanently, they proposed a twenty-five-cent addition to the annual student fee for all Berkeley students, approved by referendum in 1969. The Rolling Quads posted an appeal to fellow students for the referendum in flyers (figure 4.1) that urged their campus "BROTHERS AND SISTERS" to "VOTE YES" for funding for housing and transportation. With a figure of a scruffy man in a wheelchair, and a tall pitched-roof house, the flyer dubbed the twenty-five-cent fee "QUARTERS FOR CRIPPLES"—a reclaiming of the stereotype of the disabled beggar.[21]

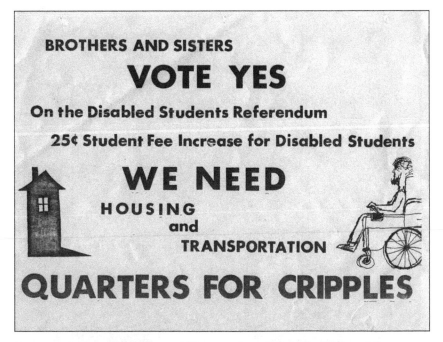

Figure 4.1. A flyer with drawings of a house and a man in a wheelchair and the text, "BROTHERS AND SISTERS—VOTE YES—On the Disabled Students Referendum—25c Student Fee Increase for Disabled Students—WE NEED HOUSING AND TRANSPORTATION—QUARTERS FOR CRIPPLES." Michael Fuss Papers, Bancroft Library, University of California at Berkeley.

A pair of images from this time shows members of the Rolling Quads attending an event at the Berkeley Stadium, sitting in their chairs at the base of the stadium's seating section. The men sit, laughing and chatting, relaxing in the sunshine. Labels on the photos help us identify some of the key figures who passed through Cowell from the late 1960s to the early 1970s: Ed Roberts and Herb Willsmore sit together (figure 4.2), both facing the camera, Roberts wearing a strap across his chest to keep him upright in his high-backed chair. In the second photograph (figure 4.3), John Hessler, a tall man with slicked-back hair and glasses, sits with Larry Langdon, a blond man a few years younger than Hessler, in a cowboy hat and polka-dot shirt. Standing behind them is Tom Wolf, a fellow student and hired attendant, shirtless in striped jeans.[22] The men's embroidered jeans, patterned shirts, beards and long hair all place them as college students of the era, although Hessler and Roberts were likely in their thirties by this time. The Rolling Quads use the sturdy, chrome

Figure 4.2. Herb Willsmore and Ed Roberts at the Berkeley Stadium, undated photograph (after 1969). Disabled Students Program Photograph Collection, Bancroft Library, University of California at Berkeley.

Figure 4.3. Tom Wolf, John Hessler, and Larry Langdon at the Berkeley Stadium, undated photograph (after 1969). Disabled Students Program Photograph Collection, Bancroft Library, University of California at Berkeley.

wheelchairs of the period, several of which have visible batteries or joystick controls.

These photos do not tell us much—we do not know what event they are attending, who else is there; we do not even know the year it was taken. The photographs can't capture the bumpy ride of battery-operated wheelchairs (one technician referred to their two speeds as "slow and very slow"[23]), or the tempo of mobility through crowds. Nonetheless, the photo is a document of the changes occurring in Berkeley in the late 1960s and early 1970s. Perhaps what is most notable is what is not in the photograph: the men are not accompanied by parents, uniformed medical personnel, or equipment such as the iron lung Roberts used for many hours of a day. Instead, they are simply appearing in public. At this moment, physical access in the town and on the Berkeley campus was limited: the stadium may have had a wheelchair ramp, but the sidewalks nearby and many campus buildings remained difficult to navigate and enter. Still, this photograph documents these disabled students' move into public space. Their presence is not overtly political, but their *being in the world* (to paraphrase University of California Law School professor Jacobus tenBroek) became the subject of political action and organizing on both local and national levels. Moreover, their entry into the public spaces of Berkeley coincided and overlapped with a range of other conflicts over control of streets, sidewalks, and parks.

The earliest expressions of group identity among the Rolling Quads and the Physically Disabled Students Program (PDSP) centered on their goals of independence in terms of control over aspects of daily life. These young people, who had come to Cowell from their parents' homes or from institutions, developed programs focused on the things that threatened to take them back—lack of accessible housing options, unpredictable or controlling caregivers, wheelchairs that were not made for such rugged use. PDSP provided attendant referral so that students could share information about reliable attendants who would not overstep the bounds of the client-caregiver relationship. Staff and volunteers surveyed the campus to assess classroom access, and drafted specifications for ramp construction.[24] They set up a wheelchair repair shop at the center of campus with their own mechanics who had experience working on the motorized wheelchairs that were still new in this time.[25] They scouted local apartments for wheelchair access, finding most to be unsuitable.[26] These activities reflected the priorities of the students and recent graduates, and the predominantly physically disabled constituency of PDSP in its first years, but also the emphasis on "independence" in terms of doing things without the assistance of charities or family members. Accessibility on campus, on the streets, and in housing were means to the end of living one's own life, a life apart from the strictures of institutions or the advice of experts. In the last years of the 1960s and into the early 1970s, this interpretation of a life on one's own terms aligned with a broader youth culture that claimed streets, sidewalks, and parks as the sites of a new way of living.

The People's Park and Sidewalks

Cowell resident Herb Willsmore recalled that "everything began happening at once" in the last years of the 1960s, as the Rolling Quads' fight for independence and mobility collided with dramatic occurrences on campus, in the city, and across the country.[27] There was a sense of urgency for Cowell residents as some students neared graduation and others felt the pressure of Department of Rehabilitation supervision. These same years of 1968 to 1970 were also moments of political turmoil that brought about a shift in the city of Berkeley's policies around street use and planning, with long-term implications for pedestrians, street musicians and buskers, bicyclists, and the newly visible population of disabled people. For the first time, the city built what it called wheelchair "ramps" in the sidewalk, eliminating the edge of the curbs at four intersections leading up to the south entrance of the university. This construction, which occurred in the fall of 1970, aligned countercultural and environmentalist interests in access to public green space and the disability rights movement's claims for access to public space in general. It also initiated the local disability community's participation in the planning and construction of accessible design—a contribution that shaped the distinct character of access in Berkeley.

The curb ramps built on four blocks of Telegraph Avenue in 1970 linked four blocks that were at the center of Berkeley's student and city conflicts of the period. Starting in 1964 and 1965, campus groups such as the Free Speech Movement and Vietnam Day Committee staged protests on the large, open plaza in front of Sproul Hall, just inside Sather Gate from Telegraph Avenue. While these protests called on national and global issues such as free speech and pacifism, they emphasized local action. In 1964 Mario Savio, the leader of the Free Speech Movement, called to his fellow students to attack the "Machine" of the university, announcing from the steps of Sproul Hall that "you've got to put your bodies upon the gears and upon the wheels, upon the levers, upon all the apparatus and you've got to make it stop."[28] Savio's physical metaphor embodied many of his peers' alienation from bureaucracy and the "multiversity" that linked academic research to governmental and economic agendas. As the historian Fred Turner has written, these were young people disillusioned with the seemingly inevitable twinning of centralized technology with the authoritative Cold War state.[29] For the Rolling Quads forming their own activist community on campus, these metaphors of the body against the institution were all the more real.

By the late 1960s, conflicts between young, free thinkers and the establishment—be it the University of California, the city of Berkeley, or the state of California—became increasingly concentrated within a specific geographic area just south of the campus, around the bustling Telegraph Avenue business district. The neighborhood was a gathering place for countercultural youth, many of whom moved to Berkeley from elsewhere in the country or the world to experience its growing radical scene. Throughout the 1960s (and on into the 1970s, and even today), protests tended to migrate from the campus's main Sproul Plaza down the avenue. In the spring of 1969, tensions mounted as a group of locals laid claim to an empty lot that the university had slated for a new building. The People's Park, as locals christened the plot, came to represent a host of issues of space and control. The university planned a soccer field and dormitories; advocates for the park opined that "the University tore down a lot of beautiful houses to build a swamp," and that the current neglected space would soon become "a cement type expensive parking lot."[30] Over several weekends, a motley crew of locals transformed the plot by planting trees, seeding grass, and conducting public speeches from one end of the land. The state of California intervened as Governor Ronald Reagan, following up campaign promises to "clean up the mess at Berkeley," sent in the California Highway Patrol and National Guard to secure the site. In clashes on the street, the Guard released tear gas and fired buckshot at protesters; one man, James Rector, died a few days later from his injuries.[31]

On May 30, 1969, with National Guardsmen in uniform standing by, somewhere between twenty-five thousand and fifty thousand people marched through the streets of Berkeley, including many more moderate citizens than those who had participated in digging up the park.[32] While the disabled community was not explicitly involved in the organization of People's Park, they saw these changes and felt their connections to local and national issues. Cowell student Catherine Caulfield recalled that during the early organizing days of the Rolling Quads and PDSP, "we had to stop the war and keep People's Park alive. . . . It was a crazy, exciting time."[33]

The People's Park crisis resonated for many people who understood the conflicts of the 1960s as relating to urban space and power. While the university was technically the adversary in the crisis, many faculty and students were involved in advocacy for the park. Members of the university's College of Environmental Design recognized the park as a site of planning driven by community needs rather than institutional authority. Faculty from the college conducted a teach-in at the park in May 1969, declaring that "trees are anarchic; concrete and asphalt are orderly and tractable." These professional planners sided with the anarchic process of spatial redevelopment rather than the "defoliation" of centralized planning.[34] After the state troops departed, the plot remained fenced until 1972, when locals pulled down the fences and reclaimed the park. The university did not actively resist, but also did not officially cede the land until 1989, when it leased the plot to the city.[35]

The People's Park crisis had a more explicit link to disability community concerns in its aftermath, when the city reconstructed parts of Telegraph Avenue. In a meeting of the city council on June 17, 1969—a month after the most violent day of clashes between locals and the National Guard—the city's Human Relations and Welfare Commission recommended that the city lease the area known as People's Park "as a citizen-planned and built neighborhood park," and also extended its attention to the nearby Telegraph Avenue district.[36] The city council resolved in June 1970 to renovate the avenue with wider sidewalks, public restrooms, trees, and sidewalk benches. The specifications also included sixteen "wheelchair ramps" to be constructed at the corners between Bancroft Avenue and Dwight Way.[37] The work was completed by October 1970.[38]

The sixteen new sidewalk curbs linked four blocks of Telegraph Avenue to create a district that was planned not only for peaceful street life, but also for wheelchair access. These ramps went beyond any code on the books to provide access to a public, civilian space rather than a government building such as a courthouse or post office.[39] Given that Telegraph was the link between the university's south entrance and the city, it also connected the campus—including Cowell Hospital and its residence for disabled students—to the adjoining district. Shortly before the city passed this sidewalk resolution, representatives of the city had attended a meeting with the Rolling Quads, the university vice-chancellor, and various representatives of campus facilities management. In the meeting, John Hessler informed these representatives of some of the major barriers for wheelchair users, including the idea of creating "routes" that would connect campus to city. Hessler pledged to work with university physical plant representatives to develop "minimum engineering standards, such as the maximum height of curb that can be negotiated in a wheelchair, which can be used to redesign points of conflict along these preferred routes."[40] The city council never recorded an explicit connection between the People's Park crisis and the Rolling Quads' demands, but in these sidewalk renovations, it paired the pressing issues of street life and wheelchair access.

The link between the eventual preservation of People's Park and the new public space of access on Telegraph Avenue can be read as coincidental, but it also predicted some of the ways wheelchair access became a part of a planning vision for equitable public space. The initial People's Park takeover suggested anarchy and chaos, a "Free for All" in which "there was no boss," as one participant wrote in the pages of the *Berkeley Barb*.[41] But this was not solely an anarchic action. The architectural historian Peter Allen points out that even in its earliest iteration, the People's Park builders planned a mixture of organized and unstructured space, including paths between cultivated areas, a stage for music and speeches, and a children's play area. Further, as professional planners from the university's College of Environmental Design supported the park, they articulated ways the park might come to represent "constructive and appropriate" community use of space and an alternative to the "archaic procedures" of planning represented by university bureaucracy.[42]

Another pair of photographs from the Disabled Students Program archive (figures 4.4 and 4.5) gives us a glimpse of a new Berkeley where the free and ungoverned space of People's Park existed alongside the newly paved swath of Telegraph Avenue. Both images show wheelchair users in People's Park: one, with a young woman perched on a mechanical wheelchair, another with a man reclining, his motorized wheelchair tilted backward in the sunlight. In both, the wheelchair users are surrounded by a crowd walking, sitting, standing, and lying on the ground. These photos capture the unstructured public use of space advocated by People's Park supporters—the "anarchic" nature of green space as opposed to the "orderly and tractable" aspect of concrete. For the wheelchair users participating in this unruly space, concrete helped to smooth the pathway there.

Figure 4.4. People's Park, ca. 1972. A man reclines in an electric wheelchair in a park surrounded by houses. Nearby, people walk, sit, and lie in the park. Disabled Students Program Photograph Collection, Bancroft Library, University of California at Berkeley.

Little has been written about the politics of the disability rights movement within the flourishing of countercultural, civil rights, and New Left ideas and lifestyles that started in the late 1960s and strongly inflected American culture well into the 1970s.[43] While the students and community members who organized as the Physically Disabled Students Program, and eventually the Center for Independent Living, shared many ideological views with their peers in radical and experimental scenes, their political agendas were not always aligned. On the one hand, the sixties ethos of questioning authority resembled the disabled community's critiques of institutional control over their lives and futures. On the other, the countercultural embrace of things "free" and "natural" often translated to an ideal of non-intervention—such as the rejection of concrete and other forms of "defoliation." In the most literal sense, disabled people needed "concrete"—as in alterations in cement and other building materials—as well as other forms of bureaucracies such as social

Figure 4.5. People's Park, ca. 1972. A woman sits in profile in a chrome wheelchair in a crowded park. Disabled Students Program Photograph Collection, Bancroft Library, University of California at Berkeley.

security and welfare. While the sixties counterculture tended toward nostalgia for an ideal of American independence in terms of rugged individualism, the disability rights movement articulated independence as something that would later be described as "interdependence," or the need for community and social supports as well as legal protections.[44] The People's Park conflict represented one moment in which the push for green space intersected with planning for disability access. For decades to follow, these agendas were often in tension. However, both movements sought to use public policy to preserve openness and "anarchic" aspects of community life. In the case of Berkeley's disability community, the agenda of access was inseparable from community input.

Access and the Center for Independent Living

The Telegraph Avenue curbs were built during a time of new organizing and new associations for the disabled community in Berkeley. With many Cowell students graduating or seeking off-campus housing, the Rolling

Quads and the Physically Disabled Students Program (PDSP) were increasingly reaching beyond the campus to consider long-term strategies around housing, attendant care, and other aspects of daily life. A new PDSP office, opened in 1970 in a second-floor office above a hot dog shop just off the Telegraph retail strip, attracted new visitors including those outside the demographic of wheelchair-using students and graduates who had formed the core of these groups. David Konkel became PDSP's first blind employee in 1970, connecting PDSP with an active blind community.[45] Another Berkeley resident, Hale Zukas, was a UC graduate who had overlapped at school with Ed Roberts, but had experienced a different college life. Due to a strong speech impairment, Zukas had not been admitted into Cowell, but instead had lived with his mother a mile south of campus.[46] Zukas's experiences navigating the city of Berkeley and engaging with left-leaning politics influenced new directions in advocacy at PDSP, including designing accessible infrastructure.

Figures like Konkel and Zukas, along with other arrivals to Berkeley who were unaffiliated with the university, brought new attention to issues outside campus life. To meet this broader community focus, the Center for Independent Living (CIL) was founded in 1972 out of a closet in the PDSP office.[47] Its initial board drew heavily from the Cowell population, with members including Herb Willsmore, Judy Taylor, Larry Langdon, and John Hessler, along with new participants, including blind members and nondisabled allies.[48] With a one-year, $50,000 grant from the federal Rehabilitation Services Administration, and ongoing (though minimal) support from the university and the city of Berkeley, CIL became a community-driven organization with national influence.[49] In its bylaws was the stipulation that it would be operated by disabled people, for disabled people: at least 51 percent of board members would have a disability.[50] Its initial goals focused around the idea of independent living in the city, including self-directed choice in housing, medical services, and other aspects of daily life. In its name and its operations, CIL asserted the fiercely held belief underlying the Rolling Quads, PDSP, and other local action groups, that "those who know best the needs of disabled people and how to meet those needs are the disabled people themselves," as Zukas summarized it.[51]

CIL's board did not explicitly name physical access as a priority at its founding, and the need for accessible buildings or wheelchair ramps is rarely mentioned in early proposals and meetings.[52] Perhaps this is because CIL positioned itself as a client-driven alternative to rehabilitation services, which worked on individual cases rather than local or national policies. Perhaps it was also that with no precedent for an accessible landscape, it was difficult to imagine consistent, widespread access. An early cover of the organization's publication *The Independent* from 1974 (figure 4.6) shows a group of wheelchair users traversing a sidewalk curb.[53] Hale Zukas, who would become CIL's primary advocate on transportation and architectural accessibility, is readily identifiable in his mechanical wheelchair and head-mounted stick. With support from his former attendant and now coworker, Eric Dibner, Zukas motors toward the right of the frame, while a woman wheelchair user is being pushed up the curb behind him. When this photograph was published in 1974, the city of Berkeley had expanded its commitment to sidewalk-level access and begun construction on dozens of successive ramps to create pathways through the city; but still, the vision of a contiguously accessible surface—a world of ramps, elevators, automated doors, and widened passageways—was far off. As Aimi Hamraie has written, the relationship of these activists to the cityscape was "frictional," not smooth. Their approach to designing access reflected these trips up and over curbs.

Berkeley's advocates for access did not propose standards as federal and state laws did, but instead approached access as a process based on immediate and potentially changing community needs. From the start, these disabled activists asserted their own expertise when it came to designing access. After the first round of curb ramps were constructed on Telegraph Avenue in 1970, Donald Lorence, then leader of the Rolling Quads, wrote to the city council expressing appreciation but also pointing out that a parking meter obstructed one of the ramps.[54] In the year following the initial Telegraph renovation, the community pushed the city to expand coverage. In 1971 a PDSP team led by Ruth Grimes, a master's student in urban planning at UC Berkeley, developed a map of 270 proposed curb renovations that would create a contiguous "wheelchair route" in the city.[55] In January of the next year, the city published a resolution ruling that all new street construction in the city would be designed to be accessible, and allocated $30,000 to curb reconstruction. Even more significant than this funding was the resolution's specification that the city manager must "consult with appropriate interested

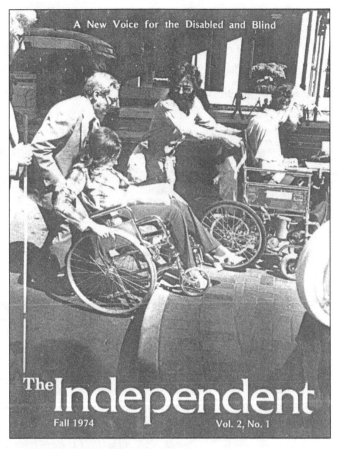

A New Voice for the Disabled and Blind

The Independent

Fall 1974   Vol. 2, No. 1

Figure 4.6. The cover of *The Independent: A New Voice for the Disabled and Blind*, Fall 1974. A group of disabled and nondisabled pedestrians traverse a curb. An unidentified woman with long dark hair and a plaid shirt is being pushed up the steep curb by a man in a suit; barely visible to the side of the frame is Dick Santos walking and carrying a white cane. At the center of the frame, attendant Eric Dibner pushes Hale Zukas in his wheelchair. Zukas wears a head stick mounted onto a cap. Center for Independent Living, Berkeley.

physically handicapped individuals in the course of implementing such design and construction work."[56]

The initial order for 125 new curb ramps was based on PDSP's "wheelchair route" map, with some specific additions based on individual requests (figure 4.7).[57] The new cuts created two districts of wheelchair

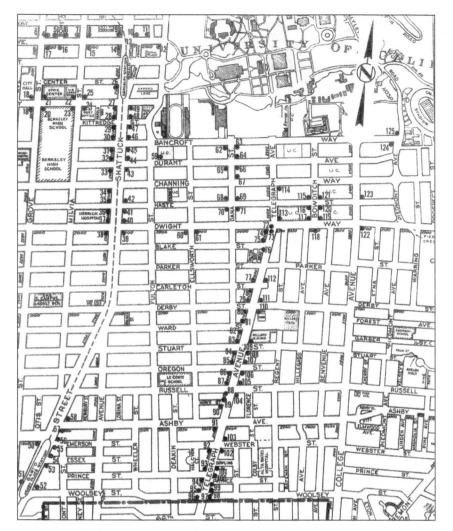

Figure 4.7. Wheelchair route mapped onto south Berkeley. Dots show additions to the initial Telegraph Avenue district, extending one mile south to Ashby Avenue, and in the downtown district to the west. Adapted from Resolution No. 45,605-N.S., City of Berkeley, February 13, 1973. City Clerk's Office, Berkeley.

access in the city. They expanded access in the initial Telegraph area to four parallel streets, including the corners around People's Park and the closest streets to Cowell Hospital. South of the immediate campus area, the cuts continued along a mile-long stretch of Telegraph to reach a major intersection at Ashby Avenue. The second grouping of cuts created an additional accessible district in downtown Berkeley around Shattuck Avenue, where the city's main governmental offices were located along with a shopping area.[58] Ashby and Shattuck were also locations of stations of the BART train line connecting Berkeley to San Francisco and Oakland, making this wheelchair route a link to accessible transit on a regional level. Other sidewalk renovations, the council noted, would be added based on consultation with local groups including PDSP and CIL.[59]

The city of Berkeley's project to create sidewalk wheelchair access was a significant departure from existing codes and processes of building physical access in the United States. As we have seen, the 1961 *ANSI 117.1* provided technical rules that were applied at the local, state, and federal level, but these measures created very slow change. The 1968 Architectural Barriers Act, which referred to this 1961 standard, was rarely followed; but even when it was, it mandated access in a piecemeal fashion, covering specific buildings and landscapes rather than contiguous areas.[60] Further, the law defined the need for access solely through the affiliation of the building, mandating access in federal government properties without jurisdiction over neighboring buildings or transportation networks. When the city of Berkeley ordered wheelchair-accessible sidewalk curbs across more than a mile of city streets, and included consultation with disabled people in planning, it laid out a very different process. Rather than setting an abstract goal of access over time, this community-centered approach focused on immediate usability.

When the city of Berkeley ordered construction of 125 new ramps, it also incorporated design feedback from the community, specifically from Hale Zukas. In the years since the first set of sidewalk curbs were rebuilt, Zukas and other local residents had observed a design problem. The ramps built on Telegraph consisted of a rounded curb that flattened into the brick crosswalk at the corner, merging the surface of the sidewalk into the street. These flattened curb "ramps" eliminated the edge of the curb entirely, making the streetscape dangerous for blind people who used canes to detect changes in terrain underfoot. To address this issue, Zukas, with construction help from his attendant-turned-colleague Eric Dibner, developed a new model for a curb cut that consisted of a pronounced dip in the sidewalk to the side of the main flow of foot traffic.[61]

The cut he designed was steep, with a six-inch drop within four feet, steeper than the 1:12 grade indicated in the 1961 standard for wheelchair ramps.[62] This design presented a more challenging slope for wheelchair users, and also required them to divert from the flow of traffic. Zukas saw this as a needed compromise to include the needs of the blind along with those of wheelchair users.[63] Zukas's design was used in Berkeley until the passage of Title 24 of the California Building Standards Code in 1989, which indicated a more gentle slope graded with lines (which Zukas deemed "virtually useless") to alert blind pedestrians.[64] In more recent years, codes have required a brightly colored, bumpy rubber strip embedded into the curb cut—a feature that can cause problems for people using crutches or walkers.[65] Zukas's design anticipated later features for multiple modes of use.

As local infrastructures of access improved in the local area, the staff on the community affairs desk at CIL often brought a disabled person's expertise to authorities who interpreted access in terms of codes and laws. Zukas articulated some of the broader social issues involved in creating access in 1975, when CIL consulted with BART on its access measures for commuter rail. From its start in 1972, BART had been a leading example of accessible public transit, with elevators, Braille signage and guides, level transfers from platform to train, and designated parking spaces integrated into its original construction.[66] After its opening, however, the transit organization observed that few people with disabilities were using the system, despite available accommodations. BART turned to CIL to gain insight. Zukas and his staff administered a survey on frequency of BART usage and attitudes within its community.[67] In his report, Zukas enumerated a variety of "discouraging factors" to disabled people using the train system. He noted the problem of taking a rail link only to find inaccessible buses and sidewalks on the other side. There was also a problem of information, Zukas noted: many disabled people simply assumed that BART would not be accessible. Finally, he observed what he dubbed "psychological barriers" within the disabled community. A population who had never had access to public transportation, he wrote, were "unlikely to have considered destinations of the sort that BART is intended to reach."[68] Encouraging BART to improve its public messaging and signage, Zukas defined access through its outcomes for disabled people, not its adherence to technical specifications. This was a difference in both method and measure from design specifications that determined access based on ramp angles or minimum numbers of accessible toilets.

The history of constructing access in Berkeley reads as something of a learning process, as the burgeoning community of disabled activists tackled first campus barriers, then city streets and sidewalks, then regional systems like BART as well as state and national agendas. Sometimes, the learning curve brought insurmountable problems, as in 1976, when the city's fire marshal ordered CIL to shut down classes or meetings in which more than four wheelchair users would be on an upper floor of the building.[69] Given the rare occurrence of large groups of wheelchair users gathering together in the 1970s, no architectural or planning guides addressed these concerns; the only technical manuals that included fire planning for people with disabilities were guidelines for nursing homes and institutions.[70] CIL proposed various improvisational fixes, including ramps connecting the rooftops of buildings and "safe refuge areas" designed to protect wheelchair users from fire danger for one hour while emergency crews could facilitate evacuation (a solution that predicted future guidelines for emergency evacuation).[71] Ultimately, though, these approaches proved unsatisfactory, and with CIL unwilling to compromise on holding its classes and meetings, it sought new office space.

In mid-1976 CIL signed a lease on a large, one-story space of a former automobile repair shop at the south end of the Telegraph Avenue shopping area, just five blocks from the University of California campus. At the new site, there was sufficient space for an expanding staff, room for groups of wheelchair users to gather without code violation, and conveniently installed car lifts that could be used for wheelchair-accessible van repair. Judy Heumann, who assumed a deputy directorship of CIL in 1975, noted that CIL "became more of a place people came to" once it opened on Telegraph.[72]

In retrospect, the office at 2539 Telegraph Avenue seems a fitting artifact of this moment in CIL history. It answered the community's need for control over its physical space and for an inclusive emergency plan, but also brought the organization into the quirky cultural environment of Telegraph Avenue. It was not built-to-purpose as an accessible site, but required creative thinking and appropriation. In this sense, it extended the improvisational survival tactics that its clients had long practiced to find their way in the inaccessible world. By 1984, the location was deeply ingrained in the culture of CIL, to the point where the poet and photographer Michael Chacko Daniels produced a book, *Going Where You Wheel on Telegraph Avenue*, paying homage to the street culture of Telegraph and its connection to an accessible community. In the book, CIL staffers and clients reflected on the possibilities open on Telegraph, an avenue where street life was unstructured and rebellious. "I can't imagine a better place for CIL to be," wrote Marty Brokaw, who reflected that she might "feel out of place in many places, but not on Telegraph."[73] Some members of the CIL community pointed out that there were, in fact, places where CIL might have been better placed, given that the proximity to the university maintained CIL's original connection to an established and elite institution, and the new location was also farther from regional public transportation.[74] Nonetheless, with its curb cuts and a growing number of friendly and accessible businesses, CIL director Phil Draper wrote, Telegraph felt like the center of the "most accessible city anywhere" during the 1970s and 1980s.[75]

The Berkeley Style of Access

As the disability rights movement grew in the 1970s and 1980s, asserting a national message around access, autonomy, and rights, Berkeley remained a central site of activism. Many disabled people found Berkeley and the larger Bay Area to be a haven of progressive politics and community. Arriving in Berkeley in 1975, the writer Simi Linton found a place "where disability seemed more ordinary," and where "curbcuts on every corner made it possible for me to go to the supermarket, to the bookstore and up to campus without having to stop someone at each corner, explain to them how to tilt my wheelchair back, take it down to the curb, and lift it back up on the other side."[76] Some of the new arrivals represented new demographics, including more race and class diversity than the initial UC Berkeley student group; others brought political experience with the civil rights and anti-war movements.[77] While this community took up political causes on a national and international scale through new organizations such as the Disability Rights Education and Defense Fund (1979) and the World Institute on Disability (1983), it also maintained a distinct local approach to accessibility. As legal battles over issues like public transportation occurred on a national stage, a quieter, quirkier design movement developed within the local disability scene— encompassing not only the clients and participants in PDSP and CIL, but extended networks of families, attendants, and architects.

As noted earlier, "access" was not a stand-alone priority for CIL in its founding documents, nor in its early organizational structure. Instead, access work fell under the purview of the community affairs desk, a division Hale Zukas defined as focused on "improving the physical and social environment for disabled people."[78] Zukas's intervention, in 1971, into the city's specifications for curb cuts proved to be the start of ongoing design work. As CIL formed, and staff developed expertise in renovations for accessibility, they advised local residents and businesses on ways to acquire funds for these projects as well as construction advice and labor. In response to requests from all corners of the Bay Area, Zukas's community affairs co-worker Eric Dibner drafted hand-drawn plans for ramps and other minor home alterations.[79] With funding from a Community Development Block Grant, CIL could offer small grants for materials or find scrap lumber for these projects as well.[80]

Berkeley's localized form of access also had an influence on architecture and planning curricula at the University of California. Given its roots in Cowell Hospital residence and PDSP, CIL had always had a connection to the university.[81] But it was not until 1972 that the organization began to engage with the department of architecture. Raymond Lifchez, a UC Berkeley professor, became aware of the vibrant local disability community after teaching Mary Ann Hiserman, who stood out in the architecture department as the only student with a visible disability (and who worked through PDSP to advocate for access on campus). Lifchez observed Hiserman sharing insights into usability and access with her fellow students, and began to extend invitations to disabled people who might contribute their perspectives. This experience fit, for Lifchez, into a broader search for alternative approaches in architecture. Rather than a technical approach to access as a set of codes, Lifchez considered the venture as a "consciousness raising" experiment, one that aimed at "disclosing an ongoing world" of disabled people living independently in largely inaccessible houses, landscapes, and buildings.[82] Lifchez published two books based on these projects: with Barbara Winslow, *Design for Independent Living* (1979), which documented the living spaces of the "consultants" who visited the class; and, with Cheryl Davis, *Rethinking Architecture* (1987), a methodological treatise that set out new goals and methods for the profession based on the UC Berkeley experiments.

Ray Lifchez's architecture teaching took a notable departure from the kind of professional design work that focused on access in terms of technical guidelines and replicable standards. Lifchez sought a new turn in architectural practice, a "New Humanism" that would bring attention to the areas left ignored in much of Modernist development; areas he cited included "regionalism, peculiar traditions, and in the realm of urban renewal of large cities, social ecology."[83] In keeping with this interest in the vernacular environment, Lifchez directed his students to observe and listen to the disabled visitors and fellow students who came into their studios, rather than jump into creating new designs. Lifchez and Winslow compiled these observations in *Design for Independent Living: The Environment and Physically Disabled People,* a volume that interspersed narratives of disabled people's life histories with documents of living arrangements. Writings and photographs depicted the independent lives of Berkeley locals, providing individual portraits that contrasted dramatically with staid design drawings that might show a wheelchair without an inhabitant or a person within abstract architectural space.[84] In fact, the book contains very little architecture or design strictly defined: there are no images of building exteriors or floor plans, and few rooms without people in them. Images of devices used by the subjects appear to be homemade and improvised, not interventions by outside designers. Some photographs show ramps or customized furniture such as a baby-changing table adapted for a wheelchair user, but most focus on the outcomes of independent living, with photos of multiple people—in couples, in groups, parents with children, indoors and outside enjoying themselves and each other.

Lifchez also introduced new practices of architectural discussion through his studio teaching. Lifchez had his students construct large-scale models with shoebox-sized parts that could be lifted from table to floor, disassembled, and rearranged during open discussion. These models provided props for students and their disabled "consultants" to discuss, arrange, reconfigure, and mark up (figure 4.8).[85] Documents of this process show students experimenting with forms beyond the wheelchair

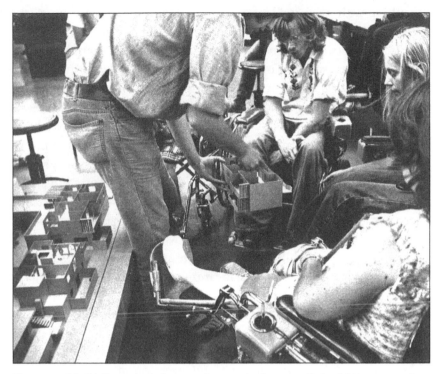

Figure 4.8. Model discussion, photograph, ca. 1987. A group of wheelchair users gathers around Raymond Lifchez, who stoops down to show them an architectural model. From Lifchez, *Rethinking Architecture: Design Students and Physically Disabled People* (Berkeley: University of California Press, 1987). Raymond Lifchez.

ramp or accessible toilet. The models incorporated approaches such as balconies and multilevel layouts, allowing interesting views and spaces within open plans. The students and their consultants taped notes to the models, identifying the benefits of features such as a "floating" stairway, which, according to a note, provided "nooks, outlooks, hiding." Other notes relayed personal responses to the spaces with the comments, "it's fun to just sit in a spacious room and relax" and "how nice is it to be a spectator and a participant!"[86] These notes filled the interior spaces, replacing the empty rooms of typical architectural models with the voices of potential inhabitants.

Lifchez and his students presented a form of accessible design that was about process, not product. Aside from the interactive models, these books provided no documentation of the work students produced after

consulting with local residents. Nor was there reference to any existing model of accessible architecture: Lifchez did not present a "greatest hits" of accessible design, nor did he include technical guidelines on
size of doorframes, height of counters, and so on.[87] These experiments
in one-to-one or small group consulting were an alternative to codes
that, Lifchez and Davis wrote, "dryly explain: 'This is a ramp, and these
are the specifications to follow for making one,' but they do not advise
how to make an intelligent decision about whether or not to use a ramp,
what kind of ramp to use for a given structure on a given site, or how
best to provide access to a given structure."[88] Later, he reflected that this
approach proved difficult to integrate into the profession as practiced.
There was a short-lived plan to replicate his studio assignments in five
other architecture schools, but it ultimately was not adopted.[89] Even UC
Berkeley's curriculum shifted to incorporate accessibility in the standard
introductory architecture studios, meaning that it was given less specific
attention and not presented as a methodological shift. Lifchez continued
to bring awareness to accessibility within the curriculum, but by the late
1980s, he lamented, there were "no more consultants, nor the big, furnished, and populated models."[90]

Lifchez's studio projects staged an intervention into the practice of
architecture, but they also had the effect of drawing attention to the architectural aspect of the Center for Independent Living's access work.
Writer and CIL staffer Michael Chacko Daniels published *Ramps Are
Beautiful: The Architecture of Independence* for CIL in 1982, compiling
writings, drawings, and photographs of Berkeley-area ramps.[91] The
title of the book suggests the effects of more than a decade of work
improving access in Berkeley: not only did the city have a more extensive infrastructure of access than any other place in the world, but
this infrastructure was infused with significance beyond the technical
accomplishment of removing barriers. That ramps could be beautiful was an architectural statement in itself, particularly given that the
ramps featured did not represent an attempt at ornamentation or camouflage. These were ramps in the Berkeley idiom: made of scrap lumber, stretched across lawns or attached to the sides of wood clapboard
houses, crowded onto lots with overgrown plants and free-form rock
gardens. Daniels explained in the introduction that the volume emerged
as a reaction to debates over plans to ramp major public sites in the Bay

Area. Specifically, Daniels wrote, a local paper had called the proposal to add a ramp to San Francisco's city hall "a form of vandalism" to the grand architectural edifice. In response, Daniels linked ramps not only to civil rights, but to theory of design in society. "Aesthetics should be in tune with the moral values of an age," he wrote; the architectural additions to update historic sites were not only a legal necessity, but a way to make the landscape fit a liberated age.[92]

Ramps Are Beautiful presented a kind of manifesto as well as an instruction book on "why ramps are needed and how to finance and build them." Where Lifchez and Winslow's *Design for Independent Living* observed the "ongoing world" of disabled people living in houses and apartments around Berkeley, Daniels's book included ruminations on the architectural qualities of the ramp—an artifact tied to the technological history of the wheel, and "a bridge" between the home and the outside world—as well as technical instructions on building one.[93] The book focused almost entirely on domestic settings, and in so doing narrated a story of access for households rather than individuals or a general public. All of the ramps in the book were additions to existing homes, and each clearly and unabashedly changed the visual appearance of the house. In most cases, the ramps were added to existing front porches or landings, creating a sharp zigzag angle away from the front door. Rather than minimizing the impact of these ramps—perhaps seen as "acts of vandalism" by architectural purists—the photographs in the book lingered on the ramps, focusing on them rather than conventional straight-on views. In several of the images, this angle of view entirely omitted the original façade, reorienting conventional angles of architectural photography.

Daniels's book also departed from the narrative of Berkeley's recent college graduates as the primary figures in the East Bay disability community. *Ramps Are Beautiful* included spotlights on households supporting aging parents with disabilities, as well as nonwhite families who reflected the larger Bay Area's demographics. Depicting working families living in rental apartments and in intergenerational households, the book's chapters provided a striking contrast to the idealized suburban single-family house that dominated rehabilitation images of the accessible home (see chapters 1 and 2), as well as the countercultural and communal settings documented in Lifchez's students' work. The more diverse array of subjects also raised different design concerns. For the Estes family, Filipino American immigrants, CIL's design assistance and a $50 grant for lumber allowed them to construct a ramp (figure 4.9) for a father who had trouble walking after a stroke. Valentina Estes described how limited access affected her husband, Marcelino's, life: he didn't feel confident going out, between having his children bump his wheelchair up and down the stairs and confronting people who did not understand his accent with his impaired speech post-stroke. The ramp provided an intermediary space for him to practice walking while still on his own property, and garnered positive attention from neighbors.[94] Another resident, an African American woman who lived with her disabled mother, noted the importance of their "properly built ramp" built with CIL's assistance, as opposed to an overly steep one that she had initially had built, which tested her own ability to push her mother up and down. "New vistas are open that were not possible before the ramp," she noted.[95] These intergenerational issues brought ramps out of isolation, redefining them from an individual's use to a household concern.

In *Ramps Are Beautiful*, Daniels and his contributors illustrated an ideal of design that is flexible and responsive to each household's needs. Ken Mineau, one of Ray Lifchez's students, contributed "Questions for users in designing a ramp" that translated some of the design conversations from Lifchez's classes for households to perform on their own.[96] Mineau suggested that readers consider who would use the ramp, such as wheelchair users, cane and crutch users, and walkers; other activities that might take place on or near the ramp, like walking or sitting; and existing features of the house that might be integrated, such as a stair or porch rail, a mailbox, or an address sign. Mineau illustrated the process of weighing these various concerns in a hypothetical scenario of a couple, "Jim and Peggy," living in a single-story rental house with a short flight of steps to the front door. Mineau sketched two possibilities, each with its own trade-offs. In one sketch, a ramp angles sharply across steps that connect the house to the driveway, cutting off the use of the porch; in another, the ramp extends to the front yard, blocking the use of the steps—which, the architect noted, made it difficult for a visiting mother-in-law who walked with a cane to enter the house. Mineau amended the plan with a third option: building out the porch to a large open space, adding a ramp to one side and leaving steps open on the

Figure 4.9. Adogbeji Oghajafor, photograph, ca. 1982. Valentina and Marcelino
Estes walking down the ramp at their home in Oakland. Marcelino grasps the
ramp handrail with one hand and his wife's arm with the other. From Michael
Daniels, ed., *Ramps Are Beautiful: The Architecture of Independence* (Berkeley:
Center for Independent Living, 1982). Michael Daniels and the Center for
Independent Living.

other (figure 4.10).[97] This ideal third way provided an open social space for both walkers and wheelchair users. Mineau's drawing, with Jim in his wheelchair tending a smoking grill among a gathering of friends, presented access as more than the sum of its parts. The beauty in this architectural form was its interpretation of access in terms of the life residents wanted to live, rather than through wheelchair access alone.

If Lifchez's studio projects and writings modeled change in the practice of architecture, *Ramps Are Beautiful* reflected the experiences of community members, most of whom were not trained architects. These books documented a local culture of residential design, largely consisting of adaptations of existing housing stock to allow for a range of

Figure 4.10. Ken Mineau, "Jim and Peggy's Ramp," drawing of a large porch with a ramp and steps, ca. 1982. A walking couple approach the ramp, while people stand and sit on the porch; Jim, a wheelchair user, tends the grill. Ken Mineau and the Center for Independent Living.

households that included disabled people. This local culture persisted—and still persists—in a community where disability was common and familiar to a degree rarely found elsewhere. This was a design culture in which designers were a secondary presence, if they were present at all. With few architects even aware of the concerns of access, let alone trained in the immersive methodology Lifchez taught, the work of constructing access in individual households was largely left to disabled people, their families, and their attendants. CIL's Eric Dibner noted that he never thought of himself as a professional, but instead an "attendant who had done good."[98] In its best form, this architectural access was approached not as a field of expertise, but as a response to listening to the needs and wants of disabled people.

Access and Independent Living

One of the more striking artifacts of accessible design in Berkeley predates the curb cuts of Telegraph. As I conducted my research, I read and heard many references to a guerilla form of access constructed when early Cowell residents such as Ed Roberts enlisted friends or attendants to install improvised curb cuts under cover of night. The image of wheelchair users and their agile assistants smuggling trowels and buckets of concrete to the side streets or campus walkways of Berkeley seems truly to capture a certain spirit of the 1960s, and of the kind of improvisation that defined living with a disability in this period. As far as anyone can determine, however, this guerilla-style accessible design did not happen: these "artifacts" of Berkeley's disability history are mythical. Save for a few patches over gaps between curb cuts and the street, there was no "nitroglycerin . . . and jackhammers in the middle of the night," reported Eric Dibner—nor were there midnight ventures to pave over curbs.[99]

Still, the myth of guerilla curb paving captures the spirit of the work that disabled people and their attendants performed in Berkeley in the 1960s and 1970s. It also suggests a search for remnants of the earliest disability rights history in Berkeley: the idea that perhaps somewhere, in a dark alley, there is a homemade curb cut that speaks to the tenacity of the Rolling Quads. This is a poignant search, given that little evidence of the earliest forms of access in Berkeley survives: neither the original curb cuts on Telegraph, nor the early office spaces of PDSP and CIL, nor even the Cowell Hospital building where the Rolling Quads made a makeshift dormitory remain standing. The myth of spontaneous curb construction is, in part, a search for a monument to the work that was done without recognition at the time.

The lack of monument to Berkeley's early era of accessible design is, perhaps, as informative as any historical marker.[100] Whether documented in Lifchez's volumes, sketched in CIL's *Ramps Are Beautiful,* or in still-standing buildings, the Berkeley style of accessible design has an ephemeral quality. Accessible housing was, and still is, difficult to find, and once found, was subject to the whims of changing real estate, landlords, and government income support. If this was the architecture of the "right to live in the world," it also materialized the contingent nature of many disabled people's living situations. In 2012, when CIL moved to a state-of-the-art new building named for Ed Roberts, it marked the end of an era on Telegraph Avenue. The new building is distinct from the university, linked instead by an elevator to the regional BART network and through satellite offices to Oakland and other less affluent parts of the Bay Area. A condominium building slated to be built on the site of CIL offices, moreover, indicates the ongoing gentrification and real estate pressures of twenty-first-century Berkeley.[101]

The purpose-built accessible architecture of the new Ed Roberts Campus building provides a contrast to the rugged, often improvised forms that characterized Berkeley's accessible landscape in the 1970s and 1980s. As the disability rights movement gained national prominence, the issue of access was often on the forefront. In 1977, in nationwide protests, disability activists asserted the need for authoritative regulations on access in transportation and public buildings. The style of this access was by necessity standardized and measurable. Its enforcement proved a challenging and public battle for the emerging U.S. disability rights movement.

5

Kneeling to the Disabled

Access and Backlash

Access became one of the primary public issues in disability rights advocacy on a national scale starting in the 1970s, particularly after the passage of the 1973 Rehabilitation Act. The act's Section 504 included, for the first time in federal law, civil rights language protecting people from discrimination on the basis of "handicap." In the ensuing years, the question of how this law should be implemented engaged a national audience on issues of access. The victories of the emerging rights movement included the first specific, enforceable accessibility requirements, issued in 1977.[1] These regulations brought about physical changes to everyday spaces in the United States, with ramps, parking spaces, and accessible toilets required at not only government buildings, but on campuses, museums, monuments, and other visible public sites. These projects, many of which required expensive renovations to architecture and transportation facilities, also became a primary target of backlash in politics and the press.

This chapter reviews the rise of accessible design as a public political issue of the 1970s and 1980s, including the increasing visibility of access as well as growing resistance to its seeming impositions. The new laws and regulations of the 1970s set in motion changes to the American landscape as well as a shift in the predominant argument that dated to the rise of rehabilitation in World War I: that technological change was a worthy investment in helping a vulnerable population and enabling disabled people to enter the workforce. Instead, critics introduced a new discourse of cost and proportion in which they weighed the relatively small number of disabled people against the cost and inconvenience of design alterations. In contrast to the enthusiasm for technological wonders of rehabilitation were new perceptions of ramps ruining historical architecture or bus lifts delaying transit routes. Accessible design, once seen as a solution that aligned technological progress with social ideals, now appeared as a form of design excess in which minor material changes could incur massive protests or lawsuits.

Given these conflicts, advocates for access defied resistance by asserting a version of disability rights that recaptured some of the rhetoric of individual salvation through technology. They did so in part by reframing the issue of access to emphasize disabled people's mobility and choice in a consumer society. The bipartisan coalition that drafted the Americans with Disabilities Act of 1990 defined disability rights anew through the logic of individual access to economic activities. They found legislative success but left intact the notion of access as a resource in limited supply, well aligned with notions of the individual citizen as a consumer and worker.

Access as a Civil Right: Section 504

Section 504 of the 1973 Rehabilitation Act provided a national agenda for a rights movement that had emerged in the 1960s in the San Francisco Bay Area, New York, Washington, DC, and other communities across the country. Section 504 was groundbreaking in terms of its wording, as it was the first legislation to use civil rights language to address disability. The key clause of the section was modeled after the 1964 Civil Rights Act:

> No otherwise qualified handicapped individual in the United States . . . shall, solely by reason of his handicap, be excluded from participation in, be denied the benefits of, or be subjected to discrimination under any program or activity receiving federal financial assistance.[2]

This explicit language of rights in Section 504 spurred a host of new debates around how this protection of rights would be implemented. Historians agree that neither legislators nor activists predicted the significance of the section as it was quickly added before the act was passed, with no open debate or discussion.[3] Within a few years of its passage, however, Section 504 had become an organizing point for a movement that defined access as a right in no uncertain terms, and sparked new arguments against government mandates for access.

Politicians, activists, and lobbying groups debated the interpretation and implications of Section 504 in the years after its passage. After the Department of Health, Education, and Welfare (HEW) published draft regulations in 1975 that would require architectural changes to sites ranging from Social Security offices to schools and college campuses, administrators of these sites raised objections not to the principle of rights protection, but to the requirement of sweeping facilities changes. The National Association of State Universities and Land Grant Colleges, for example, released a statement that argued that its members could "meet specific needs when requested" without "provid[ing] an all-enveloping system" of access. They envisioned schools attending to the needs of disabled students on a case-by-case basis ("when requested") rather than building wheelchair ramps, widening library aisles, or marking parking spaces in anticipation of their presence. Similarly, the American Council on Education argued that there was no need for "massive, costly modifications and additions to facilities" but that schools could develop access once students or employees identified the need for it.[4] Washington, DC, activist Fred Fay paraphrased these arguments as, "Well, we don't need to make things accessible. People with disabilities never come in here."[5] Under pressure from these agencies, President Gerald Ford's secretary of HEW, David Matthews, delayed signing the regulations.[6]

The non-enforcement of Section 504 gave a national agenda to a movement of groups that had already conducted community-driven advocacy on issues including housing, transportation, and attendant care.[7] The American Council of Coalitions for the Disabled (ACCD) first met in 1974, bringing together activists with experience in both congressional politics and community-based organizing.[8] The group specifically distinguished between "of" and "for" groups—that is, organizations made up of people with disabilities (such as Berkeley's Center for Independent Living or the National Federation of the Blind), rather than those working for them—asserting the importance of firsthand experience and self-advocacy to bring about effective, tangible change.[9] In early 1977, when President Carter's new secretary of HEW, Joseph Califano, suggested compromises in the drafted Section 504 regulations to allow for more waivers, longer compliance schedules, and weaker accessibility rules, the ACCD announced its intentions to mount a nationwide strike in April of that year.[10]

The largest and longest protests occurred in Washington, DC, where activists occupied Califano's office for twenty-eight hours, and in San Francisco, where protesters occupied the federal HEW building for twenty-six days.[11]

The San Francisco protest brought the kind of spatial politics that had been developing in Berkeley and other local sites to a national stage. With Berkeley CIL's Kitty Cone as a key strategist, the protest took shape as a grassroots action in the vein of anti-war and civil rights activism of the time.[12] On the eve of the protest, the 504 Emergency Coalition, which operated out of CIL offices, released a statement explaining its demands, including specific and varied elements of access:

> Disabled people will no longer accept segregation and oppression. We want jobs, accessible buildings (with ramps, wide doorways, elevators, braille signs, grip bars in the bathroom, etc.), accessible transportation, education, communication devices and interpreters for the deaf, decent health care. . . . We want basic services and civil rights to which all people are entitled. 504 is only a beginning. Disabled people are an important force in the struggle for the liberation of all people.[13]

The San Francisco protest also provided striking images of activists subverting the symbolism of the site. For those inside the building, the occupation was an active challenge to the symbolism of the grand architectural structure. In a photo (figure 5.1) by participant HolLynn D'Lil, an empty wheelchair parked alongside a mattress with people sleeping at the base of a staircase seems to deliberately juxtapose the temporary but useful objects of bodily support with the permanent and inaccessible architecture. Press photographs also captured the unexpected view of so many people with visible disabilities and disability equipment gathered in one space. One Associated Press photograph (figure 5.2) showed Lynnette Taylor standing in a room interpreting a speaker's words in sign language, surrounded by a mass of people in wheelchairs, the chrome of their chairs glinting in the flash.[14] Such a mass of persons with disabilities in public, represented as active and engaged rather than pitiful or vulnerable, marked a notable shift in media portrayals.

The Section 504 protests ended on April 28, 1977, when Secretary Califano signed regulations without the compromises requested by critics.[15]

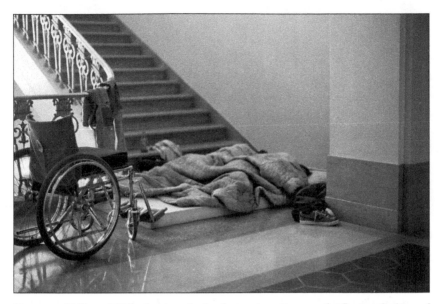

Figure 5.1. HolLynn D'Lil, photograph, April 1977. A mattress on the floor at the base of a grand staircase in the San Francisco federal building at the Section 504 occupation in April 1977. Two heads are barely visible peeking out of a blanket. A wheelchair is parked nearby next to a pile of clothing. Courtesy of the artist.

In a victory speech on April 30 on the plaza outside the San Francisco HEW building, sit-in leader Kitty Cone made clear the links between this protest movement and the causes of the time. The Section 504 actions had, she asserted, "helped to win the future for millions of disabled children who will no longer have to face no education or segregated education, or an adulthood on welfare, segregated from the rest of society." Cone invoked not only the connection between disabled people's exclusion and the race-based segregation that had been struck down by the Supreme Court two decades prior, but the spatial qualities of exclusion. She spoke for "we the shut-ins, or shut-outs," and of the struggle against "government ignorance, and inhumanity, and closed doors."[16] Likewise, Ed Roberts, who joined the victory celebration as the state of California's director of rehabilitation, called participants to remember "our fellow Americans with disabilities, to help them come out from behind, from the back wards, from the institutions, from the places, the garbage heaps, of our society. We have to stop the warehousing, the

Figure 5.2. "Handicapped Protest," photograph, April 1977. Dozens of wheelchairs pack a room at the Section 504 protest while a sign interpreter, Lynnette Taylor, stands in the center. A man stands with a camera to the side of the room. Associated Press.

segregation, of our brothers and sisters."[17] Like Cone, Roberts adopted the language of civil rights and solidarity that increasingly characterized disability rights speech. Their emphasis on collective rather than individual access became increasingly common in the rights movement as it moved beyond local actions into the national realm.

Public Transportation and the Economic Logic of Backlash

When activists insisted upon clear and enforceable guidelines to follow Section 504, they responded not only to the legislative issues at hand, but also to the condition of U.S. access laws as conflicting, uneven, and unreliable. In the field of public transportation, conflicts between local and federal authority came to the fore in the 1970s, when the U.S. Department of Transportation introduced a new program aimed at improving the nation's public bus fleet. The so-called Transbus project, which initially sought to produce a "bus of the future" that included wheelchair access among other state-of-the-art features, became the catalyst of a decade-long conflict that reshaped the meaning of access in public discourse.

In 1974 the federal Urban Mass Transportation Administration presented nine prototypes for city buses for tests in U.S. cities. The new buses, developed by three automakers under the agency's Transbus research program, represented a new design approach for public vehicles (figure 5.3).[18] Whereas motor buses of the mid-twentieth century tended to have rounded bodies lifted off the street and aluminum, "streamlined" sides that curved around a large front windshield, the new buses featured a low-to-the-ground, horizontal profile with a wide rectangular front window, smooth white vinyl with colorful stripes from front to back, and larger side windows. A three-axle design was intended to create smoother driving, while carpeted interiors, air conditioning, and more single seats promised more comfort for passengers. The buses' significant innovation over previous models was a low floor height and air-powered "kneeling" function, both of which made buses easier to board for riders who had trouble walking and climbing. Most significant to our story were the wider doors on each of the three prototypes, designed to allow for a wheelchair ramp to extend from the front door (figure 5.3).[19]

Figure 5.3. Transbus prototypes photographed at test site in North Phoenix, Arizona, 1976. A contemporary "new look" bus, far left, contrasts with the three rectilinear Transbus designs. U.S. Department of Transportation, Urban Mass Transportation Administration.

Figure 5.4. Transbus testing, 1976. Several older men and women wearing signs affixed to their chests board and step out of the prototype bus through its sliding doors. U.S. Department of Transportation, Urban Mass Transportation Administration.

The Transbus models were initially well received and dubbed the "bus of the future" for their promise of faster boarding times, easier rides, and reduced noise and smell. But by 1976, the program was in peril. The biggest of the three bus manufacturers, General Motors (GM)—which manufactured 80 percent of the country's existing buses—refused to bring its prototype to production, reporting that it would be too expensive to retool assembly lines for the new design.[20] The American Public Transit Association (APTA), an auto industry–funded group, echoed the claim that these buses would be costly, calling the new prototypes an allocation of "scarce federal resources" that "border[ed] on the ridiculous."[21] Instead, GM and the APTA began to cast the Transbus project as one of several options, asking federal administrators to allow for a modified Rapid Transit Service (RTS) bus already under development at GM. The RTS model had similar design details such as larger windows and spacious interiors, but a higher floor and optional wheelchair lifts that could be installed in the rear of the bus.[22] One of the three bus manufacturers, American Motor

Company, withdrew from the project, noting that it could not compete with GM's already-developed alternative and strong influence on the government.[23] With both GM and Rohr offering alternative designs without the accessibility features, the Transbus came to represent a design trade-off between federal demands and practicalities of production.

The Transbus program, initially hailed as an improvement in a market that had not seen significant design change since the 1950s, ended as a highly publicized design failure. In May 1977, just a month after HEW secretary Joseph Califano issued the Section 504 regulations governing access in public services, secretary of transportation Brock Adams signed a mandate requiring local transportation authorities to purchase buses that followed Transbus guidelines.[24] When automakers and local transit agencies asserted that the buses were overly expensive, Transbus became a symbol of the problems of accessibility requirements that critics linked to related rules for schools, federal office buildings, and other sites.[25] Over the ensuing years, numerous lawsuits were waged: New York's Disabled in Action sued local transit authorities who purchased inaccessible buses, while APTA moved to block federal requirements on the basis of excessive cost. As a result, by 1981, when DOT rescinded the Transbus mandate and allowed for RTS-style buses, many local authorities had not introduced new buses into their fleets in more than a decade. Media coverage tended to focus on the excessive demands of the federal government rather than the refusals and lawsuits by automakers. The libertarian magazine *Reason* specifically blamed design ambition when it called Transbus a "$28 million fiasco" that left nothing more than "rotting, futuristic buses" while U.S. cities lacked usable vehicles to put into service.[26]

The arguments over the Transbus produced a discussion of access as a public burden and a new kind of equation in which the demands of a single, small community seemed to outpace its share of public benefits. Even after the Transbus was rejected, the notion of access as excess remained. After cities adopted limited fleets of accessible buses, some reported "exceedingly low" wheelchair ridership. The industry-funded Transportation Research Board reported, for example, that St. Louis city buses carried only one wheelchair-using rider during 320 scheduled runs.[27] These reports perpetuated a sense that disabled people did not need or want public transportation and fueled city governments' arguments against the requirements. New York mayor Ed Koch called the

$1.6 billion estimated for retrofitting the subway systems "the dumbest thing imaginable" and predicted that "500 [people in wheelchairs] may use it once and maybe 10 thereafter."[28] In a time of lobbying, activism, and debate over the technical merits of the bus designs, arguments like Koch's "dumbest thing" presented the transit problem as a logical problem, as if the solution were a mere issue of calculation. In fact, as advocates pointed out at the time, underuse was a symptom of the very problem of inaccessible mass transit, given that disabled people had never had access to transportation before.[29] Riders who used the lifts and other features did so against significant odds, including the lack of accessibility in other infrastructure and poorly maintained or operated equipment. In the St. Louis case, 40 percent of lift-equipped buses were out of service at the time of the study.[30]

Even when media coverage of public transit access presented a sympathetic view of disabled people's demands, the message was still one of an overwhelming design challenge. In a *New York Times* article on the trials one woman encountered trying to bring her wheelchair on a bus, the reporter wrote that some buses passed without stopping; others were not equipped with lifts; and still others had lifts but they were out of order or drivers were unsure how to use them.[31] Stories like this only seemed to reinforce the perception of a broken system overwhelmed by demands for access, resulting in poor transportation service for the nondisabled public. Perhaps these stories bolstered the paper's editorial skepticism of access as well. After the New York Mass Transit Association (MTA) voted not to comply with federal mandates for access in 1980, the *Times* editorial board expressed concern that losing transportation funds tied to these mandates would "undermine transit for everyone—and without much help to the special group that is meant to benefit."[32] The *Times* repeated this rhetorical emphasis on the difference between this "special group" and "everyone" over several years, asking in another column, "Must Every Bus Kneel to the Disabled?"[33] Observing the strife between disabled groups, federal judges, and the MTA, a *Times* 1984 editorial called the goal of making the transit system accessible "extravagant and utopian." Echoing other arguments about the cost of the changes, the editorial's title imagined "The $2,000 Subway Token."[34]

Alongside these arguments over the relative ratio of disabled consumers to public transit budgets was the specter of an entirely separate system of "dial-a-ride" or "paratransit" vehicles. Given the complexity and expense of making transit systems accessible, paratransit promoters argued that on-call, accessible vehicles could "both provide much better service and be much less costly."[35] However, these services came with their own problems. "Dial-a-ride" has never provided the snappy or convenient service its name suggests. Rides tended to be delayed, were difficult to schedule (often requiring twenty-four hours or more advance notice), and prioritized medical visits over recreational ones. Despite these problems, paratransit fit tidily within the same economic argument levied against Transbus. Against the specter of broken-down buses and expensive subway renovation, these small, modern vehicles seemed to be a useful solution.

The failure of Transbus helped support the argument for paratransit as well. Why seek to incorporate access into the troubled bus and subway system, promoters asked, when door-to-door, on-demand service could be available? This proposal also appealed to policy makers interested in privatization of public services. C. Kenneth Orski, a former public transit administrator under presidents Nixon and Ford, proposed that reduced federal funding should provide a "blessing in disguise" by "jolting cities" toward more dramatic policy changes, specifically toward greater privatization of services. This could and should be the start of a more dispersed transportation system, Orski wrote, including private express bus systems, employer-provided shuttles between business districts, and "special on-call transportation services" for disabled riders to replace "the expensive regulatory approach."[36] This was not only an economic argument, but a technological one: Orski described privatization as a path to "innovation," as self-interested companies would generate new ideas once free of the demands of regulators. His position suggested a complete turn away from the earlier view that a federal program such as Transbus would produce industry-changing research.[37] Coming after years of conflict and delay over city transit, this view found support under President Ronald Reagan when he took office in early 1981. Within a month of his inauguration, Reagan signed an order to curb regulations, including inviting the Department of Transportation to redraft access regulations to include the option of separate vehicles rather than accessibility on standard routes.[38] New rules specifically linked paratransit to the cost of creating access on standard routes, as they allowed local authorities to substitute paratransit for accessible vehicles when costs of the latter would surpass 3 percent of the annual budget.[39]

Even as they were framed in terms of financial costs, debates over Transbus and "dial-a-ride" were both arguments about design. The Transbus presented a form of Universal Design before the term was in frequent circulation: a bus whose form addressed the needs of a variety of riders without differentiation between disabled and nondisabled riders. The low-floored bus would have advantages for older or injured riders in addition to wheelchair users, and also presented an overall design improvement as part of the "sleek" profile of the new bus prototype. The GM RTS model, by contrast, relegated wheelchair users to a separate entrance. This backdoor lift required a special request that emphasized the distance between "wheelchair user" and "general public" and reinforced the perception of accessibility features as add-ons to a standard design. Paratransit took this separation another step by providing an entirely separate vehicle for riders who were officially registered as "disabled." The vehicles reinforced the social separation of disabled people given their visible difference from public transportation, and the vehicles' resemblance to ambulances.

Disabled observers were quick to note the symbolic as well as practical differences among transportation options. Activists objected that even if paratransit services performed as promised—which they rarely did—they reinforced a separation that went deeper than the mere question of transportation. Bob Conrad, a Denver activist, identified the symbolic difference between public transit and paratransit: "I think the real difference is in what we are saying about ourselves as disabled people when we accept paratransit. It feeds into what society says about us—that we need to be pampered, and that we need to be treated differently."[40]

Just as the emerging disability rights movement used the historic architecture of government buildings as a striking symbolic backdrop for Section 504 protests, activists organized around inaccessible streets and transportation sites in the 1980s.[41] ADAPT (American Disabled for Accessible Public Transportation) emerged as a leading protest organization.[42] ADAPT was an offshoot of Atlantis, a Denver independent living organization, that came together when the APTA's annual convention was held in its hometown in 1983. The group developed a distinctive style of protest that used the visibility of wheelchairs and disabled bodies

Figure 5.5. "ADAPT Cordially Invites You to an
Uproar," flyer, ca. 1983, with drawing of a public bus
with the International Symbol of Access on it being
flushed down a toilet. ADAPT.

in nonviolent actions to disrupt APTA conventions in Denver, Chicago, San Francisco, New York, and Washington throughout the 1980s.[43] ADAPT members blocked convention hotel doorways; stopped traffic in the street; and boarded buses on their hands and dragged their folded wheelchairs up the steps, demonstrating that their physical condition was not the barrier to fuller participation.[44] Many were arrested.[45] In addition to its fearless protest approach, ADAPT developed messages that caught the eye and skewered politeness. For the 1983 Denver APTA convention, a flyer (figure 5.5) invited protesters "to an uproar," with an image showing a city bus emblazoned with the International Symbol of Access being flushed down the toilet. The flyer promised "fun and games," including a rally, hands-on training, "screaming matches & national news-making," and "wild parties." "We're gonna have a blast," it promised.[46]

For the increasingly visible and unified disability rights movement, the public transportation conflicts of the 1980s reinforced the lessons learned through Section 504 battles about the value of strong regulations and enforcement. Advocates learned to read regulations and press releases carefully and with skepticism: as Stephanie Thomas, an ADAPT organizer, later wrote, "accepted reality is not necessarily reality at all."[47]

Design definitions of access—written into bus procurement guidelines or architectural specifications—proved less than accessible in reality. The Americans with Disabilities Act, passed in 1990, did not end transportation accessibility battles, but the law showed signs of advocates' pressure. The law included an extended, and highly specific, section on public transit, including the requirement that local transit authorities who could not immediately acquire wheelchair lifts for buses must demonstrate their efforts to acquire lifts, and set a specific date by which they would comply.[48]

In the 1970s and 1980s, the rise of a strong disability protest movement and the subsequent backlash against accessibility regulations created new political meaning for the issue of access. Whereas postwar rehabilitation programs had produced strong rhetoric and images of the promises of technology to aid disabled people, in the era of enforceable regulations the artifacts of access became more controversial. Arguments over the extent and cost of creating access in architecture and transportation expressed a tension in U.S. political culture between the greater provision of rights protections and measures of public inclusion. Transportation conflicts bolstered the idea, as C. Kenneth Orski put it, that public services such as transportation and infrastructure were best seen as a "joint responsibility of the public and private sectors" rather than a public amenity.[49] The tension between these principles also shaped the landmark Americans with Disabilities Act before its passage in 1990.

Toward Independence: The Americans with Disabilities Act

The backlash against accessibility mandates in public transportation and architecture suggested significant barriers to broad-based federal action. And yet, a bill was proposed in 1988 with bipartisan support that extended these requirements even further, encompassing private sites as well as the federally funded services. The success of this new act was due in part to advocates' appeal to an interpretation of civil rights in terms of individual achievement and economic participation. Disability rights advocates managed to maintain support for accessibility laws and other rights protections in the 1980s with an emphasis on appealing, individual faces of disability, not the abstract population of "the handicapped."

The ADA was a late addition to the twentieth-century cordon of civil rights laws, coming decades after race- and gender-based discrimination protections in the Civil Rights Act of 1964 and Title IX of the Education Amendments Act of 1972. As such, it reflected new positions on rights from a conservative standpoint. In the 1980s a new wave of conservatives, including President Ronald Reagan and commentators William F. Buckley and James Kilpatrick, argued for "color blindness" as a guiding civil rights principle as opposed to "special privileges" for minority groups. Nancy MacLean characterizes these claims as a way for conservatives to play two sides of the civil rights debate: opposing specific civil rights policies, but avowing support for "equality."[50] Hugh Graham describes this new civil rights ideology of the period as "rights claims in collision." Conservatives, Graham notes, framed their opposition to minority and women's rights as defenses of other rights: the rights of women against the rights of unborn fetuses in abortion cases, the right to compensation for past injustice against the right to opportunity for others when it came to affirmative action.[51] These "rights in collision" also informed disability rights issues, including the cost arguments relating to accessibility. Shortly after Reagan took office in 1980, Vice President George H. W. Bush's Task Force on Regulatory Relief instructed local authorities that "regulatory action shall not be undertaken unless the potential benefits to society for the regulation outweigh the potential costs."[52] This Reagan-Bush compromise upheld the basic premise of accommodations, but gave credence to claims of competing rights by local authorities and businesses.

As policy historian Edward Berkowitz writes, even considering controversies over physical access, the disability rights cause remained politically "safe" in the 1980s. Advocates could count on a certain level of bipartisan support given ongoing association with veterans' benefits, as well as the fact that the dominant image of disabled people remained, in Berkowitz's terms, "the antithesis of the stereotypical, menacing members of the underclass" vilified in race- and poverty-related discussions.[53] The image of the striving, white, middle-class disabled person that dominated rehabilitation narratives did much to shape this perception and downplay intersections of disability with race and poverty. This image was reinforced as a number of disabled people took posts in the world of politics. The National Council on Disability, a Reagan-appointed committee, included participants in the Independent Living movement, such as Lex Frieden, the founder of the Coalition of Texans with Disabilities, as well as representatives of more conservative constituencies such as Joni Earickson Tada, an evangelical Christian who promoted international mission work among disabled populations.[54] Also on the council was Kansas senator Robert Dole, Reagan's rival in the 1980 presidential primaries, who was also a disabled veteran of World War II.[55] These professionals and public leaders represented the successes of rehabilitation among educated, white Americans.

Media stories, too, depicted a more sympathetic view of individuals with disabilities, in contrast to the conflicts over accessibility and overt activism. Even as major newspapers vilified "handicapped rights" on their editorial pages, they ran more sympathetic descriptions of the everyday lives of disabled people in the back pages, in culture and "lifestyle" sections. In contrast to *New York Times* editorials that called the project of making subways accessible "utopian," one *Times* writer set a scene of frustration over physical barriers in the cosmopolitan setting of an Italian restaurant on the Upper West Side. The writer described lack of access in terms of cultural exclusion, describing a scene in which "a table of customers sipped wine, ate linguini and idly looked out a window at passers-by. Outside, Paul Campos could only stare back. His wheelchair could not cross the restaurant's seven-inch concrete step."[56] The *Times*, the *Washington Post*, and the *Wall Street Journal* ran periodic articles during the 1980s on the business sector's actions to approach disabled people as a consumer group: business districts pitched in to provide accessible sidewalks, while travel agencies provided advice for disabled travelers.[57] In this coverage, the papers moved away from the competitive language of cost and benefit in favor of describing a lack of access to consumer culture.

The image of a disabled consumer seeking to participate in such activities as going to restaurants or traveling with their families was central to the National Council on Disability's narrative as it proposed a legislative agenda for disability rights. In 1986 a nationwide poll reported that out of a thousand people with disabilities surveyed, two-thirds had not gone to a movie, three-fourths never went to live theater or music, and two-thirds had not gone to a sporting event in the preceding year.[58] The National Council cited this poll as a primary reference in a report,

Toward Independence, that argued that federal policy overemphasized the segment of the disabled population who relied on public income support. The council advised the federal government to "issue minimum guidelines for universal accessibility and other standards for the removal of architectural, transportation, and communication barriers in facilities, vehicles, programs, and activities covered by the equal opportunity law for people with disabilities."[59] This recommendation was the first official call for public accommodations laws to apply to all public facilities, not just government buildings. As a part of the Americans with Disabilities Act (ADA) first drafted by the council in 1988, this requirement gave the same public protections to people with disabilities in public accommodations as to groups protected on the basis of race, gender, religion, and national origin.

Republican supporters presented the ADA as legislation in keeping with the new conservative interest in "equality," highlighting its benefits in terms of individual choices and opportunities, rather than dependence on public support. W. Bradford Reynolds, Reagan's chief civil rights lawyer and a noted opponent of affirmative action, described the act in terms of "the difference between giving a man a fish and teaching him to catch his own."[60] Likewise, on the eve of its passage, Republican Congressman Steve Bartlett referred to the act as a part of a push for "programs or laws that empower people to control their own lives. You empower parents to choose their own child care, you empower parents and students to choose their own education. . . . Without the whole array of federal regulation, you empower people to purchase a home or housing, to live where they want to live." Through a policy that emphasized civil rights through economic participation, he asserted, "you take the power away from government and give it to individuals."[61]

The passage of the ADA, as many commentators have since observed, signified a precarious success for the disability rights movement. By extending many of the provisions of Section 504 to the private sector, the law met with some of the same resistance.[62] Once again, physical changes for access provided a visible target for critics. Philip K. Howard, a conservative lawyer, wrote a best-selling book that presented these overreaching regulations as part of a lawsuit-dependent "culture of complaint." Howard described what he saw as the most ridiculous examples of accessibility requirements: a homeless shelter forced to close rather than install a $100,000 elevator, a hockey rink required to make the scorer's box wheelchair-accessible.[63] By filing lawsuits under the ADA, Howard wrote, the "disabled lobby is waging war against every other citizen."[64] Perceptions of the excess of disabled people's "complaints" informed the enforcement and litigation of the ADA as well. In his book *Bending Over Backwards*, Lennard Davis recounts the story of a failed lawsuit over an office worker's request to have the office-kitchenette sink lowered so that she could use it from her wheelchair. Her employer rejected the request, arguing that the accessible bathroom sink was available. This argument—as Davis puts it—gets at the "difficult positions" of disability in a post-ADA world, when rights are established but arguments remain over the *extent* of these rights.[65]

The design debates that took place throughout the last decades of the twentieth century, whether in response to Section 504 requirements or the ADA's attention to private businesses, consistently focused on the question of the extent of rights disabled people should expect. Starting with the first accessibility standard in *ANSI 117.1*, guidelines were organized around a design minimum that defined access as a quantity: a certain width of clearance for doorways and passages, a certain grade for ramps, a set number of parking spaces, signs, or units within the whole of a building or site. Opponents of accessibility regulations also focused on quantities in their objections, comparing high construction cost estimates to the low numbers of riders, residents, or participants. These metrics appealed to the fiscal conservatism of public policy, but they also drew on cultural associations of design with luxury. Failed projects like the "bus of the future" and the seemingly "utopian" plans to renovate entire urban infrastructures left a lasting impression of access as excess, or a demand over and above "regular" design. As the next chapter reveals, the consumer design world—not affected by legal regulations—provided a small but influential arena for creative thinking about disability and design. Arguments for "Universal Design" successfully used the visual, tactile, and functional appeals of consumer product design to avoid the negative associations of government-mandated accessibility. The products and plans that followed this argument transformed design discourses around disability, but also removed some of the political messages about rights and inclusion.

6

From Accessible to Universal

Design in the Late Twentieth Century

In the last decades of the twentieth century, disability rights reached the mainstream of American culture with conflicting success. On the one hand, disabled people were increasingly present in the public view: organizing in political groups, taking up leadership roles in government and social service agencies, and speaking for themselves in media venues that had previously focused a pitying or "inspiring" lens on disabled subjects. On the other hand, as disability issues came to the fore, so did backlash against the causes of inclusion and civil rights. Accessible design was an easy target for criticism. Some of the earliest public measures for access involved difficult and awkward renovations of public buildings—such as courthouses, train stations, and libraries—which were otherwise perceived as grand and stately forms of architecture.[1] In public transportation, decades-long renovation projects similarly provided a poor public face for the cause of access. The regulations of the 1970s and 1980s were unevenly enforced and often confusing for architects and builders: with differing timelines of enforcement coded in the fine print of accessibility regulations, government specifications were not widely embraced, and by the time of the passage of the Americans with Disabilities Act (ADA) in 1990 there were few elegant or monumental examples.[2]

The designers who worked to promote and improve accessible design were dismayed by its poor public image. After the passage of the ADA, Ronald L. Mace, an architect and longtime advocate of accessible design, lamented having to defend "this stuff . . . being put out as what it means to comply with the ADA," given that "the buildings end up looking like hell." For Mace, one of the few American architects of the 1970s who used a wheelchair himself, it was the "ultimate frustration" to see buildings where architects and engineers tacked on access features only when they realized the need to comply with government regulations. These buildings "ended up being discriminatory after all," Mace argued, because this "added on" access usually did not work well, if at all, and seemed to reinforce the message that people with disabilities were a marginal afterthought.[3]

For decades before the passage of the ADA, Mace had argued that design that included disabled people did not need to be an unattractive and expensive addition to "standard" design. After completing his architectural training at North Carolina State University in 1966, Mace consulted first with local, then federal agencies to develop guidelines for accessible architecture, and often performed the architectural work of planning renovations for public agencies after the laws went into effect.[4] While his work often focused on helping local agencies meet legal guidelines, he argued that these requirements were just a starting point for well-considered design. Mace is credited with coining the term "Universal Design," an ideal of design that is "usable by all people" rather than the kind of separate facilities often employed to provide access.[5] The term gave a name to the idea that many designers, engineers, medical specialists, and individuals with disabilities had articulated for years—namely, that designing for people with disabilities was not so different from designing for everyone else.[6]

Ron Mace first publicly used the term "Universal Design" in the interior design magazine *Designers West* in 1985, when he characterized it as an approach to designing "for everyone" rather than for a limited group of people with identifiable disabilities.[7] The concept proved useful for many within and outside the disability rights movement to argue that attention to disability was not an added burden, but instead would align with broader goals in planning and design. When he spoke directly to his fellow design professionals, Mace presented Universal Design as a solution to the problem of perceived cost and inconvenience of designing for access. As he wrote in a 1998 guidebook, this approach was a response to the perception of accessible design as a separate category of features, "'special', more expensive, and usually ugly."[8] Instead, he and his collaborators advocated simple, easy design solutions found among the supply of "less expensive, unlabeled, attractive" hardware and materials—such as lever-shaped door handles, which were easier for people with manual impairments, but were not visually or conceptually associated with disability. In the best-case scenario, he imagined a form of Universal Design that would disappear into its surroundings: he noted that, from the standpoint of accessibility, "the best door is no door at all," suggesting a minimal, elegant solution rather than a search for complex or high-tech installations.[9]

The designers who actively explored disability through design in this period were scattered, and they showed little sign that they associated their works with a defined "movement"—in fact, only some adopted the term "universal" to describe their work (at least initially). Still, there are common concerns that thread through a range of experiments and products of the 1970s to the 1990s. A number of these design works were not finished products, but tools and processes: charts, handbooks, and guidelines for designers to address a new set of human concerns. There was a sense among many designers that addressing the population of disabled users would prompt new perspectives, new definitions of human concerns, and new parameters for the very activity of design. Design publications, including *Humanscale*, an ergonomic guidebook that incorporated the latest anthropometric research on disability, as well as Mace's own early work publishing guidelines to the state of North Carolina's building code, sought to translate new information on disability into a design process. For others, exploring disability was a prompt to depart from existing rules, to experiment personally and professionally. From a designer who dressed as an elderly woman for several months' research, to student groups imagining entirely new criteria for accessibility, designers embraced disability for its possibilities to disrupt existing practices and introduce better ones.

This work also produced new aesthetic approaches in product design. Universal Design was not a unified style, but its products echoed Ron Mace's arguments that designs for disabled people need not "look like hell." One of the most significant commonalities among Universal Design efforts is that they bear the marks of careful design attention. Oversized buttons, curvaceous handles, and uncluttered interiors made for a kind of late twentieth-century streamlining, an attempt to smooth away difficult object encounters and transform the everyday. This smoothing, however, also brought new contradictions of its own. Consumer products including the Cuisinart food processor, designed in 1978, and the 1989 OXO Good Grips line of kitchen tools both incorporated awareness of disabilities to produce successful products, but in both cases, disability was a silent contributor, to which marketers made no overt mention.

This gloss over disability in favor of aesthetic and functional appeals became a characteristic of the commercial version of Universal Design. The measure of success of the strategy to incorporate knowledge of disabilities into mainstream products seemed to be the possibility of selling these products without mentioning disability at all. The notion of seamless design for multiple user groups without distinction was an ideal, but the subtlety of working toward this ideal was often lost on design companies and design media. Much of the public discussion of Universal Design focused on areas in which disability features most easily contributed to appealing and functional design, leaving aside more difficult discussions of how to address specialized user needs.

The concept and practices of Universal Design transformed design discourses around disability and its place in economies of mass production and consumption. By linking disability with aesthetic and functional innovation, these design works provided an alternative to the political backlash against legal accommodations. For some, Universal Design suggested a powerful public role for design in adjudicating social injustices. The market successes of products like OXO Good Grips helped bolster an argument that the neglect of disabled people was not only a moral shortfall but also a missed opportunity for market competitiveness. As I argued in the previous chapter, the legal arguments around the ADA produced a contradictory message as the act framed disability rights as the right of the individual economic actor, particularly as a consumer. Similarly, disability-informed design works of the same period presented individual products with an autonomy of their own: stand-alone successes that obscured the collective and community work behind them.

Designing for People

When designers began to address a variety of body shapes, sizes, and capabilities in the 1970s, they redefined parameters for design that had been established in key moments of modern design history. Foundational figures in European and American Modernism of the early twentieth century put forward an ideal of machine efficiency that often abstracted, simplified, or simply omitted reference to the human body. In 1925 Le Corbusier wrote that human needs "are not very numerous; they are very similar for all mankind." He proposed an approach to design in terms of "type-objects," standardized objects and buildings that would respond to these uniform "type-needs" of humans. This new design, he noted, would have no room for the "sentiment-objects" of custom craftsmen: to design for "the fat man, the thin man, the short, the long, the ruddy, the lymphatic, the violent, the mild, the utopian, and the neurasthenic" would be "an impractical impossibility" in the rationalized modern world.[10]

Even for designers who might have been interested in the human experiences and categories dismissed by Le Corbusier, there were few technical guides that acknowledged a varied human body before the mid-twentieth century. Le Corbusier himself offered a new system for measurement, called Le Modulor, which he rendered as a broad-shouldered, slim-waisted man with a single arm raised, as the physiological basis for uniform—thus "harmonious"—architectural proportion.[11] This "universally applicable" figure, he claimed, could be used as a basic building block for estimating space and distance, bridging competing systems such as metric and imperial measures.[12] Other standardization systems similarly presented a single male figure as the basis for furnishings, interiors, and buildings: as Lance Hosey writes of *Graphic Standards*, the United States' primary technical architectural reference, "bodies are constructed as abstractions; idiosyncrasies are ignored in favor of generalizations."[13] *Graphic Standards* presented a simplified outline of a figure based on a statistical average of white American men as the definitive "Dimensions of the Human Figure" from the 1941 edition through the revision of 1981.[14]

A significant exception to Modernist generalizations came in the field of ergonomics, where designers attended to variations, rather than simplifications, of the body. Primary among designers who addressed a variety of body types was Henry Dreyfuss, a prolific American industrial designer of the twentieth century, who presented statistics on human bodies as a crucial tool for developing appealing and functional products, furniture, and interiors. Drawing from ergonomic methods he had observed during World War II military research, Dreyfuss asserted that designers could account for the majority of human bodies by using standard and adjustable designs. He outlined this methodology in his 1955 book *Designing for People*, in which he included a series of charts of male and female figures that he suggested could be used as the basis for more user-friendly designs. Unlike Le Corbusier's Modulor and other systems that selected a single set of measurements, the charts' figures, which Dreyfuss dubbed "Joe and Josephine," incorporated data from the 2.5 to 97.5 percentile sizes of men, women, and children. So popular were these charts that he published them in expanded form under the title *The Measure of Man* in 1960 (figure 6.1), supplying what he saw as the three most important measurements—the 2.5, 50, and 97.5 percentile, which he saw as a range that could be accommodated within a single design. A proper design, he wrote, "must strike a balance that provides all 3 with reasonable fit."[15]

By allowing for a range of body types, Dreyfuss departed from the standardized "type-needs" of orthodox Modernism. Dreyfuss also brought design attention to disabled users when he took up a prosthetic limb design contract from the National Research Council as part of the post–World War II push to provide improved limbs for disabled veterans.[16] Dreyfuss described the project in *Designing for People* among dozens of other anecdotes on designing irons, tractors, and the interiors of submarines. Like many of his other stories, this one described the time spent observing the users of these devices. Initially, he reported, his staff attempted to analyze the problem of artificial limbs by strapping them on themselves, but quickly recognized that they could not get beyond "the taken-for-granted magic of sound arms and legs." They invited a group of amputees to the office, where the staff marveled at "how they co-ordinated their muscles to operate the steel substitutes for what they call their 'meat hands.'" Dreyfuss recommended a fairly moderate intervention, altering the limbs to improve weight distribution, all to support the wearer "to further develop this remarkable ability."[17]

When Dreyfuss presented his story of designing the prosthetic limb within *Designing for People*, he seemed to use this example to establish the terrain of designing "for people." In his chapter introducing Joe and Josephine, he emphasized the importance of sensitivity to the body: an iron should be seen "as an extension or an appendage of the arm," he wrote in the paragraph preceding the prosthetic limb story.[18]

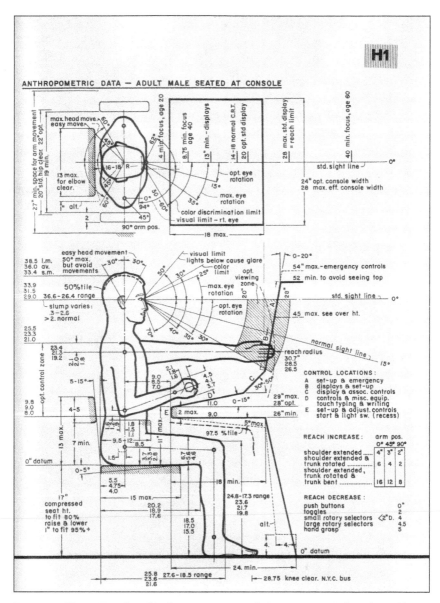

Figure 6.1. Henry Dreyfuss, "Anthropometric Data" chart, 1960. Dreyfuss charted his male character "Joe" as an outlined figure seated at a desk. Dozens of numerical annotations surrounded the figure with measurements of height, reach, visual field, and work surface. From Dreyfuss, *The Measure of Man: Human Factors in Design* (New York: Whitney Library of Design, 1960). Henry Dreyfuss Associates.

He included a photograph of the arm in his catalog of three decades of work. The stainless steel cuff and split-hook hand, shown dressed in a crisp, white man's dress shirt and holding a pen (figure 6.2), appeared, as David Serlin has written, as a "'civilized' alternative to the otherwise painful and traumatic representations of amputees and prosthesis wearers that were displayed in public."[19] Printed alongside images of clocks, thermostats, and tractors, the image presented the prosthesis as more product than body part. In this sense it is not unlike the hand charts Dreyfuss included in *The Measure of Man* (figure 6.3), where three hand outlines, lined up vertically, showed various configurations for

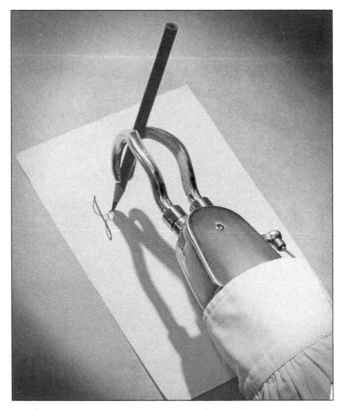

Figure 6.2. Henry Dreyfuss, "Mechanical Hand," 1948–1950, for the National Research Council. A metal split-hook prosthetic hand dressed in a man's dress shirt signs a name. Henry Dreyfuss Associates.

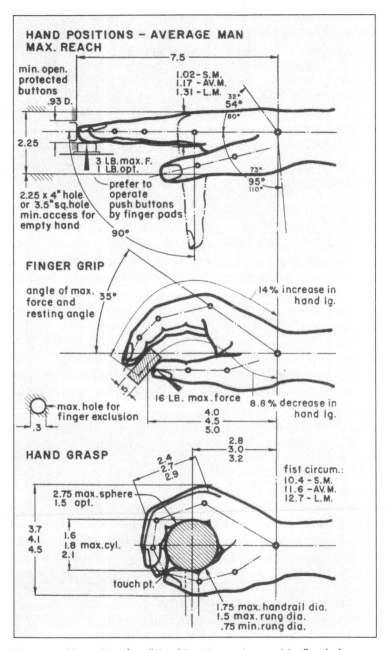

Figure 6.3. Henry Dreyfuss, "Hand Positions—Average Man," with three outlines showing hands in positions of reach, finger grasp, and a full grasp around a ball. Henry Dreyfuss Associates.

product interaction: one with fingers extended, poised to push buttons or keys; one gripping a small object like a toggle switch; and one grasping a round form to represent a handle or railing.[20] In these drawings the hand is an ergonomic problem to be considered in relation to the world of objects. Dreyfuss wrote that the task of the industrial designer was "to improve . . . a world of non-designer people, non-designer machines and non-designed things"[21]—a statement that seemed to allow for both the imperfect person and the imperfect thing. Whether the hand was "meat" or metal, Dreyfuss's primary interest was how it interacted with objects of design and how he might improve that interaction.

Even as he integrated disabled bodies into his process of "designing for people," Dreyfuss also set them apart. Amputees, with their "remarkable ability" beyond the knowledge of nondisabled designers, were not accounted for in the "Joe and Josephine" charts, nor were any other bodily variations beyond the range of 2.5 to 97.5 percentile sizes of men, women, and children. If the story of the prosthetic limb helped define the practice of "designing for people," it was the exception that proved the rule of Dreyfuss's attention to users' bodies. Other designers, too, cited disabled bodies as a sort of boundary line for user-centered design. Thomas Lamb, a handle designer, designed a crutch for disabled veterans in the post–World War II years, hoping, as so many designers did, to contribute to the war effort. Lamb, like Dreyfuss, developed a semi-statistical approach to design, measuring the hands of hundreds of friends and strangers to inform a sculpted handle (figure 6.4) that could be used by a variety of hand sizes and shapes, and by left- and right-handed people. His crutch was never produced, but the grip that he developed became a successful handle applied to luggage, hardware, and the widely sold Cutco knives—a product advertised as the "world's finest cutlery" with "the exclusive Lamb handle."[22] For these consumer-focused designers, the disabled body was an instructor as much as it was a client, providing insight into technological use and possibility that could then be transformed into market-ready products for everyone else.

Dreyfuss and Lamb integrated an awareness of disability into a modern design practice that used the human body's variation as a starting point, rather than something to be rationalized or eliminated. As disability and human variation became more visible in design practice, disabled people themselves remained in the shadows, part of a group of

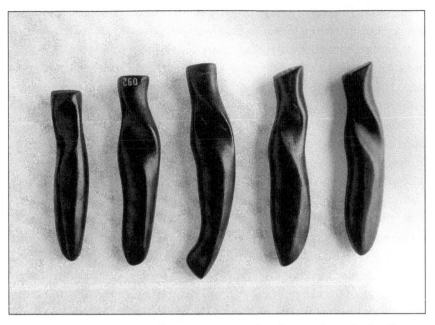

Figure 6.4. Thomas Lamb, handle prototypes. Five shapely, carved wooden handles. Hagley Museum and Library.

special users (still almost exclusively identified as veterans) for whom the government would provide design attention. In the 1970s and 1980s, a new generation of designers would follow Dreyfuss and Lamb in proposing ways of designing for people in their variation, rather than as standardized abstractions. They departed from Dreyfuss's and Lamb's models, however, when they sought to address disabled people as a part of the mass market rather than as a statistical rarity or functional curiosity.

Design Meets Disability in the 1970s

In May 1974 the magazine *Industrial Design* presented a twenty-page article titled "The Handicapped Majority." Rather than discuss design for "the handicapped" as a niche or specialized concern, the provocative title suggested the commonality of disability among the general population. Header images, borrowed from Dr. Howard Rusk's Institute for Physical Medicine and Rehabilitation, showed people with impaired hands wrestling with everyday products—a cracker box, a milk carton, a paintbrush in a blister pack. These photographs, in stark contrast to the staged product portraits featured elsewhere in a typical issue of *Industrial Design*, put the disabled subject at the center of the conversation. The article text suggested changes in designers' perspectives on the subject. As one designer noted, "a 'normal' person is liable to fall on a polished floor, slip in the bath, or trip over a threshold. . . . He has limitations of reach, and can only see over a limited distance." An awareness of disability, it seemed, suggested a change in perspective, not only on design, but on users, and even on oneself. One design student asked, "How many of us are really normal?"[23]

In the early 1970s a number of publications and projects addressed the topic of disability, broadening the otherwise specialist literature that primarily focused on "barrier-free" architecture in the vein of *ANSI 117.1* or the design of rehabilitation facilities and devices. Outside the design world, it was a time of political shifts, as the passage of the Rehabilitation Act of 1973 and its crucial civil rights language in Section 504 brought new legal power to the disability rights movement. Within the design world, publications on disability also reflected changes in the professions themselves. In response to political and social upheavals of the 1960s, many designers sought ways to define their fields beyond a purely commercial act, considering instead the social and political functions of design. The argument of "The Handicapped Majority" and other publications of this time was that disabled people represented more than a specialized market for assistive devices or a new category of legal requirements. Instead, disability promised to change the way that designers saw the world by moving the focus from a Modernist ideal of the standard body to a deeper understanding of human lived experience. The very definition of concepts like "normal" and the "majority" were under question, opening new areas of exploration for designers in a variety of fields.

Two books published in 1974 highlight the different ways that designers presented disability within changing design practices of the period. In that year, furniture designer Niels Diffrient published a revision of his mentor Henry Dreyfuss's *Measure of Man*, retitled *Humanscale,* which included a set of charts showing data on "the handicapped and elderly."[24] The book was not a reflection on principles of disability rights or inclu sion, but a statement of the many variations in the body that designers could consider in constructing functional spaces. In a very different context, Ron Mace published *An Illustrated Handbook of the Handicapped Section of the North Carolina State Building Code*, a work that interpreted the accessibility portion of the state of North Carolina's building code in architectural drawings. Mace's handbook also made a statement on how designers could respond to a new form of information—this time, the legal requirements of new accessibility codes. For Mace, the question was not so much about finding a place for disabled people in design, but asserting the need for *design*—with all its connotations of function and form—in disability accommodations. Together, these very different books capture a moment of reckoning with the disabled figure in design. Each book presents an attempt to depict, summarize, and determine the implications of the disabled user for the design of consumer products and public spaces.

Humanscale, produced under the aegis of Henry Dreyfuss's office but under Diffrient's authorship, and published two years before Dreyfuss's death, expanded upon the original work in form, breadth, and depth. In this edition, the "Joe and Josephine" data were presented on plastic boards with rotary wheels that turned to show data for Dreyfuss's percentile groups (identified as "large male," "average male," "small male," with the same for "female" and "youth" figures) in tiny windows set into the charts (figure 6.5). These interactive charts were now organized into three categories: "Sizes of People," "Seating Considerations," and "Requirements for the Handicapped and Elderly." The "Handicapped and Elderly" charts showed the familiar "Joe" figure seated in a wheelchair, standing with a cane, and in seated and standing postures with indicators of limited eyesight and reach. While the other *Humanscale* charts focused primarily on aspects of the environment directly touching the body (seating, work surfaces, controls, handles), the "Handicapped" charts set parameters for the placement of light switches, size and coloring of signage, and use of icons.

Humanscale replicates some of the contradictions of the Dreyfuss originals, which embraced a diversity of human bodies while also summarizing them through a visual presentation of a normative figure of a single, seemingly unblemished male body.[25] While Dreyfuss admitted that others mistook his figures for "average" types, Diffrient provided so

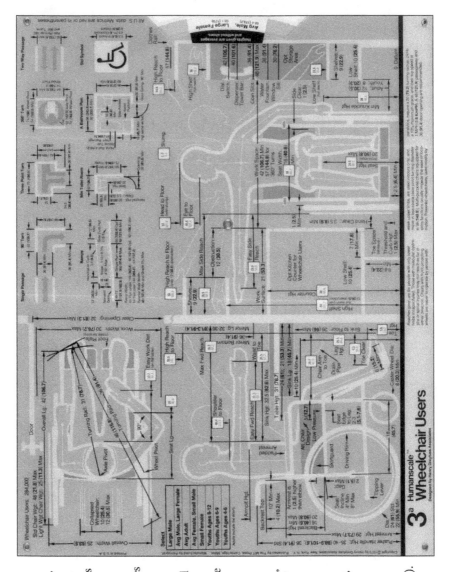

Figure 6.5. Niels Diffrient, Alvin R. Tilly, and Joan C. Bardagjy, "Wheelchair Users" chart. On a printed rectangle of plastic, three white outlines of male figures indicate measurements for bodies using wheelchairs. The figures are seen from above, front, and sides, in proximity to shelves, telephone booth, and desk surfaces. A round disk inserted into the chart (visible to the right side) allows the reader to reveal measurements for figures including "average male," "large female," and so on. From Diffrient, Tilly, and Bardagjy, *Human-scale 1/2/3: A Portfolio of Information, 1. Sizes of People, 2. Seating Considerations, 3. Requirements for the Handicapped and Elderly* (Cambridge: MIT Press, 1974). Henry Dreyfuss Associates.

much information that it is impossible to imagine a single reading of a "normal man" from these charts. In his introduction to the book, Diffrient discussed the challenges of interpreting the ever-expanding data on the human body. He noted the shortfalls of both an "average" metric (which would not work for "large and small" people) and a metric that focused on "the extremes—the *very* large and small people." He found that it was "nearly impossible to cover this range without jeopardizing the comfort, efficiency, or safety of the majority." Thus, he concluded, "it is necessary to decide on what percentage of the group should be considered."[26]

Diffrient's suggestion that the designer calculate a percentage of certain groups to be considered takes a similar logic to statements weighing the cost and inconvenience of accessible design against the perceived small population of disabled people, as in the public transportation battles of the later 1970s. However, the overall effect of *Humanscale* is one of abundance, not limitation. The translucent plastic sheets took Dreyfuss's charts, with their carefully noted numbers floating around the outlines of Joe and Josephine, to a new level of precision. The charts were now crammed with information: not just measurements of the reach of an arm, but a range of qualifiers: service counter posture, typing table posture, standing work posture; "most efficient" work area versus the larger periphery extending to the "limit of work area." The rotating wheels in the charts introduced a new aspect of interactivity, suggesting an active role for the designer in reading the relevant information for a given task, rather than Dreyfuss's idea of a single "proper design" to fit a range of human measurements.

In Diffrient's own work, this abundance of information led to the development of furniture that offered minute adjustments to fit different body types. Soon after the publication of *Humanscale*, he wrote of the ideal of chairs "bought to fit individual bodies" in the way shoes are purchased.[27] As a contractor for Knoll furniture and then as the lead designer at a company called Humanscale, Diffrient contributed to the first generation of "ergonomic chairs" with complex systems of levers and springs to allow for adjustment to fit.[28] For Diffrient, this kind of adaptability filled a missing link in a world where technological advance had as often created new problems for individual users as it had resolved them. In this world, he wrote, "rudimentary science is not in enlightened use among designers," with the result that "counters and tables, let alone shelf heights, generally prevent small people from comfortable use. . . . Controls on automobiles and appliances are in different and conflicting locations. . . . Stairs and ramps often ignore dimensions of stride, and cause accidents."[29] Much had changed since Dreyfuss's musings on the industrial design task of improving "non-designer things" and "non-designer people": Diffrient shifted the emphasis to the possibility of designing with the understanding that people's bodies were and would always be variable.

Humanscale is an artifact of a design profession increasingly aware of disability but unsure of how to integrate this information into a standard design practice. In design fields not affected by legal requirements, disability represented one way to think about how standard designs failed users. For Diffrient, adding more information was a way to guide designers away from stylistically driven work or from using their own subjective experiences as a metric. Ultimately, the charts presented disability as a component of a closely researched design practice, but Diffrient left open the question of why or how designers might produce work responsive to disabled people. With an insistence on the "science" of ergonomics, Diffrient did not engage in thinking about inclusion in terms of design ethics, but instead defined disability solely through empirical data on the built environment.

In contrast to *Humanscale*, which presented the figure of the "handicapped" through the outline of a male figure sitting in a wheelchair, reaching a shelf, or standing in a doorway, Ron Mace's *Illustrated Handbook of the Handicapped Section of the North Carolina State Building Code* supplied a more multifaceted interpretation of disability in architectural space.[30] The *Illustrated Handbook* was a state code publication, not a work where one might expect to see expressive design and layout. The code itself was typical of local standards of the time that adopted specifications from the 1961 *ANSI 117.1* guidelines (see chapter 2), but Mace's graphic interpretation put the rules into a new context. Mace, at the time a young architect and principal of his own firm, called Barrier-Free Environments, was invited to advise the North Carolina Governor's Study Committee on Architectural Barriers, and to produce this handbook as a way of improving architects' understanding of the code. As one member of the committee recalled, "After we printed the code [in 1969], the architects were grumbling about how to comply when it was so hard to figure out what all those words really meant."[31] Drawings of the features in context, Mace wrote, would allow architects, engineers, planners, and contractors to see "quickly and clearly exactly what the code requirements mean."[32]

Mace's *Illustrated Handbook* is a work both fitting to the clarity and specificity required of code writing and surprising in its subtle additions to the form. The illustrations presented written legal requirements as a starting point for a variety of design options in public architectural work. Most of the pages included, in horizontally oriented two-page layouts, a typed item from the Handicapped Section of the building code juxtaposed with an illustration or set of illustrations that interpreted the text. For example, on a page detailing specifications for parking spaces (figure 6.6), Mace drew two parking spaces viewed from above, showing the measurement for a "handicapped space" alongside a "regular" one, and explaining the rationale for the larger space: wheelchairs would not

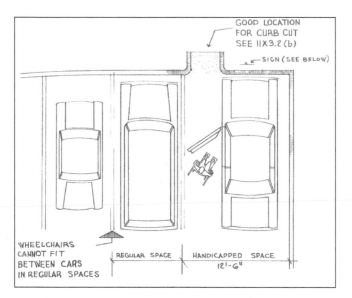

Figure 6.6. Ronald L. Mace, "Parking Lots," drawing, 1974. Line drawing showing three parking spaces with cars. Between two "regular spaces" there is a note indicating that wheelchairs cannot fit between the two parked cars. In the "handicapped space," Mace places a wheelchair next to a car's open door, showing the space needed to maneuver. Ronald L. Mace.

fit between cars in standard spaces. He also included "preferred" additions: in this case, he noted that doubling the size of designated spaces would be an improvement on the minimum requirement.[33]

Mace's drawings did a number of things for the original, un-illustrated code. First, they added visuals to the lists of measurements, angles, and requirements for markings and signs. These not only clarified the design specifications, but also offered variations, suggesting that the code could be a start, not an end, to design. With the specifications for curb cuts, for example, Mace sketched three different arrangements (figure 6.7). With a basic, broad sidewalk cut and two different examples of a "radiused cut" with raised curbs on either side, the *Illustrated Handbook* showed the variety of design arrangements that could comply with the code.[34] Second, Mace included in the drawings a crucial presence that the written codes

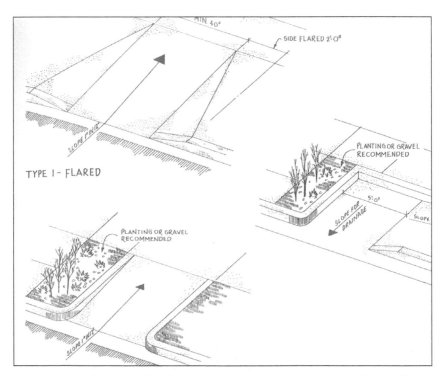

Figure 6.7. Ronald L. Mace, "Curbs," drawing, 1974. Line drawings show three different curb cuts: "flared," with a central slope and two slanted edges; "radiused" (preferred), with a defined curb next to the slope, and planting or gravel; and "parallel," with the ramp parallel to the street and planting on one side. Ronald L. Mace.

did not: people. Mace often illustrated the effect of various specifications by including the figure of a disabled person, generally a wheelchair user. These figures answered some questions about the reasoning behind the specifications—for example, showing that the requirement for space on a landing was needed so that a wheelchair user could back up when the door opened.[35] But they also redefined the subject of the code: while it was about buildings, it was also about the *use* of those buildings, and for a specific group of people. Given that architectural drawings and blueprints rarely include images of the humans who will use them, this was a departure from the otherwise technically oriented style of the manual.

The most surprising addition to the *Illustrated Handbook* was a series of abstracted, manipulated photographs that appeared in the margins or between sections and chapters. The front cover and inner-cover illustration juxtaposed two illustration styles (figures 6.8 and 6.9): the outer

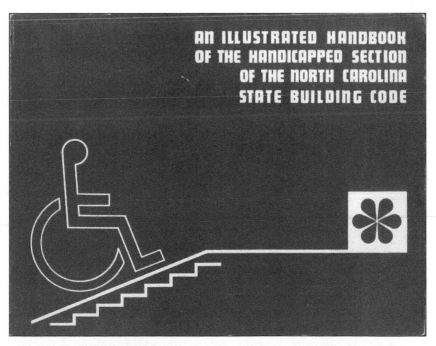

Figure 6.8. Ronald L. Mace, cover illustration of *An Illustrated Handbook of the Handicapped Section of the North Carolina State Building Code*, 1974. On a dark ground, a white outline figure of the International Symbol of Access sits on a diagonal ramp drawn on top of steps. At the top of the ramp, a flat line leads to a geometric flower or star form. Ronald L. Mace.

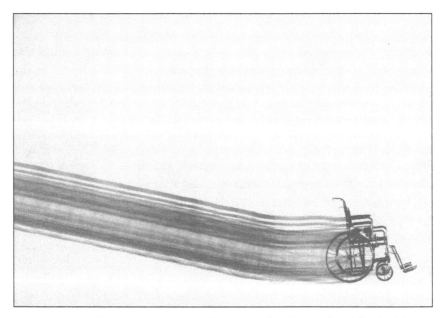

Figure 6.9. Ronald L. Mace, inner cover illustration, *An Illustrated Handbook of the Handicapped Section of the North Carolina State Building Code*, 1974. A metal 1970s-style wheelchair moves, riderless, across the page, with a photographic trail extending behind it. Ronald L. Mace.

cover presented the stick-figure-in-wheelchair of the International Symbol of Access, poised motionless on an angled surface seemingly laid over a stair, as if translating the meaning of the symbol into its most commonly affiliated architectural feature. On the reverse side of this two-dimensional layout, on the inner cover of the book, was a very different image: a parallel view of a wheelchair, this time without a person in it, zooming down a slight slope into empty space. Whereas the cover represented the wheelchair as its graphic sign, the inner illustration is a photograph of an actual wheelchair, with ghostly multiples trailing behind it in a kind of slow-motion, slow-shutter-speed trajectory.

In a number of other photographs scattered throughout the book, Mace repeated this stop-motion style, providing images of motion in contrast to the static line drawings. Opposite the illustration of curb cut variations was a close-up photograph of a wheelchair negotiating a

Figure 6.10. Ronald L. Mace, stop-motion photograph of a wheelchair riding over a curb, 1974. Ronald L. Mace.

curb, with the user's grip on the wheels framing overlapping versions of the chair as it wrenches from street to curb (figure 6.10). Elsewhere, there were similar layouts of wheelchairs rolling up ramps and being dragged up stairs, as well as of a woman walking with elbow crutches. These photographs recall stop-motion images used in industrial management, as well as photography used in medical observation of walking and other movements,[36] but here, the practice seems to be reclaimed to clarify the motions that wheelchair users performed in order to surmount existing barriers. While Mace avoided any overt political statement in the *Illustrated Handbook*, his graphic layout implied an answer to the question of why these codes were necessary in the first place. They recall the *Toomey J Gazette* and the off-road adventures of students at Berkeley as evidence that disabled people were present in public spaces, and were active in community life, despite the architectural barriers they faced. They also presented a reality that Mace himself already knew well to audiences of architects, builders, and administrators who did not.

Mace's illustrated code integrated standard drawing practices of his profession with new approaches to representing disability. It is significant for adding any images to the code, but the variety of images, including photographs of disabled people in public, made a statement about visibility. The International Symbol of Access, immediately familiar to any reader today, was relatively new in 1974. While accessible design itself was most clearly developed in the United States, the symbol was not. It was the product of a Swedish student design workshop of 1968, after which it was adopted by Rehabilitation International (where an official added a head to what was intended to be a pictogram of a wheelchair).[37] While U.S. agencies adopted the symbol for changes made to government properties to follow the 1968 Architectural Barriers Act, the push for a visible symbol for disability access was distinctly European. As Elizabeth Guffey has chronicled, American advocates of access such as Timothy Nugent of the University of Illinois did not propose clear signage, instead insisting on the integration of accessible features with as little visual distinction as possible. In contrast, the British architect Selwyn Goldsmith argued for the need to clearly mark and identify accessible features and routes, specifically repudiating what he saw as "an almost secretive, 'self-help' design culture" in the American approach to access in favor of one that frankly and visibly identified disability.[38] That Mace's efforts to make accessible design clear to architects also included a more visible disabled subject seems to indicate a similar response. It is no surprise, perhaps, that both Goldsmith and Mace were themselves wheelchair users and thus brought a perspective on disability and its frank representation free of an outsider's politeness or bias.[39]

We cannot credit any of these works of the early 1970s for single-handedly revising their professions' views of disabled people. *Industrial Design*'s "Handicapped Majority" was a major commitment from the field's primary periodical to coverage of disability; while we cannot know how many designers read it or took its lessons to heart, the magazine continued to run product reviews and methodological articles throughout the 1970s and 1980s.[40] Diffrient's edition of the Joe and Josephine charts in *Humanscale* is less known and cited than Dreyfuss's original, but a version of the "Handicapped" charts were included in the 1981 edition of *Graphic Standards,* the primary technical reference for U.S. architectural practice.[41] Mace's handbook is much less known or reproduced: today, while Diffrient's book is in nearly four hundred libraries worldwide, Mace's is in only thirty-six. Neither comes close to Dreyfuss's *Measure of Man*, with multiple editions and revisions published from 1960 to 2002. Together, though, they document the state of design knowledge and perception of disability at a moment when legal requirements for design were still fairly new and untested, only a year after the passage of Section 504 of the 1973 Rehabilitation Act and three years away from meaningful federal regulations to support it. Both suggested the new possibilities that could come from inclusion. Full information on the human body, Diffrient seemed to suggest, could lead to design that truly fits all; for Mace, the "preferred" approach reminded the reader that compliance with the law need not be the end point of designing for access.

For this new generation of designers, disability research offered new territories of exploration that allowed for both the immediacy of functionality and the horizon line of experimentation. From the mid-1970s into the 1980s, disability grew as an area for experimentation for designers, particularly in the product field where regulation did not apply. The methods designers took up to explore disability topics show the desire to understand the deeper social purposes of design beyond commerce and superficiality. At the same time, designers also aligned the task of understanding the disabled user with the market purposes of design. Commercial products introduced a new discourse that positioned market success as a possible benefit of disability research.

Disability and the Real World

While Diffrient and Mace sought to integrate new information about disability into their design fields, other designers explored disability as a part of a larger quest to transform the very profession of design. In bestselling book *Design for the Real World*, Victor Papanek excoriated his fellow industrial designers as a "dangerous breed" who engaged in designing "a whole new species of permanent garbage" in the form of "tawdry idiocies" like mink carpeting and electric hairbrushes, not to mention "criminally unsafe automobiles."[42] If design was often the culprit for the world's commercialized glut of products, it could also be the salvation, Papanek argued. He identified several "areas of attack" for more responsible design activity, emphasizing those overlooked by commercial marketing: the poor, the developing world, and "the retarded, the handicapped, the disabled, and the disadvantaged."[43] Having spent a brief time in his early career working in the world of mass-market industrial design, Papanek spoke with disdain of the job of selling more stuff. At best, it was a waste of creative energy; at worst, "murder on a mass-production basis."[44] Instead, he suggested, designers should work independently from corporations to serve a broader public.

Papanek often used disability to illustrate the ways a commercially driven design world misunderstood human populations. In his 1983 book *Design for Human Scale*, he wrote about his mother, who, at four foot eleven, found that "being so short was quite a handicap" given the difficulty of reaching sinks, shelves, and counters. He recounted telling his boss at a corporate design office about his mother's situation. The boss laughed at the problem, saying, "There are more important things for our office to worry about than helping a few little old ladies."[45] In response, Papanek performed a series of calculations of the world's population of smaller people, guessing at 100,000 "little old ladies," plus 100,000 male counterparts, then adding millions in the world affected by malnutrition, and finally wheelchair users and children. "By this time it seemed frivolous to try and compute their number," Papanek concluded. "It now remained to convince the design establishment that we were trying to help nearly three billion people rather than just a few little old ladies."[46]

Papanek's calculation of the number of people for whom standard counters, cabinets, and shelves were unreachable was not so much a literal plea for revised statistics, but a suggestion that mainstream designers held limiting views of target users as affluent, able-bodied, Western consumers. The limited assessment of the human population was an outcome of a market focus (feeding "product addiction" in Papanek's terms), rather than a dedication to design as a human service. Casting design as an anthropological activity, apart from the context of modern industrial capitalism, Papanek cut across time and space to present tableaux of functional objects, many from his personal collection, as object lessons. He presented four objects to introduce "human scale": a Japanese bamboo tea whisk, a bentwood horse-racing carriage, a Shaker meeting-house bench, and a motorized wheelchair. These objects all seemed to stand for a core function of design as relating to the body; on a page with the simple lines of the whisk, carriage, and bench, the wheelchair seemed to stand for a similar humanity, as if disability marked one of the parameters of this "human scale." As Alison Clarke has written, Papanek's references to vernacular cultural objects, many of which came from his own collection, aligned with a new interest in anthropology in the design world. Folk art and non-Western cultural objects, Clarke suggests, offered strong examples of "non-capitalistic creativity" as well as downgrading the attention to individual artist-makers.[47] In Papanek's writing and practice, disabled people, too, represented design's potential virtues. The equipment made for them held a certain mystique for Papanek akin to the animal-powered vehicle or culturally specific tea whisk.

Another industrial designer, Patricia Moore, likewise took up an adventure of observing the world of objects from the standpoint of "human scale," also resulting in a published work arguing for change in the design world's priorities. In 1978 Moore took a leave from a position in the office of Raymond Loewy, a prominent New York designer, to study and explore design apart from commercial practice.[48] Interested in the everyday design experiences of the elderly, Moore disguised herself as an older woman, with latex wrinkles, padded joints, and a cane. Attending a design conference in her disguise, she noted that friends and colleagues, unaware of her true identity, simply ignored this older person in their midst. An eighty-five-year-old woman among the young design professionals "was not the object of hostility or resistance," Moore wrote, "it was just that she didn't count."[49] Moore saw responding to the experiences and needs of older consumers as a missed opportunity for designers. A "young-is-beautiful" bias, she wrote, dominated American design. Her argument for greater attention to this population rested on both economic and moral grounds. She wrote that the culture lost a certain wisdom when it ignored older people, but also asserted a market opportunity as "the companies and merchants who catch the vision of designing specifically for older people will reap rich rewards for their efforts."[50]

Moore's experiment marked the beginning of more than thirty years of work on design related to an aging population, but in its initial form, it was as much a personal experience as a professional study. Her 1985 book *Disguised* described in detail her advance planning, the process of applying her disguise, and her worries about truly passing as an older woman. Her accounts of dressing, of traveling, of her own self-awareness in the disguise affirm more recent critical writing about "disability simulations" in which nondisabled people "try out" aspects of disabled life by using a wheelchair or wearing a blindfold. Social scientists have noted that these exercises, still common in many teaching and design environments, can produce an over-exaggerated sense of the environmental effects of impairment and the "tragedy" of disability.[51] The social isolation Moore reported, for example, was certainly a product of encountering her own social environment (a design conference) in a new guise. Her narrative highlighted the personal effects of this exercise, as she described the project as a "turning point" in her career, "a mental catalyst which triggered an entirely different way of looking at [her] work."[52]

Moore and Papanek each explored disability as a kind of object lesson for the failures of design in their time, and as a marker for what creative opportunities might emerge from a shift in focus in the design world. Both authors emphasized the shared characteristics among "disabled" or marginalized groups and the general mainstream—from Papanek, with his hypothetical recalculation of the number of people who shared something with "little old ladies," to Moore, who offered the suggestion that "by designing with the needs of older consumers in mind, we will find that the inevitable result is better products for all of us."[53] In both cases, these designers approached disabled subjects with a similar distance to Henry Dreyfuss's observations of amputee veterans. Disabled people were mysterious to these designers, similar to the historical and cultural others whose tools Papanek collected. Their written works similarly revealed a design profession eager to explore and appropriate the experience of disabled people for their own learning, but they gave no indication of an awareness of a disability rights movement or other accessible design advocacy. As a result, the lessons they drew from work on disability reflected back on themselves as nondisabled people. Their emphasis on the benefit of disability awareness "for us" countered the arguments of the period that access was too expensive to justify, but it also left unexamined the marginal status of disabled people overall.

At the time of Moore and Papanek's early writing, the term "Universal Design" was not yet in circulation, but some designers and accessibility advocates had already begun to assert the claim that designing for and with disabled people was a holistic design change, not a specialized or legal concern.[54] In the 1980s, this concept drove a new wave of product developments that drew on the kinds of disability research indicated by these early publications. Commercial designers who adopted Universal Design strategies echoed Papanek and Moore's claims that disability was an under-studied arena for design and a positive social direction for the profession, and they also incorporated (to varying degrees) personal or professional experiences with disabled people. The position of actual disabled people in relation to this work, however, was often as design influence or research subject rather than as the primary imagined user.

Commercial Universal

The forays designers made into disability research in the 1970s, whether in educational, commercial, or advocacy realms, began to materialize into product ideas by the end of the decade. Many who took up projects investigating disability questioned assumptions about the size or relevance of the disabled population to mass-market work. Instead of calling to discard the commercial values of design, as Papanek did, these designers asserted that overlooking disabled users was a missed market opportunity. One designer's research on disability in an educational setting contributed to one of the most iconic consumer products of the 1980s, the Cuisinart food processor.[55] In 1978 the American company Cuisinarts hired Marc Harrison, a professor of industrial design at the Rhode Island School of Design, to give a design update to the professional-grade food processor it had first introduced in the United States in 1973.[56] Harrison had explored disability issues in his teaching, but the company did not specifically request that these issues be included in the design of the food processor.[57] He designed an off-white block, with low, flat buttons, a columnar plastic handle, and boldface brand name; removed visible air vents; and gave the appliance a more monumental profile. Rolled out in 1978 as the DLC-7 (for its seven-cup capacity), this new Cuisinart became an icon of 1980s housewares design and a cultural reference point for gourmet chefs and cosmopolitan consumers.[58]

Harrison gave a nod to his Modernist training as an industrial designer with the plastic monolith and sans serif, block lettering of the Cuisinart, but he also drew on an awareness of disability issues.[59] The Cuisinart is an assemblage of basic three-dimensional forms, with a cylinder atop a solid block, without any added element that is not functional. As one design commentator of the 1980s described the Cuisinart, it was among a wave of American-made products that mimicked "sleek imported goods" to appeal to "status-conscious upwardly mobile" consumers with "Europeanized tastes."[60]

The same features that marked the Cuisinart as "European" and chic also reflected Harrison's research on physical impairment. Through the 1960s and 1970s, Harrison had directed student design projects including specialized furniture for a rehabilitation center and a full-scale, wheelchair-accessible model house for an industrial trade group.[61] Harrison transferred the knowledge he had gained through these student projects into his private work for Cuisinarts, shaping specific design

Figure 6.11. Cuisinarts "Fruit Dessert" advertisement, 1986, with handwritten notes by Marc Harrison noting the accessibility features of the design: "Large handle. Large paddle-like controls. (Gross motion vs. fine-finger acuity). Large white letters on dark field for maximum contrast. Lettering on controls at angle of view when using product." Marc Harrison Papers, Hagley Museum and Library.

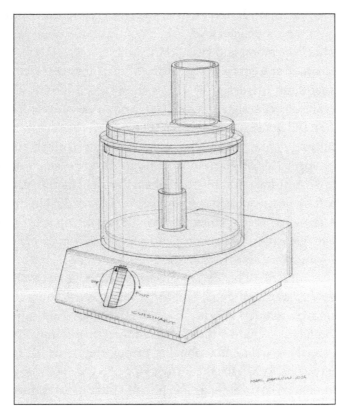

Figure 6.12. Marc Harrison, food processor drawing, 1978.
Alternate design for Cuisinart with large rotary dial as control.
Marc Harrison Papers, Hagley Museum and Library.

features to improve usability for the hand and eye. Harrison explained the disability-related features in handwritten words across the bottom of a Cuisinart advertisement (figure 6.11): "Large handle. Large paddle-like controls. (Gross motion vs. fine-finger acuity). Large white letters on dark field for maximum contrast. Lettering on controls at angle of view when using product." This was the language of rehabilitation and occupational therapy, reflecting design research on arthritis, Parkinson's, and limited vision.[62] He used a similar approach in a range of products for Cuisinarts, from a kitchen scale with large print and rubberized, solid base, to cookware with carefully beveled handles to prevent sharp contact with the hand. In preliminary sketches for the Cuisinart (figure 6.12), he had explored alternate design themes, such as a round dial control and variations on the bar-shaped lever.[63] Each of these, too, was planned for "gross motion" operation and visual clarity.

The Cuisinart presents a design story of disability research gaining greater traction in the design world of the 1970s, but with some ambivalence. The object design reflected Harrison's awareness of functional usability, but did not register as a disability-related product for the general consuming public. Although inclusive design had become something of a specialty for Harrison through his work as an educator, Cuisinarts' advertising never mentioned anything about physical impairment. The food processor was simply "the best," according to marketing messages as well as media coverage.[64] With marketing success paired to an image of cosmopolitan, European sophistication, associating the Cuisinart with injury, weakness, or disability would not seem to fit. Harrison himself described his design process as meticulous, including "a review of every part and detail and form" in terms of "human factors and ergonomic and safety considerations."[65] Consulting anthropometric research on hands including those affected by arthritis and Parkinson's, Harrison sought to define functionality through the disabled body, not the normative one. While the final marketing of the work made no reference to disability, Harrison made it explicit in interviews and reports on his design process.[66]

Tools You Can Use: OXO Good Grips and Other Handles

In the 1980s and 1990s, other designers followed similar paths to Harrison's in developing products that took manual and visual impairment as a starting point for mass-market appeal. Perhaps best-known among these products was the OXO Good Grips line (figure 6.13), developed in 1989 by a retired kitchenware designer and his wife as a more comfortable set of tools for persons with arthritis.[67] Sam Farber, retired as design director of his family's company, Copco, and his wife, Betsey, conceived of the line while vacationing in France in the late 1980s. Betsey had arthritis in her hands, and had difficulty with the old-fashioned metal kitchen tools in their rental house. Sam and Betsey together devised clay models for a larger, more forgiving handle, and when they returned to New York they worked with the up-and-coming design

Figure 6.13. Sam Farber/SmartDesign, OXO Good Grips vegetable peeler, 1989. Sharp metal blade with a wide rubber handle with small fin-like grips on either side and a large hole at the bottom. OXO International.

firm SmartDesign to develop the OXO Good Grips line of kitchen tools, with Patricia Moore as an additional consultant.[68] The oversized rubber handles with rippling "fins" at the top were applied to twelve initial products, including a vegetable peeler, can opener, pizza wheel, and citrus zester. The tools share a common physical vocabulary, with thick, bar handles, oversized curves to protect the hand from sharp blades, and a name that can be read upside-down or backwards. These features simultaneously responded to an awareness of a spectrum of physical abilities and gave the products a distinctive look that set them apart from standard, lower-priced models. While the Cuisinart's geometric, sleek lines projected an image of professionalism and sophistication, OXO's grips suggested familiarity and reliability. The design team purposefully chose a shape and texture that would resemble bicycle grips, so that users would intuitively sense their sturdiness and soft grip.[69] As Farber described them, the handles "say 'I'm special. Come feel me and you'll see how special I am.'"[70]

Although OXO Good Grips never marketed its products using specific reference to arthritis or hand pain, the brand name and image hinted at the design's origins without making the message explicit. In an early press kit for the products (figure 6.14), for example, a variety of hands demonstrated the firm, steady grip of the tools, around a bold tagline reading, "Gadgets You Can Grip Are Tools You Can Use." Hands in the images were both male and female, and suggested a range of ages; one hand sported a Band-Aid, suggesting injury. In squiggly lines running around the products, the text presented the idea of a personalized product, promising that the user could "hold the tools the way you want to hold them, not some way you're forced to hold them," and that "the grip is as unique as your fingerprints." The main text of the advertisement employed the buzzword that was increasingly familiar to designers: "a *universal design* makes Good Grips easy for everyone to hold on to and easy for everyone to use" [my emphasis].[71]

OXO used the term "universal" as a clue to knowing insiders, signaling the term's currency in the design world as a sign of innovation, without the stigma associated with disability. By this period, the design world had begun to recognize the possibility of design exploration among a minority population as a key to new approaches to mass-market design. For some manufacturers, this avenue of research became just one of many possible tools for product development. The research and design team at the American division of Fiskars scissors, for example, seeking new models in the early 1990s, developed a concept for "Golden Age" scissors, with features that aimed to relieve pressure and strain in the hand. The scissors sprang open automatically, while the handles' unconventional angle, jutting up from the blade, allowed users to rest them on the tabletop as they cut. After focus groups of various demographics responded well to the new model, the Golden Age line was renamed Softouch, emphasizing the product's benefits without making explicit reference to just one ("golden") age group.[72] In products developed for older consumers, for example, attention to manual impairment seemed, in the words of their designers, simply "common sense."[73] This lesson was presented as an optimistic outcome, in contrast to political controversies around legal mandates of the same period.

Design for All: Universal Design's Rise and Critique

By the 1990s, the term and concept of Universal Design were established enough to raise new debate around their implications. Fully

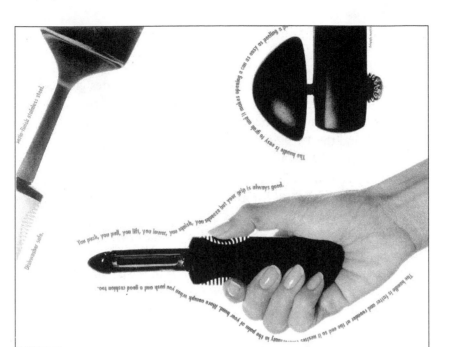

satin-finish stainless steel.

Dishwasher safe.

The handle is easy to grab and it makes opening a can as easy as peeling a p...

The handle is easy to grab and...

You push, you pull, you lift, you lower, you squish, you squash but your grip is always good.

The handle is fatter and rounder at the end so it nestles ......ctively in the palm of your hand. More ... enough when you push and a good cushion too.

Use your whole hand and cutting is a breeze. Relax your grip—they spring open for another squeeze.

GADGETS YOU CAN GRIP ARE TOOLS YOU CAN USE.

Gadgets are gadgets but Good Grips are kitchen tools. The difference is in the handle. A universal design makes Good Grips easy for everyone to hold onto and easy for everyone to use. After all, ergonomics aren't just for automobiles and office chairs.

Good Grips get the job done, whether it's peeling, coring, zesting, melon balling, cheese planing, pie serving, pizza wheeling, pot brushing, straining, grating, bottle opening, grapefruit cutting, flipping, spooning, balling, skewering, skimming, measuring, scissoring, garlic pressing, or simply opening a can.

Good Grips are everything that an everyday tool should be. They're comfortable. They're durable and functional. They're attractive and easy to use. And best of all, they're affordable. Because good quality doesn't have to be expensive.

Hold the tools the way you want to hold them, not some way you're forced to hold them.

Figure 6.14. OXO Good Grips catalog, ca. 1990. A series of fair-skinned hands grips a variety of kitchen tools: scissors, pizza cutter, and vegetable peeler. One hand holding a white-handled pizza cutter, sports a white patterned bandage. OXO International.

incorporated into the design world, Universal Design came to represent a great success for a more conscious approach to design: one that lent design interest to products and conveyed a sense of positive social ambitions. Articles in the lifestyle sections of the *Boston Globe*, the *New York Times*, and the *Washington Post*, and in design magazines including *Metropolis* and *Popular Mechanics* told the story of how designers were "taking a cue from designs for the disabled" in pursuit of "making products that are practical for all consumers."[74] These stories emphasized the benefit "for all" when research into physical disability led to visually appealing, sensuous objects. "It's a paradoxical truth that an elegant solution for a specialized user often makes an inspired product for everyone else," mused a *Boston Globe* reporter in 1993; a *New York Times* observer of a 1999 housewares trade show commented that "thick, black, easily gripped rubberized handles seemed to be on every implement, a la Oxo's Good Grip [*sic*]. What originated to help people with arthritis cope in the kitchen has gone mainstream."[75]

Coverage of Universal Design products presented disability research in terms of the added value it brought to the companies and a broader public. The media's overall conception of disability did not depart from conventional views of a specialized user apart from the mainstream marketplace. While disabled bodies taught designers how to improve products "for all," their own contribution was repositioned as need for "help" by design. As Universal Design products moved into the mainstream, disabled people made only rare appearances in images and writing about the approach. Emphasis, instead, shifted to the potential market for these goods—often encapsulated as a group who would be disabled in the future (the "baby boomer" generation as they aged) or those considered "temporarily disabled" due to injury or simply because they were carrying groceries or had slippery hands. These hypothetical populations seemed to take precedence over disabled people whose design concerns might be more difficult to see, discuss, or resolve.

Universal Design gained significant acknowledgment in the mainstream design world in 1999, when the Cooper-Hewitt, the Smithsonian's National Design Museum in New York, mounted an exhibition called *Unlimited by Design*. The exhibition indicated some of the distinct qualities of Universal Design as it took hold in the world of mainstream industrial design. Guest curators Bruce Hannah, an industrial designer, and George Covington, a writer who was blind, described Universal Design as both socially progressive and commercially viable, an "outgrowth of contemporary culture's emphasis on diversity" as well as an important move toward addressing the large "postwar baby boomer" market segment.[76] In its efforts to emphasize the relevance of "diversity" to mainstream design, the museum made few overt references to disability. The exhibition graphics (figure 6.15) incorporated whimsical line

Figure 6.15. *Unlimited by Design* graphics, 1999. Six white outline drawings on a dark ground, showing cartoonish hands, bodies, and animals. Cooper-Hewitt, National Design Museum Publications, Smithsonian Institution.

drawings that corresponded to themes in the show—"demographics," "economics," "senses," "generations," and other key terms, none of which made explicit reference to disability. The line drawings, including an oversized hat worn by several people ("demographics"), a hand with facial features ("senses"), and a chicken laying an egg ("generations"), represented human bodies and body parts without apparent disabilities. In representing the widespread applicability of "universal" concepts, the exhibition homogenized the audience for design, imagining a user group that was only slightly more diverse than the "typical" bodies imagined in standard design reference books.

One of the centerpieces of the *Unlimited by Design* exhibition was a "Universal Kitchen" designed by Marc Harrison in collaboration with his students at RISD. With products including adjustable-height countertops, lever-shaped faucets, and a layout designed for several members of a family to work at once, the Universal Kitchen employed a number of familiar approaches to designing for disabled users. The kitchen featured counter surfaces electronically controlled to adjust in height to accommodate wheelchairs or any other height requirement. Other features included multiple "stations," such as a mini-refrigerator and an island for snacking, that made certain functions readily available for any user, including children, older family members, or others performing specific tasks. The kitchen also included a number of futuristic gadgets developed in partnership with Frigidaire, such as a pasta pot that drained from the bottom (eliminating the need to tip its hot, heavy contents into the sink) and a cutting board that retracted over the sink for quick disposal of trimmings.

Text accompanying Harrison's Universal Kitchen repeated the overall exhibition's emphasis on the benefits of Universal Design "for all," with only faint reference to disability. The brochure for the Universal Kitchen featured a primary image of a family using the kitchen, with younger, older, male, and female characters cooking, eating, and preparing food. None of these figures had a visible disability, although a single, offset separate image—showing the model of a smaller, modular version of the kitchen for modest budgets—featured the figure of a wheelchair user.[77] In the brochure for the project, Harrison presented these design solutions as new benefits for a population currently using substandard design—writing that "physically able human beings are remarkable in their ability to adapt to poor design"—rather than a necessity for a population not served by mainstream design at all.[78] In this iteration of his work, Harrison represented disability research as a way of diagnosing design shortfalls to which nondisabled people had "adapted."

In contrast to the vague references of the Universal Kitchen display and poster, one reviewer brought a very specific disability viewpoint to the exhibition. "Is anyone opposed to universal design?" Robert Samuels asked rhetorically in the disability community publication *New Mobility*. The version on display at the Cooper-Hewitt disappointed him. "Much of what I saw offers elaborate and expensive solutions to problems others have already fixed more simply and cheaply," he wrote. A display of a bathroom with a perforated floor offered no improvement over his own, where a threshold-less, tiled floor sloped to a drain in the floor, leaving only one place for debris and soap scum to collect. He ridiculed many of the Universal Kitchen gadgets—such as the pasta maker that drained through its base—as "Rube Goldberg" gadgets: "unlikely, complicated and costly."[79] As an exhibition geared toward showing the commercial applicability of disability-related research, the lesson seemed to be that marketing had surpassed usability as the ultimate goal.

In recent decades, designers, consumers, and critics have echoed some of Samuels's critiques. With marketing that makes little reference to disability and media depictions that emphasize benefits "for all," designers and companies that embrace Universal Design often end up removing disabled people from view. For many in the disability community, questions of audience remained: were these truly products for "all users," including disabled people, or were they "inspired" by disability, only to serve an assumed nondisabled mainstream? Who was included in the "Universal" ideal, and who was left out?

The successes and trade-offs of Universal Design revealed new concerns about the applications and purposes of accessible design at the end of the twentieth century. While the cause of disability rights had made significant gains by establishing disability as a category of civil rights protection, legislation had limited effect on the image of disability in American culture. Universal Design signified the latest in a series of attempts to employ the tools of invention and design to reconcile the mis-fit between the disabled body and the world of mass-produced things and standardized spaces. It simultaneously opened new avenues in design for addressing disability and reflected a politics of access in which design was positioned as a scarce resource not to be over-extended to disabled people. As the final chapter shows, in the decades since the emergence of a disability rights movement and the passage of the Americans with Disabilities Act, some designers continue to explore the possibilities of design not only as a "barrier-free" move, but as a gesture of style and personality. In contrast to the minimum clearances of regulation, as well as to the seamlessness of Universal Design, a more expressive, personalized form of design makes new statements about the possibilities of design to reflect more recent politics of disability.

7

Beyond Ramps

Cripping Design

In this book, "access" has been a keyword describing the alignment of disability rights with design. From the midcentury efforts at rehabilitating veterans, to the rights movement's claim to "the right to be in the world," to the ultimate codification of access as a right of citizenship in the 1990 Americans with Disabilities Act, design became a mechanism to fulfill American values of mobility, autonomy, and economic participation. In the years following the passage of the ADA, and into the twenty-first century, the civic role of design remains a topic of ongoing redefinition in relation to disability inclusion.

The ubiquity of accessible design generated its own politics, as both proponents and resisters of disability rights used its artifacts in arguments about the rights and responsibilities of citizenship. Critics of government regulation focused on things like expensive renovations or seemingly unnecessary accessible features to lampoon a "nanny state" that was a threat to free markets and common sense. Among disability rights advocates, accessible design was a necessity but not an end point. Marta Russell wrote of a politics "beyond ramps" in a 1998 book by the same title.[1] Subtitling her book of essays "A Warning from an Uppity Crip," Russell signaled her resistance to celebratory post-ADA statements on inclusion. Ramps, for Russell, represented the 1990s "leaner, meaner" approach to rights, one that accepts physical changes such as ramps but avoids deeper, systemic change that would alter the social and economic status of not only disabled people, but poor and minority groups as a whole. The ADA was, Russell wrote, a product of "free market civil rights in a public relations era," and images of successful, taxpaying wheelchair users zipping up ramps concealed a host of issues when it came to true inclusion for disabled people.[2]

Russell's critique of ramps (or more accurately, ramps alone) speaks to the status of accessible design in the era after the political successes of the disability rights movement in the 1980s and 1990s. Even as disability groups celebrated the passage of the ADA and insisted on its enforcement, they also pointed out how much is left out when access is defined solely in terms of measurable architectural elements. From a design perspective, the kind of access that came out of the first wave of regulations was unwieldy and unsubtle. Addressing access under the law meant designing for a broad population all at once, through standards and guidelines that often led to uneven forms of access, awkwardly installed or badly maintained. Architect Ray Lifchez's critique in the 1980s of his profession's approach to access with little regard or awareness of the lives of people with disabilities still holds, as architectural training programs largely define access through regulatory codes.[3] The argument for a politics "beyond ramps" is itself a comment on the transformation of the wheelchair ramp from a virtually unknown object—something described, but not illustrated, in the 1961 *ANSI 117.1* that offered the first technical guidelines for accessible architecture—to a standard feature in the U.S. material landscape. But ramps, too, were a particular kind of architectural symbol, one that suggested smooth transitions and easy mobility. In contrast, as Aimi Hamraie has written, the processes that brought about access were characterized by friction and compromise.[4]

If ramps performed a rhetorical role in Russell's critique of a neoliberal approach to disability rights, recent works of art and design also reassess ramps as symbols of the conflicted accomplishments of disability rights. In 2002 the artist Stephen Lapthisophon presented a bright green ramp (figure 7.1), installed facing a wall, at Chicago's Gallery 400. Fellow artist Joseph Grigely described the bright green wedge as "so beautifully symmetrical, solid and minimal that it could have been made by Ellsworth Kelly," but also as a visual metaphor. For all its minimalist solidity, its run into the wall signified the "beautiful progress to nowhere" of disabled people despite the successes of the rights movement.[5]

Grigely's reference to the abstract artist Kelly gives the ramp an art historical place, but its bright color and clean-lined form also suggest the world of design. Giving the wheelchair ramp this aesthetic attention sets it apart from other ramps in look, not only in (mis)function: we come to

Figure 7.1. Stephen Lapthisophon, detail from *Within Reasonable Accommodation*, Gallery 400, Chicago, 2007. Viewed from above, a constructed ramp (green in the original installation) sits on a hardwood floor facing a white wall. Courtesy of the artist.

wonder why so few ramps have a color. This green ramp came to mind for me when I visited the Ed Roberts Campus (figure 7.2), the building opened in Berkeley in 2014 to house a number of disability-related organizations, including the Center for Independent Living and its offshoots, the World Institute on Disability, the Disability Rights Education and Defense Fund, the Center for Accessible Technology, and others. The building, hailed as a model of accessible and Universal Design, is organized around a single, large, red ramp circling the lobby and leading to the second floor. The ramp recalls both conventional public buildings with grand staircases and Frank Lloyd Wright's central ramp at the Guggenheim Museum. Its exaggerated visibility also provides a discursive space to consider the many less-visible forms of accessible design in the building, such as open spaces for circulation, audiovisual tools built into community meeting rooms, and an advanced HVAC system to reduce the building's effects on people with chemical sensitivities. The bright ramp provides a cue to visitors to pay attention to accessibility features usually not considered design highlights: oversized elevator buttons placed at floor level for foot operation, for example, or unified typefaces and sizes on signage throughout the building to avoid overstimulation or confusion.

Figure 7.2. Leddy Maytum Stacy Architects, Ed Roberts Campus, Berkeley, CA, 2014. A view from a balcony into the spacious lobby of the Ed Roberts Campus building, with white walls and ceiling and a central ramp leading to the second floor. Photo by Tim Griffith.

While the red ramp at the Ed Roberts Campus offers a more optimistic view than Lapthisophon's ramp to nowhere, both suggest a new self-consciousness in accessible design of the last several decades. This chapter surveys a spectrum of experimental, commercial, and public projects in which artists and designers offer complex and subjective interpretations of access and inclusion. These works redefine design "beyond ramps": that is, thinking not only in terms of functional access, but also in terms of concepts prized in the broader design world of beauty, style, and conceptual provocation. In a variety of arenas, from the high-design world of fashion to the mass-produced wheelchair, a new visibility characterizes this form of design in a post-ADA world. While these examples differ in a number of ways, they share an approach to disability that is direct, visible, and generative of conceptual and creative power.

Cripping Design

With the rise of disability studies as an academic field since the 1990s, and a greater recognition of disabled people in the arts and culture, representations of and responses to disability have become increasingly layered and complex. Scholars and critics have, in recent decades, identified distinct "disability cultures," given that disabled people and those whose lives are affected by disability contribute distinctive perspectives and works, whether they be literary, artistic, or simply everyday life experiences that shape communities and cultures. The idea of disability culture suggests a reversal of the medical or charitable construction of disability as a lack—or, as Petra Kuppers writes, the "radical assertion of difference as positive value versus the need to catch an accessible bus."[6] While there is a long history of disabled people who produced art and design, disability culture provides a new category of cultural works and artifacts that can be studied, collected, preserved, and valued.

For design, interest in and engagement with the particulars of disability experience and culture point to outcomes other than accessible or universal design. Disability has been a marginal concern at best through most of modern design history; at worst, designers' visions of "ideal form" have aligned with eugenic notions of streamlining human bodies to eliminate disability or difference.[7] In the late twentieth to early twenty-first century, however, disabled people moved to the center of design practice in examples we might call "crip design"—borrowing from the "crip culture" practices that arise from a self-aware disabled perspective and interrogate underlying claims of the legitimacy or "normalcy" of able-bodiedness.[8] If design itself has multiple valences, referring to the planning and organization of production as well as the products of those plans, the opportunities for "cripping" design are multiple.

To "crip" design is to challenge the premise of much of twentieth-century accessible design that framed disability as a kind of imposition or an interference in the accepted norms and standards for the built environment. Throughout decades of argument over the legal right to accommodation, advocates nearly always framed their cause in terms of minimum impact, emphasizing that improving access would involve minimal cost and disturbance to existing design plans, or that it would benefit the "general public" in addition to persons with disabilities. Even the Universal Design approach that acknowledged the commonality of disability has often been reframed as common sense or "good design" without reference to disabled people.[9] In the post-ADA world, when the primary means of enforcement for access regulations has been individual or class action lawsuit, the perception of access as excess has merged with public skepticism about personal litigation. In the broader culture of consumption and marketing, however, *design* tends to imply something greater than mere function. As John Heskett has written, design "sits uncomfortably between . . . two extremes" in contemporary culture, nothing less than "one of the basic characteristics of what it is to be human," and yet also associated with the most frivolous, prepackaged, unnecessary objects and messages.[10] In discourses around access and design, advocates are quick to trumpet associations with the former, highlighting the extent to which design can improve life or provide access. On the other hand, when it comes to the seemingly frivolous—the fashionable, the customized, the expensive or luxurious—requests for design to accommodate these concerns are more suspect.

In direct repudiation of the perception of access as an excessive demand, since the 1990s a number of designers, manufacturers, and consumers have embraced a more elaborate and expressive style in functional objects and devices that fall outside the regulatory realm. But unlike the market-oriented arguments for a "universal" design whose value is tied to its appeal to nondisabled people, "crip design" speaks plainly and directly to disabled people. Brightly colored, sporty frames of late twentieth-century wheelchairs, for example, stand out not only for their high-tech functionality but for their unquestioning embrace of the wheelchair as a part of a person's daily self-presentation—somewhere between technology and fashion. Current-day models of customized prosthetics and fashionable walkers and canes similarly stake claims to a style-conscious, individually focused form of design that goes beyond "need" to embrace desire, choice, and whimsy. The recent wave of design and art works that take a more experimental, hypothetical approach mark an even more dramatic departure from the minimums of regulation. When designers imagine "what if?" scenarios around the design of assistive technology and accommodations, they subvert (consciously or not) the premise that accessible design must not disturb the status quo. Their outcomes are artifacts not only of current disability and technology discourses, but also of the possibilities of design as a generous, attentive process available to disabled people as both makers and users.

Athletics and Style

One major contributor to a more style-conscious design in assistive technologies was the field of athletics. The history of sport as a public, and professional arena for people with disabilities runs as a thread through modern disability history. Initially introduced in rehabilitation contexts, athletic activities including wheelchair basketball, wheelchair racing, and a host of adaptive sports developed as increasingly competitive fields over the late twentieth century. The Paralympic Games grew from a local contest for World War II veterans at Stoke Mandeville Hospital in London to an international event with major media coverage and corporate sponsorship by the late twentieth century.[11] While some commentators observe that the Paralympics and other disability-specific sports competitions still take a "second-class" position compared to "regular" sports, there is no doubt that these activities created a distinctive image of physical achievement and power. In recent years, some of these athletes have become prominent public figures, challenging mainstream notions of capability, beauty, and the normative body.

Just as high-performance athletics provided a new avenue in public discussion of disability, the equipment associated with it also departed from the medicalized, institutionally oriented assistive technology that was widely available in the mid- to late twentieth century. Starting in the 1980s, several entrepreneurs developed new wheelchair designs based on a sports aesthetic, with bright colors, high-performance materials, and an overall speedy look. These specialists were descendants of the long-established tradition of technicians and inventors who developed equipment based on their own experiences of disability, from nineteenth-century amputees who became prosthetists, to Herbert Everest, whose wheelchair that could easily fold to fit in the trunk of a car became the standard modern wheel-chair design.[12] Newer designs of the late twentieth century introduced a new aesthetics and rhetoric around disability influenced by the rights movement and changes in disability culture. These were the first genera-tion of liberated wheelchairs, free to shape- and color-shift to match their users' personalities.

The most prominent developers of new, sporty-styled wheelchairs were themselves wheelchair athletes. Bob Hall, the first wheelchair racer to compete as an official entrant in the Boston Marathon in 1975, pro-duced his own chair as a reconfiguration of standard sitting posture, for better leverage when hand-propelling. The chair was low to the ground, with the rider's legs sticking out in front to reduce wind resistance.[13] The wheels and tube on Hall's self-built chair were initially repurposed bicycle parts, along with custom-fabricated elements. Hall was not the first athlete to customize a chair in this way, but he was among the first to found his own shop (New Hall's Wheels) that manufactured made-to-measure chairs, including a racing wheelchair available in customized colors.[14] He produced his Hallmark chair for everyday use, employing the same methods and materials, but in a standard model. It was lightweight, made with aircraft aluminum, with bars simplified and moved in as close as possible to the user's body.[15] Compared to the standard boxy, chrome chairs available at the time, Hall's chairs were lower in profile, with nothing rising above a low back support. Without a high back or handles for pushing from behind, the visual emphasis falls below the waist, and the chair becomes more clearly self-propelling. Whether in racing photographs or images of people using the Hallmark and other "everyday" chairs, the person appears more prominently than the chair.

Perhaps the person with the single greatest impact on wheelchair design in the last half century was Marilyn Hamilton, who, like Bob Hall, parlayed a custom chair for sports into a wheelchair enterprise. Hamilton was injured in a hang-gliding accident in 1978, and worked with hang-glider manufacturers to create a lightweight, brightly col-ored chair using bicycle and hang-glider parts. She founded a company, Quickie, to produce these chairs with options for adjustability and a full color spectrum.[16] The wheelchairs sold well, and Hamilton sold

Quickie to Sunrise Medical, staying on as a consultant as Quickie became a best-seller in a market otherwise dominated by hospital-style,
chromed chairs such as Everest & Jennings' models.[17] The bright colors
of Hamilton's chairs translated the aesthetics of sports into the consumer realm; with her signature yellow wheelchair (figure 7.3), she became a tennis champion, but her yellow wheelchair was also available
as a choice for all users.

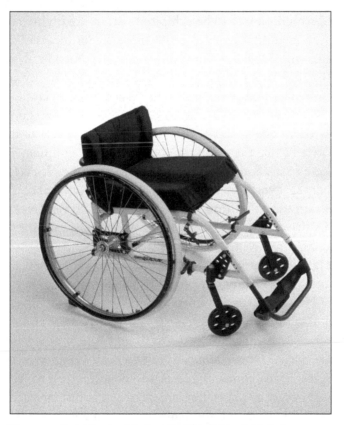

Figure 7.3. Quickie wheelchair, 1983. This lightweight chair was
developed by Marilyn Hamilton in consultation with hang-gliding
manufacturers. Its black cushioned seat barely extends above the
yellow-painted frame and wheels, giving a sleek profile with no
handles to push from behind. Division of Medicine and Science,
National Museum of American History.

The aesthetics of chairs like New Hall's Wheels and Quickie introduced a new element of style and personality into the market for wheelchairs and other assistive devices. Their stylistic innovation garnered attention not only among wheelchair buyers, but also within the design world. In 1986 the Museum of Modern Art gathered a number of sleek, sporty chairs in what seems to be the first exhibition of assistive devices in a mainstream art and design museum. Included in the show were several of Hall's chairs, along with colorful European walkers equipped with brakes and shopping baskets.[18] For equipment associated with disability to be exhibited within the premiere institution for modern design signaled a new presence for topics of disability on the high-cultural ground of fashion and art. Outside the doors of MoMA, the New York City government and many of the city's business interests were resistant to the mandates of accessibility law. Inside the museum, however, the style and elegance of these chairs and walkers suggested an engagement with the everyday aspects of disability through style. While the exhibition presented the equipment in standard museum style, on platforms and podiums, the objects evoke a new idea of the stylish, savvy disabled consumer. Several of the products shown in the exhibition also went into the consumer market at the MoMA design store, a true mark of acceptance into the realm of high design.[19]

Hall, Hamilton, and other disabled athletes challenged the paradigm of design serving or "helping" disabled people as they took up the role of creator and entrepreneur. In the 1990s, Paralympic sprinter Aimee Mullins brought new attention to issues of style and disability from a consumer perspective as she took up a role of competitive athlete, model, speaker/writer, and collaborator with designers, artists, and technologists.[20] After competing as a sprinter at Georgetown University and the 1996 Paralympics, Mullins emerged as a public figure in the late 1990s, when she presented—perhaps more than any individual figure in modern media—disability as a source for creative empowerment and opportunity. Her self-presentation was aligned with a third-wave feminist embrace of beauty culture, consumption, and self-fashioning. In a single photo spread for *Sports Illustrated for Women*, she embodied figures of athlete, model, and "everyday" woman at once: in the photo spread she appeared running (figure 7.4), her two blade-like sprinting

Figure 7.4. Lynn Johnson, photograph, 1997. Aimee Mullins in mid-hurdle, wearing black sprinting legs, white leggings, and a black Nike sportsbra. Ohio State University.

legs ("like upside down question marks") flying through the air as she approached the finish line in a race; in sweatpants bunched up above the struts and springs of her everyday-wear legs and sneakers; and in a bathing suit and low heels as she tried on rubber, life-like legs made by a custom designer in England.[21] Her multiple legs seemed to represent the multiplicity of her personae.

In public talks and collaborations with limb makers over the last two decades, Mullins has suggested the possibility of a design that seamlessly incorporates technical function with aesthetic and stylistic distinction. In a 2009 TED talk titled "My 12 Pairs of Legs," she happily flaunted the possibility of swapping out legs to be taller, or to change into shoes either fabulous, informal, or athletic.[22] Her collection of legs also spans categories of production, including the areas of high fashion and contemporary art. In 1998 Mullins appeared as part of fashion designer Alexander McQueen's *No. 13* collection runway show wearing a stitched-leather bodice and lace skirt above ash wood legs that resembled shapely, tightly fitted knee-high boots.[23] After this experience, in 2002 Mullins appeared in the artist Matthew Barney's *Cremaster Cycle* films as characters including a cheetah-woman with the lower legs of the animal, and a domineering queen-figure whose molded-resin legs were nonfunctional, terminating in a tangle of tentacle-like threads.[24] In both of these collaborations, Mullins wore legs that had little to do with walking or even standing, and instead embraced the instability and non-humanness of the prosthetic as a bodily accessory.

As she changes limbs and makers from the commercial to the avant-garde, Mullins brings together her varied public personae into a single discourse on the possibilities of disability as a generative force for design and style. In her public presentations, Mullins emphasizes the benefits of variety, not the search for a single, optimal limb. She uses her experiences as a design participant to reveal mysteries of the design and fashion worlds. She presents herself, a tall, beautiful woman on the stage of the TED tech conference, as relatable when she reveals the indulgence of being able to choose between legs that make her five feet six or five feet ten, and jokes that this choice makes her non-amputee women friends envious.[25] In an interview at the time of a retrospective on McQueen's work at the Metropolitan Museum, Mullins remembered the difficulty of the catwalk, where she had to steel herself much as she had before running a challenging race. The boots, unlike her prosthetic legs, did not bend at the ankle, and with the straight posture required for the catwalk she could not look down to see where she was walking. She reflected that this seemed fitting, as McQueen's work "has always been very sensuous, and I mean the full gamut of that. So hard and strict and unrelenting, as life can be sometimes."[26] Her comments are in line with the dark psychological themes of McQueen's work, but by relating her embodied experience of wearing the legs, she also asserts her own design perspective, and resists the possible interpretation of her appearance as another instance of design's appropriation of otherness.

Mullins's public discourse on prosthetics "crips" design at some of its most visible and provocative sites—in the worlds of models, fashion designers, superstar contemporary artists, and the recently glamorous tech innovators of TED. Her argument seems to be that disabled people, too, can and should be subjects and objects of desire. She plays the line between familiarity and distance well as she stalks the runway for McQueen but also points out the discomfort of her shoes at the *Cremaster* premiere. Vivian Sobchack notes how Mullins brings her individual legs into the category of the trope: that is, that they come to represent an idea or genre in disability presentation, but also, in their variation, suggest the role of the individual. Mullins is not a typical amputee or disabled person, but—like other fashion models—she can represent the aspirations of the everyday consumer/user.[27] Her argument in TED or other interviews is always that her "12 pairs of legs" represent an underexploited possibility in prosthetics design, that these specialized legs should be available to all wearers.

Mullins's discourse on variety and choice in prosthetics has been realized in recent design practices that produce customized limbs with greater consciousness of style.[28] Bespoke Innovations, a company founded in 2009, offered a service akin to clothes tailoring for prosthetic limbs. These limbs used new applications of 3-D scanning to fit limbs to individual bodies, and then built their limbs according to the style preferences of the individual user.[29] During its relatively brief period of activity, the company presented its products in magazine-style photo shoots that matched the limbs to clients' profiles. The athletic Chad, an athlete who appeared in the reality show *Survivor*, modeled a highly structural leg, with geodesic hexagons providing a lightweight but strong construction. By contrast, Deborah, photographed perched on an Eames side chair (figure 7.5), wore a leg "meant to be seen," a sinuous, silver-edged white leg-piece with imprinted lace patterns and a strip of tattooed leather. When the company was acquired by a 3-D printing company in 2012, the acquisition left the future of these customized

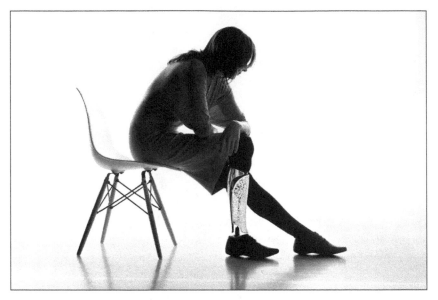

Figure 7.5. "Deborah," publicity photograph for Bespoke Innovations, 2014. A woman sits on the edge of a white fiberglass side chair. With her face obscured behind her hair, the focus is on a white prosthetic leg with a lacy perforated surface. Scott Summit.

limbs in question. The purchaser, 3D Systems, noted the potential applications of Bespoke's proprietary scanning technologies, and continued to produce experiments in prosthetic limbs for both animals and humans.[30] But these new projects appeared as one-offs, ways to publicize the technological capability of 3D Systems' advanced scanners and printers, not a client-focused business in itself.

While Aimee Mullins's "12 Pairs of Legs" and the Bespoke models respond to a contemporary sensibility of self-expression, they also recall some of the rhetoric around prosthetics and other technologies of the twentieth century. Veterans returning from World War II made the argument for not only the best prosthetic limbs, but a choice among them: in a 1948 congressional hearing, one amputee, Sergeant Lon Carberry, compared selecting a prosthetic arm to shopping for a suit, telling the House Committee on Veterans' Affairs, "I don't want to look at only one suit."[31] Half a century later, the new models of wheelchairs and prosthetics in varied colors, materials, and styles present a similar solution of choice. In both cases, the choice of prosthetic is about more than provisioning—in fact, it presents a tacit acknowledgment that a single device will not be a miraculous cure-all. Instead, these design producers and commentators unquestioningly champion variety and market choice as a means of addressing the breadth of human needs and desires.

Exploring over Solving

The will to find improvement through material change is, as some design theorists have argued, a fundamental definition of design in the modern period. Judy Attfield, for example, articulated design's particular connection to "a modern mentality that turned its back on the past and believed in the possibility of progress through change."[32] The push for improved access rests squarely within this history of design, as architects, policy makers, and activists alike argued for the benefits to disabled people of design change. Some contemporary designers, however, question this paradigm of "problem solving," emphasizing instead the possibilities for design to explore alternative outcomes, and question assumptions about products as they are or will be.

The genre dubbed "critical design"—a term coined by its most prominent practitioners, British designers Anthony Dunne and Fiona Raby—asks the question "what if?" with designed responses to future scenarios of environmental and technological change.[33] Many critical design works address the hopes and pitfalls of media and technology with a tongue-in-cheek, even sardonic perspective. One example is Dunne and Raby's "Technological Dreams" series of sleek domesticated robots, each of which requires distinctive treatment, such as a prolonged, intimate stare for retinal recognition, or the highly anxious robot prone to agitation, which might be adopted as a security device.[34] In recent years, some designers have adopted a similar speculative or critical approach to designing for disability. Their work, more earnest and optimistic than that of Dunne, Raby, and their collaborators, uses the speculative mode to consider disability outside the paradigms of existing markets or legal requirements.

The most explicit call for an approach to disability within the vein of critical design came from Graham Pullin, a British industrial designer whose 2009 book *Design Meets Disability* departed from a design literature that almost exclusively addressed disability through technical

solutions.[35] Pullin suggested that design "meet" disability as a theoreti-
cally challenging concept worth exploring beyond literal functionality.
What this meant for Pullin was questioning the underlying values of the
market for assistive technologies and accessible design. Among these is
the aversion to fashion, as Pullin noted that the creators of assistive and
accessible design often reject the trendiness and fleeting desire underlying fashion. Many products related to disability are distinctive for their
lack of distinction, such as arm or leg braces cast in bland, normatively
white "flesh" tones, or hearing aids made to be as invisible as possible.
Universal Design, too, embraced a certain kind of invisibility, with ideal
products and installations that are indistinguishable from standard
designs.

For Pullin and the few designers who explore disability in experimental, critical terms, this kind of practice departs from current expectations in consumer and assistive products and from the emphasis on
single, "revolutionary" solutions. Even for those products that do veer
from the blandly quiet designs of many medical technologies, Pullin
observed, one style tends to sweep in and dominate an entire category,
such that the athletic-style wheelchair "replaced one stereotype . . . with
another—a frail older woman for an athletic younger man."[36] In 2001
Pullin organized an exhibition of design projects that probed the issue
of style and "types" of users, focusing on the hearing aid. All efforts to
redesign the hearing aid have, he noted, pushed toward the invisible—
even at the cost of the ability to pick up ambient sound. The new design
collection, exhibited in partnership with the British Royal National Institute of Deaf People, was dubbed "HearWear": hearing devices fashioned for style, akin to "eyewear" as a fashion-conscious segment of the
eyeglasses market. The pieces in the collection, including a pop-art set
of protective headphones available in a variety of graphic patterns and
a snake-like silver and gold hearing aid designed by a jeweler, not only
explored stylistic departures but also considered a spectrum of possible
auditory needs other than amplification.[37] The prototypes imagine disabled people primarily through the lens of personal style, rather than
proposing the "hearing aid of the future" or any single solution for all
users. In the case of the headphones, we can imagine a context—such
as the loud music event—where one might select a visible, fashionable
form of ear protection, a statement of stylistic affinity that also broad-

casts one's preparedness for the intense sensory experience. The options may prize style over function, even: the jeweled option's necklace-like form would likely capture ambient sound with less attention to individual conversations—perhaps an apt approach to certain formal-dress social events.

Many of the projects Pullin discussed took the visibility of disability as a creative starting point rather than a problem. He recruited the Japanese designer Tomoko Azumi, whose work shows a honed attention to surface and proportion in furniture, to address the portable step as a common tool used by those with short stature, such as people with dwarfism. In keeping with Pullin's goal to create "conversations" around these projects, Azumi did not produce a specific step stool but instead offered a series of sketches proposing the kind of design that might best provide on-the-spot access. From her own commercial work, in which she has designed multi-purpose sets of furniture, Azumi borrows what she calls the "enjoyment of transformation."[38] For Pullin's hypothetical project, she imagined an object that might facilitate "a cough and a lift"—a discreet means of getting attention, then the means for a physical boost. The act of unfolding an intriguing, beautiful folding step, Azumi imagined, might allow the user to make their presence clear in a "pleasant, elegant" way, rather than an obtrusive one. If the unfolding is the "cough" that alerts people to one's presence, the beauty and interest of the object provide a "lift"—both emotional and physical.[39] Azumi's proposal remained hypothetical: the outcome was not an object, but a kind of design journal that suggested the possibilities that might occur if more designers had the opportunity to "meet" disability.

In other recent works, designers and artists have adopted similarly critical and exploratory approaches to the public forms of accessible design. Sara Hendren, a Boston-based designer and professor, defines her work in terms of design, research, and writing. Hendren shares Pullin's interest in experimental practice, framing her work in terms of the "artist as amateur," or a beginner, a non-expert unafraid to ask questions or propose impossible actions.[40] Like Pullin, Hendren is acutely aware of the limitations of many conversations around disability and design. In response, she borrows from the visual languages of art, high design, and forms of guerilla or protest culture to explore alternatives. Her work ranges from the hypothetical to the individual, the pedagogical, and the public, encompassing and self-consciously commenting on previous iterations of accessible design.

In 2009 Hendren embarked on an experimental project that led her to greater engagement in the mainstream of public design. In collaboration with Brian Glenney, Hendren developed an "edit" for the International Symbol of Access (ISA), the familiar stick figure in a wheelchair first developed after a design competition in 1968.[41] Looking at other stock figures on signage, Hendren noted that other figures are often engaging more "energetically" with their environment—walking, reaching, running, pushing, and so forth. Comparatively, it seemed that in the ISA "the posture of the figure is unnaturally erect in the chair. . . . There's something very mechanical about that."[42] The new icon instead depicted the figure "leaning forward in the chair," giving "a clear sense of movement, self-navigation through the world."[43] Hendren and Glenney developed a transparent sticker with the new icon that could be applied to existing signs (figure 7.6), so that both icons could be seen at once.

Figure 7.6. Photograph, 2014. A "Reserved Parking" sign for disabled drivers. An orange figure of a wheelchair user leaning forward is placed over the standard blue square with white wheelchair user. Courtesy of Sara Hendren. Photo by Brian Funck.

Hendren described the project as a part of her larger thinking about an "edited city," a space of intervention by both designers and amateurs. The transparency of the sticker—allowing the original icon to show through—would ideally "draw attention to the old image (since it's one of those that's at once familiar and utterly forgettable)—and to suggest its becoming something else."[44]

After stories in the *Boston Globe* and a number of blogs and newspapers, the new icon began to take on a life of its own. Hendren and Glenney developed a version that would align with existing standard icons and could be easily stenciled on signs and pavement (figure 7.7). With local activists promoting the icon, several towns, colleges, and companies adopted it for official use. In June 2013, New York City announced that it would use the icon in all new accessibility signage in the five boroughs, with a specially adapted version for accessible taxis showing the active wheelchair-riding figure with an arm extended to hail a cab.[45] With more press coverage, the icon also received some negative feedback. Some commentators questioned the new, "leaning in" symbols,

Figure 7.7. A black line figure of a wheelchair user leaning forward, as if in motion, against a white field. The wheel appears as two juxtaposed curves with a break in the middle to allow for easy conversion to a stencil. Accessible Icon Project.

pointing out that many wheelchair users do not propel themselves with arms raised for momentum, not to mention the larger issue of representing the category of disability through the wheelchair alone. Some of these comments expressed suspicion of the sporty look of the icon: "Why does everyone have to be in such a hurry?" noted one Internet commenter, while another called the symbol an example of a "'mountain dew' aesthetic."[46]

The Accessible Icon Project—from its origins as a deliberate "editing" of urban signage to its official adoption in municipalities and companies—is a critical design project that crossed over into the "real" or non-speculative world, and with that shift came new realities. The criticisms of the project as well as its very adoption as an official symbol seem to give Hendren pause. In early 2014 she reflected on the successes of the project as a "re-branding" effort in the vein of commercial logos. The best results of the project, she insisted, could not be measured in numbers of press stories or official adoptions, but instead the "publicness and action around changing signage"—including the objections to it—that maintain the "restless and unfinished conversation I consider to be the living pulse and grounding of the work."[47] Hendren echoed the credos of critical design in insisting against the project as a finalized work or a commercial product. Her position, however, suggested more than a conceptually driven designer's resistance to commercialization; instead, Hendren articulated a position for critical design specific to disability topics, and perhaps other fields of socially oriented design. "Re-branding," she wrote, suggested a marketing approach, and with it, a "smoothness," or an easy resolve around complicated issues. When it came to rights concerns, Hendren wrote, this "smoothness" did not suffice: instead, she embraced "the hard stuff, friction, a willingness to embody and suspend *un-resolve*."

The ambiguity and "friction" in the projects Sara Hendren and Graham Pullin proposed in the early twenty-first century are familiar qualities of the world of art making, as opposed to the problem-solving focus of design. Indeed, some of these tactics of exploration and recategorizing also drive the work of contemporary artist Park McArthur. McArthur, an artist who uses a wheelchair, creates installations and performances that respond to the lived experience of disability using the material and conceptual language of post-minimalist art. In a 2014 installation at

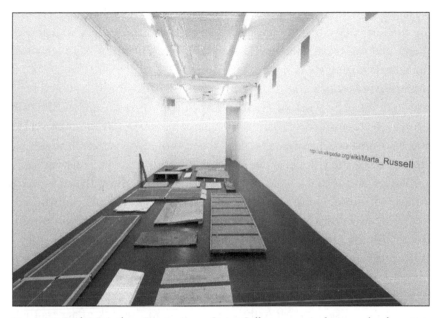

Figure 7.8. Park McArthur, *Ramps*, Essex Street Gallery, 2014. A photograph taken at the entrance of an art gallery featuring portable wheelchair ramps placed in an uneven grid on the floor. The ramps are different sizes, colors, and materials. On the gallery's right side is an unencumbered pathway to the back of the room, with black vinyl lettering reading "https://en.wikipedia.org/wiki/Marta_Russell" adhered to the gallery's right wall. Above the vinyl letters hang five blank, blue handicap parking signs with white borders and no symbols or text. Image description by the artist.

the Essex Street Gallery in Manhattan, McArthur assembled an array of ramps from institutions around New York (figure 7.8).[48] Ranging from the improvised (a worn fragment of plywood, no more than two feet long) to the official (sleek, rubberized folding ramps with yellow traffic stripes), the ramps came together in a kind of archive or collection: assembled together, they call attention to their distinctions and oddities, rather than their similarities from a legal standpoint. Many of the ramps, the gallery reported, had been expressly made or ordered in response to McArthur's own requests for accommodation, a point that calls even more attention to their distinctiveness as a personal archive of accessibility in the New York art world.[49] The installation suggested some of the trade-offs of both accessible design and art making, as the ramps were removed from their institutions for the exhibition, and replaced with signs indicating that there was no wheelchair access during that time. Five blank, blue signs hung high on the gallery wall above them, making clear reference to standard "handicapped" signage with the wheelchair figure removed.

Park McArthur's *Ramps*, Hendren's icon, and Pullin's staged encounters, like the work of Stephen Lapthisophon a decade earlier, all addressed the unresolved nature of accessible design in the post-ADA era. Each project involved specific, material objects, yet also called the viewer to consider the broader issues of disability, social construction, aesthetics, and legality. In McArthur's installation, above the mosaic of ramps, an Internet address was printed on the gallery wall, pointing to the Wikipedia entry for Marta Russell, the author of *Beyond Ramps*—an entry that McArthur herself originated on the crowd-sourced site.[50] With this reference, McArthur hinted at a firmer political stance than the otherwise unlabeled ramps might suggest. *Beyond Ramps* critiqued the culture that created ramps in a search for singular resolutions to the "problem" of disability. McArthur's ramps—and the lack of access that they left behind when she assembled them at Essex Street—pointed beyond themselves to larger issues of incomplete access and unresolved design standards.

As a contemporary artwork and a temporary installation, McArthur's *Ramps* is distinct from the market-oriented products and critical works I have called crip design. Nonetheless, it featured a disabled person as a producer of culture, whether through conventional materials of art making or through processes like the request for a ramp. In another work, McArthur left the heaters she required to be comfortable in the Chisenhale Gallery in London during installation onsite for her exhibition *Poly*.[51] The heaters, which created a noticeable spike in temperature for viewers, were another of McArthur's gestures of using the accidental or improvised aspects of her own access as a central element of the work. The project also captured the simultaneous, often conflicting impulses of critique and optimism that exist in so many moments in the history of accessible design and seem to come to play in crip design. This work, along with other speculative efforts in recent design, centered on both the inadequacies of public accommodations and the possibilities for more ambitious approaches.

What Design Knows

This assemblage of disparate works I have called crip design indicates some of the ways disabled people came to the center of design practices in the later twentieth and early twenty-first centuries. When disabled people became producers, such as Bob Hall and Marilyn Hamilton, or models and commentators, such as Aimee Mullins, or when designers and artists explored disability experience without the aim of "solving" a problem, they called into question the assumption that design is a seat of expertise—particularly, of rational or neutral expertise. The practices of design under Modernism, in particular, exerted the authority of knowledge through planning, statistical analysis, and standardization. In a postmodern era, knowledge and power become more diffuse.

These projects deployed disability as a form of knowledge in itself that might supplant or at least reorient existing standards of value. Disability studies scholars have offered the concept of "cripistemology" (combining the reclaimed "crip" with "epistemology") to describe disability as a way of knowing the world.[52] This knowing operates in contrast to the forms of knowledge imposed onto disabled people through medicine, social services, and marketing campaigns.[53] Cripistemology informs disability culture work, which revises existing representations of disability to "stare back" at visual conventions such as medical photography, freak shows, and the charitable telethon.[54] A design version of "cripistemology" might include the vernacular access work of *Toomey J Gazette* readers and Berkeley disability rights activists: work made by disabled people and for disability communities in resistance to the lack of disability knowledge in mainstream and public versions of design. But does it apply to the recent, style-conscious crip designs covered in this chapter?

I suggest the possible application of the concept "cripistemology" with hesitation. Design—whether we consider it an act of shaping form or a category of stylish things—is never far from the powers of capitalism or the hegemonies of mass culture. To suggest that design can capture the queer, post-structuralist notions of crip culture is to imagine a version of design apart from or at least self-conscious about

the marketing functions of design more broadly. Scholars who artic-
ulate cripistemology or other notions of crip knowledge that "exceed
and make detours around capital," as Jack Halberstam suggested in
a 2013 roundtable, do not account for the figure of the disabled producer within commercial culture. The moves to design with and from
knowledge of disability frequently indulge in the excess and luxury of
design—of being designed for, of having choices that fit, of having the
cultural power of the fashion model or the economic power of the entrepreneur. At a 2011 session at the Society for Disability Studies, Sumi
Colligan raised the question of "Crip Fashion Justice," suggesting both
the liberating aspects of having the right clothes, even flaunting them,
and the vexed nature of any participation in the global systems of fashion production that exploit workers as well as consumers in the production of desire.[55] In these projects of crip fashion, crip knowledge
necessarily merges with other forms of design knowledge, including
knowledge of marketing and signification that may reify the powers of
capital as much as they exceed or evade them.

The more visible, varied design that emerged in the last decades of
the twentieth century, and continues in new creative and critical areas,
questioned the premises of accessible design as it had been established
in the twentieth century. To the extent that these works subverted accepted standards of beauty or discretion, and posed questions instead
of providing answers, they departed from precedents of government-
sponsored or mass-market designs. They engaged with the underlying issues of rights as crystallized in design and design experience: the
question of whether civil rights includes the right to desire, to luxury,
or to variation makes these more than just superficial frivolities of design. In Colligan's question about the possibilities of a Crip Fashion Justice, she links the disability rights concerns of inclusion and access with
contemporary awareness of fashion's social costs. Her formulation suggests that as disability takes a more prominent place in design culture,
it produces new awareness of the implications of design's effects—be
they visible or invisible, knowable or unknown. If, as I have argued
throughout this book, accessible design introduced new roles for design in the shaping of society, more recent developments in crip design
extended these roles again to include critical lenses on disability and
design themselves.

Conclusion

Design for All?

Recent experimental art and design work on ramps, prosthetics, and other disability technologies seem to come from a world far from twentieth century scenes of veterans testing prosthetic limbs, polio survivors typing at home, or activists who designed curb cuts and occupied the Department of Health, Education, and Welfare building in San Francisco. Compared to the subtle commentary on how a ramp works in space or what promises might come from treating a hearing aid as a fashion statement, early work to introduce access into existing environments seemed to be more about establishing the category than defining it. Much of this early work was a response to a lack—no ramp for a wheelchair, no cut in a curb, no kneeling buses. In the crowded material landscape of the mid-twentieth century, accessible design was a novel category, whether introducing features that had never been seen or adding new requirements and meanings for basic architectural forms.

As this history shows, however, from the start, those who designed and used accessible products and buildings discussed them in terms of varying qualities of design, and what those qualities meant. Disabled veterans of World War II rallied around the poorly performing limbs they first received in military hospitals; when they found the sympathetic audience of congressional veterans' supporters, they detailed the problems of limbs cutting their clothes or fitting uncomfortably. Their testimonies about personal choice in prosthetics helped them lobby for more support, leading to the cars and houses that became part of veterans' benefits. The administrators of rehabilitation programs, too, became design commentators as they prepared people to enter an inaccessible world. For Timothy Nugent, who translated work making the campus of the University of Illinois accessible into the first national standard on access, the firm message that his students would have to succeed in an inhospitable environment influenced a form of access that took built-in barriers for granted. The priorities set by Nugent and others for acceptability and inconspicuousness would characterize government-mandated design throughout the twentieth century.

Disabled people's own interventions into everyday designs presented a parallel and sometimes divergent story line for access alongside the history of government mandates. In the relatively isolated contexts of home life in inaccessible places, with difficult-to-use appliances and housewares, people documented creative practices of adapting, repairing, or inventing technologies of access. These design projects were forerunners of the more consciously political moves of disabled activists in the 1960s and 70s, many of whom also came from the same generation who had been "rehabilitated" in polio hospitals and other medical institutions. In Berkeley, the notion of self-advocacy informed a distinctive style of access that prized independence as a personal pursuit, not one defined by outside authorities. Here, "access" rarely stood alone from a broader project of advocacy, but instead was a process of involving disabled people in aspects of planning, building, and policy making.

The accessible features that increasingly appeared in public in the United States were forms of design without designers, constructed with little input from the design professions: whether codified by program administrators like Timothy Nugent or designed through family and community work, the earliest ramps, curb cuts, and parking spaces were additions to already-designed environments, rarely meant to occupy attention as works of design or architecture in themselves. When these features did capture public attention in the form of controversy over federal mandates, detractors identified what they saw as awkward form and government overstep. In the public transportation debates of the 1980s, opponents of federal mandates used design as an argument against access. The principle of aiding this "special" population, opponents suggested, could not outweigh the cost and inconvenience that subway and bus alterations would incur to the general public. This argument was a design statement in itself, as they identified the "public" for public transit in exclusion of disabled people. Even as mandates were expanded under the Americans with Disabilities Act, many advocates depicted a sympathetic individual consumer or taxpayer rather than a collective mass requiring public resources.

If design was a scarce resource for critics of accessibility regulations, it also appeared as a salve against political turmoil at the end of the twentieth century. Proponents of Universal Design presented a more optimistic and generous vision of design that could not only improve function, but also transform the image and meaning of disability. Ron Mace, who disseminated the term during a career spent writing federal accessibility regulations, considered it not as an alternative to accessible design, but an explanation that removing barriers could have a host of possible benefits. Shapely consumer products and fashionable assistive devices revamped the image of disability to bring it into a vision of an attractive *and* equitable "good design." Engagement with the consumer marketplace brought its own treacherous terrain, but these developments reoriented debates over the validity of disabled people's claim to design inclusion.

* * *

In the fall of 2016, just months before the end of President Obama's last term in office, the White House held a Design for All Showcase, a fashion show and panel discussion highlighting "inclusive design, assistive technology, and prosthetics." Organized by Maria Town of the White House's Office of Public Engagement, with the Office of Science and Technology, the show featured clothing and personal devices on the market or in development, modeled by disabled people.[1] The show included jeans designed for seated wheelchair users, with added stretch and side closures; prosthetic arms and legs of a variety of vivid designs; and elegant braces sculpted for the body by 3-D printer. Some products suggested widespread possible use, such as shirts with magnet closures to avoid the use of buttons, while others responded to a more specific need, such as a line of T-shirts designed with fused seams and ultra-strong fabric that had been co-designed by MIT researchers with a young autistic woman who picks and frays her clothing apart. There was no single strategy of "universal" or mass-market appeal at the showcase, although this value was certainly on display with products such as an alternative system for lacing shoes from Nike, developed by an intern with cerebral palsy. As the celebrity guest announcer described each product, certain familiar

tropes recalled the history of accessible design: the notion that a prosthetic leg allowed a veteran to "pursue his dreams," or that clothing with
easy closures created "independence" for its wearers. The language of
rehabilitation was less present than the language of consumption, from
the fashion show format to personal statements by individual users
dressed up and performing for the spotlight.

Instead of a unifying aesthetic or design strategy, the organizing
theme of the Design for All Showcase was the experience of disabled
users. As each model spoke into the microphone, they tended to define the role of design in relation to a sense of identity. Blogger Annette
Lamont started the show, rolling up in her wheelchair wearing ABL
Denim adaptive jeans and stating that "fashion is my passion, and inclusive designs . . . provide ease of comfort without compromising my
style." Others spoke from the perspective of makers as well as users: a
goth-styled figure named Peregrine said of his 3-D printed, open-source
arm from Enabling the Future, "I wear this design because I designed
it, I made it, and it's me." For others these design moves were part of
professional identities. Sarah Fernandez, a lawyer modeling a leopard-
print wrap dress from Kathy D. Woods's collection of fashions for people with dwarfism, said the garment gave her "the extra oomph to let
people know I mean business." Whether the clothes and devices were
understated or elaborate in style, they presented design as a catalyst for
new ways of thinking about disability. Kyle Garcia, an ex-Marine on his
way to becoming a lawyer, said that his custom-designed leg cover in a
matte black with orange details "shifts the conversation from disability
to design."

In this showcase, this shift "from disability to design" never departed
from a focus on disability as a presence and design impetus. The show
firmly positioned disability as a source for innovation. The venue of
the White House also suggested that this form of inclusion was a part
of civic identity and national industry. The Obama White House had
made a particular point of showcasing disability in its public pro-
gramming. In 2015 the president marked the twenty-fifth anniversary
of the Americans with Disabilities Act with a meet-and-greet that included signed, typed, and video conversations, while the following year
the White House's South by South Lawn technology festival featured
an exhibit of Sara Hendren's work on critical design around disability

technology.² Nowhere in the fashion show or the South by South Lawn festival did the White House identify disability-related technologies as a product of legal requirements. These projects were not "boldly going where everyone else already goes," as the ADAPT bumper sticker suggested in 1990. Instead, this was accessible design presented as a part of the technological future.

The Design for All Showcase exhibited a hopeful techno-futurism that at once recalls post–World War II prosthetics trials and also speaks to a current-day investment in design as part of the tech industry. What is striking here is that disability is positioned as an aid to design and a research area that leads designers to new technological discoveries. In her work on access, Tanya Titchkosky asks us to reconsider the common understanding of access as a form of asking—a "space of questions surrounding who belongs where, under what auspices or qualifications."³ Instead, she asks us to consider disability itself as a form of access, "a concept that gives us access" to people, to experiences, and to relations among people. In the case of the Design for All Showcase, disability applications gave access to a positive future vision of technology supporting the body in all its differences.

Titchkosky defines access in terms of relations between bodies—human and human, human and institutional, human and architectural—in a way that goes beyond the purview of the single object or building. My own definition is rooted in the artifacts of material change in the historical period of the mid- to late twentieth century, when people developed specific physical forms in response to the rise of rehabilitation, redefinitions of rights, and the late twentieth-century backlash against social entitlements. As this book goes to press, the disability rights movement has returned to the national spotlight as activist groups, especially ADAPT, agitate to oppose changes to Medicaid and the proposed repeal of the Affordable Care Act under President Trump. On one hand, these arguments reveal historical changes, as an organization once called "American Disabled for Accessible Public Transit" now uses the simplified moniker ADAPT to address a range of political issues of exclusion. Still, the U.S. health care debates reveal deep and unresolved issues of the last half century around disability rights. Namely, the notion of access in terms of physical change in isolation has proved an impossible design scenario. Concrete cracks, elevators break, and, as Berkeley activists showed in the 1970s, initial design installations may need revision. Likewise, physical change without support in policy enforcement—as with the non-enforcement of Section 504 of the 1973 Rehabilitation Act after its initial passage—or broader social supports such as attendant care will amount to a design shortfall. Discussions about health care in U.S. society often center on questions of individual cost weighed against the overall social benefit; as in the public transportation conflicts that ADAPT first organized to protest, truly inclusive policy requires an acknowledgment that disability is an expected part of human life, not a tragedy or "special" consideration. Designing an accessible America—still a vision left unfulfilled—requires embedding design in systems that can support rights and equality in ways that go beyond the material.

ACKNOWLEDGMENTS

I could not have written this book without the help of numerous advisers, funders, and friends. I began studying this topic in the University of Delaware's history department, where I found my footing among fellow explorers of American material culture and the history of technology. My adviser Arwen Mohun encouraged my questions about the grand plans of designers, as well as the less visible actions of users and caregivers. Her attention, in her own work and in comments on mine, to questions of agency and motivation proved essential. Faculty including Katherine Grier and Susan Strasser allowed me to link my earlier training in design history to a rigorous tradition of interrogating historical objects and sources. Before arriving in Delaware I was fortunate to study with David Brody, whose guidance and honesty have carried me through a number of professional moves.

As my research developed, I received institutional support to travel to collections and dedicate time to writing and research. Support included fellowships from the University of Delaware, the Lemelson Center for the Study of the History of Innovation at the Smithsonian's National Museum of American History, the Baird Society at the Smithsonian Libraries, and the University of Southern California Library's Wallis-Annenberg Fellowship. The Hagley Museum and Library's Du Pont Dissertation Fellowship allowed me to explore its collections in the history of industrial design with the support of Lynn Catanese and her staff at the Soda House. In my final year of graduate school, the Mellon-ACLS Dissertation Completion Fellowship allowed me to work full-time on my research, while the Chemical Heritage Foundation's Beckman Center in Philadelphia offered me office space and membership in its community of fellows.

With no formal training in disability history or disability studies, I found friends and colleagues in this remarkably open and generous field. Sarah Rose first introduced me to many of the historians whose work would prove significant to mine; Susan Burch, Cathy Kudlick, David

Serlin, Beth Linker, Susan Schweik, Mara Mills, and Rosemarie Garland Thomson were among those who welcomed me to the conversation at conferences, in journals and publications, and in their classrooms. Katherine Ott, whose work as curator at the National Museum of American History has fueled a cohort of material culture and disability scholars, shared her files with me and pointed me in new directions at several key points. Emily Smith Beitiks, Aimi Hamraie, Wanda Liebermann, and Elizabeth Guffey, scholars who roam similar scholarly terrain, have proved vital colleagues and collaborators. Finally, in completing this work, I pay tribute to Paul K. Longmore, a foundational figure for the field of disability history, who advised the early stages of this project. Paul's essays in *Why I Burned My Book* changed the way I think about welfare, academia, and historical work, and his own personal stories, narrated during walks and chats around the southern end of San Francisco helped me connect my archival research to the lives of disabled activists and scholars.

During graduate school and in my recent life as a professor, I relied on the encouragement and accountability of writing friends and colleagues. Janneken Smucker, Jennifer Fang, and Jen Moses read conference papers, chapters, and drafts of the book; Hillary Mohaupt, Alice Marwick, Stephanie Tuerk, David Brody, Aimi Hamraie, and Emily Smith Beitiks answered last-minute calls for help in the final stages. In Chicago, my writing partners Debra Riley Parr and Annika Marie supplied deadlines, marginalia, cocktails, and critical perspectives on writing and academia. Liz Jackson was first a Twitter friend and now a friend whose insights on "designing with" disability fueled the completion of this book. My colleagues at the School of the Art Institute of Chicago have provided impressive models of intellectual adventure and productive writing. I am especially thankful to Michael Golec for his mentorship as a fellow design historian at the school.

Finally, I dedicate this work to my grandmother Phil Asher Gates, with whom I shared a love of art, fashion, and writing, and whose insistence on living a free life with an unruly body shaped her and her descendants' lives. Thanks also to my mother, Kathe Gates Williamson, who proofread several drafts and called to check on my book-writing progress even when I was reluctant to discuss it. Last but not least, thank you, Wayne, for believing in this work and also for caring about things other than it. Our lives with Nate and Frank go beyond any map I ever charted alone.

NOTES

INTRODUCTION

1 Architecture built with the wheelchair in mind dates to the earlier twentieth century, but was concentrated in medical facilities and segregated schools for disabled children and adults. Franklin Delano Roosevelt's polio rehabilitation center was one site of significant pre–World War II access, where architect Henry J. Toombs designed ramps and accessible spaces and shared these plans with patients to use at home. Rogers, "Race and the Politics of Polio"; Henry J. Toombs, "Architectural Suggestions—Ramps and Steps," *Polio Chronicle*, August 1931, Disability History Museum, disabilitymuseum.org.

2 United Nations Convention on the Rights of Persons with Disabilities.

3 Stiker, *A History of Disability*, 121–36.

4 Winner, *The Whale and the Reactor*, 19–39.

5 Ibid., 22–24.

6 tenBroek, "The Right to Live in the World."

7 Scott, *Seeing Like a State*.

8 The story of the individual household as the dominant site for feminized technological consumerism is told in Dolores Hayden, *The Grand Domestic Revolution: A History of Feminist Designs for American Homes, Neighborhoods, and Cities* (Cambridge: MIT Press, 1981); Susan Strasser, *Never Done: A History of American Housework* (New York: Pantheon, 1982); and Ruth Schwartz Cowan, *More Work for Mother: The Ironies of Household Technology from the Open Hearth to the Microwave* (New York: Basic Books, 1983).

9 Dolores Hayden, "Model Houses for the Millions: Architects' Dreams, Builders' Boasts, Residents' Dilemmas," in *Blueprints for Modern Living*, ed. Elizabeth A. T. Smith and Esther McCoy (Los Angeles: Museum of Contemporary Art, 1989), 197–212.

10 Davis, *Bending Over Backwards*, 124–25; Siebers, *Disability Theory*, 179–82; Kittay, "Dependency," 54–57.

11 Johnson and Shaw, *To Ride the Public's Buses*, 77.

12 Howard, *The Death of Common Sense*; Davis, *Bending Over Backwards*, 124–25.

13 Stanton, *WALL-E*.

14 Latour, *We Have Never Been Modern*, 3.

15 Deetz, *In Small Things Forgotten*.

16 Marks Adjustable Folding Chair Co., *The Marks Improved Adjustable Folding Chair*. Examples of this chair are in the collections of the Metropolitan Museum, Brooklyn Museum of Art, and the Art Institute of Chicago.

17 The nineteenth-century innovation of spring seats was also recognized for its potential for "invalid" sitters. Grier, *Culture & Comfort*, 133–34.

18 Shapiro, *No Pity*, 211–36.

19 Guffey, "The Scandinavian Roots of the International Symbol of Access"; and Guffey, *Designing Disability*; Fritsch, "Beyond the Wheelchair."

20 Kudlick, "Disability History."

21 See, for example, the controversy surrounding the depiction of U.S. president Franklin Delano Roosevelt sitting in his wheeled chair. The Washington, DC, monument is the only public monument to Roosevelt that visually depicts his disability. Parsons, "The Public Struggle."

22 Thomson, *Extraordinary Bodies*, 22–24; Russell, *Reading Embodied Citizenship*, 4–7.

23 Day, *The Crow's Nest*, 44.

24 Ibid., 48.

25 Upton, "White and Black Landscapes in Eighteenth-Century Virginia."

26 Ott, "Disability Things."

27 Ott curated the online exhibition *EveryBody: An Artifact History of Disability in America*, Smithsonian National Museum of American History.

28 Edwards, "Constructions of Physical Disability," 41; Wilson, *Living with Polio*, 2.

29 Rose, *No Right to Be Idle*.

30 Cowan, "The Consumption Junction"; Garvey, *The Adman in the Parlor*.

31 Cogdell, *Eugenic Design*.

32 Gorman, "Educating the Eye."

33 Herschbach, "Prosthetic Reconstructions."

34 Linker, *War's Waste*, 99–101; Serlin, *Replaceable You*, 21–56.

35 On the depiction of prosthetics in pop culture and postmodern cultural theory, see Katherine Ott, "The Sum of Its Parts: An Introduction to Modern Histories of Prosthetics," in Ott, Serlin, and Mihm, *Artificial Parts, Practical Lives*, 1–43; Sobchack, "A Leg to Stand On."; and Kafer, *Feminist, Queer, Crip*.

36 Wilson, "Need for and Development of Aids for Handicapped People." Even recent reports suggest that only about half of arm amputees use artificial limbs. "An Open-Source Approach to Better Prosthetics," *Fresh Air*, WHYY, November 10, 2009.

37 Franklin Delano Roosevelt campaigned from the back of a convertible as part of a public life of private disability. Gallagher, *FDR's Splendid Deception*. Stories abound of people shipping themselves or family members to Roosevelt's Warm Springs spa via freight car. "FDR's Little White House a Healing Retreat," *Deseret-News.com*, May 23, 2004, www.deseretnews.com.

38 On the removal of disability from statistical research, see Hamraie, *Building Access*, 44–50. On their removal from streets, see Schweik, *The Ugly Laws*.

39 Nugent, *Design of Buildings to Permit Their Use by the Physically Handicapped.*

40 Guffey, *Designing Disability*, 87–90.

41 The hashtag #saytheword was initiated by Lawrence Carter-Long. Barbara J. King, "'Disabled': Just #SayTheWord," NPR, February 25, 2016, www.npr.org; Jamie Davis Smith, "Perspective: My Daughter Doesn't Have 'Special' Needs; She's Disabled," *Washington Post*, September 28, 2017, sec. On Parenting, www.wash ingtonpost.com. See also National Center on Disability Journalism, "Disability Language Style Guide," accessed May 31, 2018, http://ndcj.org.

42 Ratto and Ree, "Materializing Information."

43 Among the many who have discussed the very breadth of the category of design are Heskett, *Toothpicks and Logos*; and Attfield, *Wild Things.*

44 Attfield, *Wild Things*, 33.

45 Douglas Baynton notes that nineteenth-century terms linking disability to slow time—"retarded," "handicapped"—denoted disability's challenge to the perceived forward arc of history. Baynton, "'These Pushful Days.'"

46 Scholars of design studies often point to Herbert Simon's definition of design as "devis[ing] courses of action aimed at changing existing situations into preferred ones." Herbert Simon, "The Science of Design," in *The Sciences of the Artificial*; Margolin, introduction to *Design Discourse*, 3; Fuad-Luke, *Design Activism*, 4–5.

47 Hamraie, *Building Access*, especially 68–70.

48 Ibid., 72–78.

CHAPTER 1. PROGRESS THROUGH PROSTHETICS

1 Sobchack, "A Leg to Stand On"; Ott, "The Sum of Its Parts."

2 Linker, *War's Waste.*

3 Serlin, *Replaceable You*, 24–25.

4 See, among others, Pursell, *Technology in Postwar America*; Adas, *Dominance by Design*; and Cohen, *A Consumers' Republic.*

5 A number of writers of the period discussed the problems of disabled veterans as a subset of the veteran population in general: Cartwright, "Re-Education of the Returned Soldier and Sailor"; Covalt, "The Medical Rehabilitation Program." David Gerber notes that many mainstream veterans' groups used disability issues as a way to influence veterans' policies overall: David A. Gerber, "Introduction: Finding Disabled Veterans in History," in Gerber, *Disabled Veterans in History*, 35–36.

6 This skepticism has especially accompanied any form of social need, from begging to welfare entitlement. Schweik, *The Ugly Laws*; Paul Longmore refers to the "institutionalized system of social humiliation" aiming to limit welfare to the "truly needy" who would endure such treatment. Paul K. Longmore, "Why I Burned My Book," in *Why I Burned My Book and Other Essays on Disability*, 240.

7 Cohen, *A Consumer's Republic*, 138–42.

8 Onkst, "'First a Negro . . . Incidentally a Veteran'"; Canaday, *The Straight State*; Cohen, *A Consumer's Republic.*

9 David Serlin situates prosthetic limbs among a range of "medical procedures used to rehabilitate or alter the human body" that "enabled a new alignment of civic goals and national imperatives." Serlin, *Replaceable You*, 1, 21–56.

10 Ott, "The Sum of Its Parts," 5–7; Kafer, *Feminist, Queer, Crip*, 103–28.

11 Serlin, *Replaceable You*, 22.

12 Stiker, *A History of Disability*, 121–90.

13 Ibid., 151–52.

14 Ibid., 152.

15 Gerber, "Introduction: Finding Disabled Veterans in History"; Linker, *War's Waste*, especially 98–119; Sauerborn, "Advances in Upper Extremity Prosthetics"; Ott, "The Sum of Its Parts"; and McDaid, "'How a One-Legged Rebel Lives.'"

16 Jennings, "'An Emblem of Distinction,'" 14–16.

17 Furman, *Progress in Prosthetics*, 11–13.

18 "Shoulder-Operated Artificial Arms and Hands"; House Committee on Veterans' Affairs, *Artificial Limb Program*, 7.

19 Rusk, *New Hope for the Handicapped*, 47.

20 Kessler, *The Knife Is Not Enough*, 106–8.

21 *Servicemen's Readjustment Act of 1944*, 3.

22 Rusk, *New Hope for the Handicapped*, 18.

23 Serlin, *Replaceable You*, 21–56; Gerber, "Heroes and Misfits"; Schweik, "Homer's Odyssey." Bilateral upper-limb amputees (those who had lost both arms) were particularly visible in postwar media, even though the government counted only 63 men with this specific injury out of a total disabled veteran population of over 100,000. Reister, *Medical Statistics in World War II*, 23.

24 United States Army, Signal Corps, *Meet McGonegal*.

25 Wyler, *The Best Years of Our Lives*; Gerber, "Heroes and Misfits."

26 Gerber, "Heroes and Misfits," 561–62; Schweik, "Homer's Odyssey," 24–25.

27 Thomson, *Staring*.

28 Gerber, "Heroes and Misfits," 567.

29 Gerber observes that the film takes a "moral stance . . . : women are responsible for the welfare of men and by caring for men, contribute greatly to social harmony." Ibid., 555.

30 "Armless Man of 1918 Will Inspire New: Pilot, Father of Two Sons, to Tour Hospitals with Wife," *New York Times*, February 3, 1944.

31 Gerber, "Introduction: Finding Disabled Veterans in History," 5.

32 House Subcommittee on Aid to Physically Handicapped, *Aid to Physically Handicapped*, 1575.

33 Ibid., 1596–1601.

34 "Artificial Limb Program" (typescript, Department of the Army, Public Information Division, May 13, 1948), 1–2, Division of Medicine and Science, National Museum of American History.

35 "Artificial Limb Program."

36 Howard A. Rusk, "Prosthetic Devices Exhibit Will Aid Disabled Veterans," *New York Times*, September 7, 1947, 51.

37 Furman, *Progress in Prosthetics*, 11, 18–22.

38 House Committee on Veterans' Affairs, *Providing Automobiles*; House Committee on Veterans' Affairs, *Artificial Limb Program*.

39 House Committee on Veterans' Affairs, *Artificial Limb Program*, 7–8.

40 Ibid., 16–17.

41 Ibid., 6.

42 Ibid., 10–11.

43 Rusk, *New Hope for the Handicapped*, 39.

44 H. Walton Cloke, "Amputees Excel at 'Driving Clinic,'" *New York Times*, January 13, 1946; "Cars for Veteran Tests: Disabled Men to Be Helped to Obtain Drivers' Licenses," *New York Times*, August 25, 1945.

45 United States Army, Signal Corps, *Meet McGonegal*; War Department, *Helpful Hints to Those Who Have Lost Limbs*.

46 Howard A. Rusk, "REHABILITATION: Bill to Provide Automobiles for Amputees Called Bonus and a Threat to Current Veterans' Pension System," *New York Times*, July 28, 1946.

47 "New Cars Limited to Eight Groups; Others May Buy Only Used Autos," *New York Times*, March 15, 1945; "Sale of '45 Autos Will Be Limited at First to 'Essential' Drivers: List Will Be Expanded When Output Rises, Says OPA," *New York Times*, July 17, 1945.

48 "Cool to VA's Giving Autos to Amputees," *New York Times*, March 25, 1946.

49 Society of Automotive Engineers, *Vehicle Controls for Disabled Veterans*.

50 "Cars for Veteran Tests."

51 Society of Automotive Engineers, *Vehicle Controls for Disabled Veterans*, 9.

52 Rusk, "REHABILITATION."

53 Rankin, "Authorizing the Payment"; "GI Amputees Get Huge Auto Fund: $30,000,000 Appropriation to Provide Automobiles for 20,000 Former Soldiers," *New York Times*, August 3, 1946.

54 House Committee on Veterans' Affairs, *Providing Automobiles*, 42–43.

55 Rankin, "Authorizing the Payment," 2.

56 Weatherford, *American Women during World War II*, 393–94.

57 Rogers, "Authorizing the Payment," 1–2.

58 "Autos for Amputees of All Wars Favored," *New York Times*, July 2, 1947; "15,353 Autos for Amputees," *New York Times*, September 10, 1947.

59 "Special Parking Forms Available for Disabled," *New York Times*, January 29, 1947.

60 "Warns on Giving GI Cars: Bradley Says Stop Must Be Made Somewhere in Program," *New York Times*, May 9, 1947.

61 Ibid.

62 "Disabled GI's Make Congressman Flee," *New York Times*, July 31, 1946.

63 "Two Veterans Get Government Cars: Disabled Veterans Get Government Purchased Cars," *New York Times*, September 24, 1946.

64. Gerber, "Disabled Veterans," 904; Berkowitz, "The Federal Government and the Emergence of Rehabilitation Medicine." With life expectancy from one to five years, as one paraplegic veteran put it, medical personnel "made short and sweet of the fact that there wasn't a damn thing that could be done for us but keep us alive until we died." Paralyzed Veterans of America, *An Oral History of the Paralyzed Veterans of America*, 1.

65. An estimated 2,500 paraplegic veterans of World War II were alive in 1957, according to S. Berns et al., *Spinal Cord Injury*, 1.

66. Paralyzed Veterans of America, *An Oral History of the Paralyzed Veterans of America*.

67. Ibid., 5–6.

68. House Committee on Veterans' Affairs, *Providing Housing Units*.

69. Rusk, *New Hope for the Handicapped*, 40–41; Robert M. Carrere et al., "Housing Units for Paraplegic Veterans," *Progressive Architecture*, February 1947, 70–71.

70. House Committee on Veterans' Affairs, *Providing Housing Units*, 12.

71. Ibid.

72. Ibid., 6–7.

73. Ibid., 16–17.

74. *Servicemen's Readjustment Act of 1944.*

75. *An Oral History of the Paralyzed Veterans of America*, 27–28.

76. Paralyzed Veterans of America, "Legislative Program," 9.

77. Boatwright, "The Social Adjustment of Eleven World War II Veterans to Paraplegia"; I am grateful to David Gerber, whose citation led me to this source. Gerber, "Introduction: Finding Disabled Veterans in History," 48, n. 72.

78. Boatwright, "The Social Adjustment of Eleven World War II Veterans to Paraplegia," 44–45.

79. Ibid., 45–46.

80. Ibid., 34.

81. Ibid., 48.

82. Ibid., 51.

83. Ibid., 1.

84. Canaday, *The Straight State*, 15, 137–73.

CHAPTER 2. DISABILITY IN THE CENTURY OF THE GADGET

1. The earliest accessible "campuses" were rehabilitation facilities and specialized schools for disabled students, many of them built during the Works Progress Administration era. The first documented example of multiple public wheelchair ramps were several curb cuts constructed in the downtown area of Kalamazoo, Michigan, which were requested by a local veteran who sustained a spinal cord injury during World War II. Urbana-Champaign combined the two with an accessible campus as well as coordinated curb cuts in the neighboring towns. Serlin, "Cripping the WPA"; Brown, "The Curb Ramps of Kalamazoo."

2. Gritzer and Arluke, *The Making of Rehabilitation Medicine*; Brandt and Pope, *Enabling America*, 1–45; Rusk, "Rehabilitation: The Third Phase of Medicine."

3 Rose, *No Right to Be Idle*, 314.
4 While aspects of what came to be known as "rehabilitation medicine" were practiced during World War I, policy makers maintained a clear distinction between
physical treatment and the broader social and vocational goals of social services.
Gritzer and Arluke, *The Making of Rehabilitation Medicine*, 46–52. The different
strains of practice were once again joined in the World War II era, for servicemembers as well as for civilians under the Barden-Lafollette Act of 1943, which
funded a new Office of Vocational Rehabilitation to consolidate scattered medical
and social support programs for disabled workers into a single, independent
office. Jennings, *Out of the Horrors of War*, 49–51.
5 Rusk, *A World to Care For*, 9.
6 Ibid., 58.
7 Rusk, *New Hope for the Handicapped*.
8 Berkowitz, "The Federal Government and the Emergence of Rehabilitation Medicine"; Redkey, *Rehabilitation Centers in the United States*, 18, 81.
9 Rehabilitation institutions of the interwar years tended to be industrial in focus
and mostly male in patronage. The New York Institute for Crippled and Disabled
Men, for example, opened in 1917 with support from the American Red Cross. Its
services focused on physical training combined with skilled work on industrial
machinery adapted for use by individuals with disabilities. Faries, *Three Years of
Work for Handicapped Men*; Institute for the Crippled and Disabled, *Rehabilitation Trends*.
10 Patterson, "Points of Access."
11 Brown, "Breaking Barriers"; Rose, "The Right to a College Education?"
12 Skocpol, *Protecting Soldiers and Mothers*; Gordon, *Pitied but Not Entitled*; Boris,
"Contested Rights."
13 Mittelstadt, *From Welfare to Workfare*, 11–15; This disability metaphor for social
inferiority also infused discussions of women's rights and immigration. Baynton,
"Disability and the Justification of Inequality."
14 Oscar H. Ewing and Jewell Swofford, "Research Facilities for the Vocational
Rehabilitation of the Blind and Other Severely Disabled Individuals," September 24,
1947, 17, Mary Elizabeth Switzer Papers.
15 Mary E. Switzer, "Statements on Vocational Rehabilitation [Prepared for Mrs.
Mae Thompson Evans]," November 17, 1949, Mary Elizabeth Switzer Papers.
16 Rusk, *New Hope for the Handicapped*, 80–85.
17 "Institute of Physical Medicine and Rehabilitation" (Fundraising brochure, May
1958), Rusk Institute of Rehabilitation Medicine Archive.
18 Rusk, *New Hope for the Handicapped*, 80–81.
19 Rusk's institute served patients from a range of class and geographic backgrounds,
due in part to labor union funding: among the first of his patients, for example,
were a group of coal miners brought in through the United Mine Workers. Rusk,
A World to Care For, 142.
20 Institute for the Crippled and Disabled, *Rehabilitation Trends*.

21 Rusk, *A World to Care For*, 112.

22 Deaver and Brown, *Physical Demands of Daily Life*.

23 Rusk, *New Hope for the Handicapped*, 82–83.

24 Ibid., 90–92.

25 Ibid., 171.

26 Zimmerman, "Accent on Progress," 19.

27 Rusk and Taylor, *Living with a Disability*, 10–11.

28 Howard A. Rusk, "Research in Developing Techniques and the Equipment for Them Held Needed," *New York Times*, July 13, 1947, 25.

29 Rusk, *New Hope for the Handicapped*, 144; Lancaster, *Making Time*, 317.

30 Lancaster, *Making Time*.

31 Ibid., 4–6, 214–58.

32 The undated photograph represents either the original kitchen that Gilbreth designed for the institute in 1948, or a replacement kitchen constructed later; regardless, it replicates Gilbreth's design suggestions.

33 Lancaster, *Making Time*, 317.

34 Elspeth Brown, "The Prosthetics of Management: Time Motion Study, Photography, and the Industrialized Body in World War I America," in Ott, Serlin, and Mihm, *Artificial Parts, Practical Lives*, 249–81.

35 Puaca, "The Largest Occupational Group."

36 Gilbreth, "Building for Living," 48–49.

37 Ibid.

38 "The House That Rosati Built," *Evening Independent*, May 20, 1962; Rusk, *A Functional Home for Easier Living*.

39 William Pahlmann, "Imagination and a Few Cans of Paint" (typescript, November 19, 1972), William Pahlmann Papers; Rusk, *New Hope for the Handicapped*, 80–81.

40 Howard A. Rusk to William Pahlmann, March 19, 1964, William Pahlmann Papers; "The House That Rosati Built."

41 Rusk, *A Functional Home*, 1.

42 Ibid., 1–2.

43 The brochure's title and style echoed design advice literature of the time, such as Russel and Mary Wright's modern design guide, which likewise suggested open interiors and clean-lined furniture. Wright, *Mary and Russel Wright's Guide to Easier Living*.

44 The first major revision of the standard was published in 1980, with added subject research and illustrations: American National Standards Institute, *ANSI 117.1–1980*. The 1990 Americans with Disabilities Act regulations made reference to this standard as the basis for its accessibility requirements. See Hamraie, *Building Access*, 158–60.

45 Clark, "'The Two Joes Meet.'"

46 Rose, "The Right to a College Education?"

47 The program was not officially linked to the Veterans Administration, but paraplegic veterans represented a new and visible population whom the university

readily recruited. Brown, "Breaking Barriers"; Rose, "The Right to a College Education?"

48 Timothy Nugent, "Founder of the University of Illinois Disabled Students Program and the National Wheelchair Basketball Association, Pioneer in Architectural Access," 19–24, interview conducted in 2004–2005 by Fred Pelka, Disability Rights and Independent Living Movement Oral History Series, Regional Oral History Office, Bancroft Library, University of California, Berkeley; Patterson, "Points of Access."

49 Nugent, "Founder of the University of Illinois Disabled Students Program," 42, 45–46.

50 Weller, *100 Years of Campus Architecture.*

51 Rose, "The Right to a College Education?," 39–42.

52 Nugent, "Founder of the University of Illinois Disabled Students Program," 112–18.

53 Nugent, *Design of Buildings to Permit Their Use by the Physically Handicapped*, 55.

54 Brown, "The Curb Ramps of Kalamazoo"; "Paraplegias Go to College," *Journal of Paraplegia*, January 1952, 12, 16.

55 Brown, "Breaking Barriers," 173. While other universities enrolled disabled students at this time, they largely limited acceptances to students who did not require significant accommodations, such as amputees and blind or deaf students. Wheelchair users were typically relegated to off-campus housing, and required to choose classes based on the availability of first-floor or elevator-accessible classrooms. Rose, "The Right to a College Education?," 42.

56 Nugent, *Design of Buildings to Permit Their Use by the Physically Handicapped*, 57.

57 Ibid., 59.

58 Nugent, "Founder of the University of Illinois Disabled Students Program," 66–67, 76.

59 Over time, Nugent did allow some students who required personal attendants to enter the program. Starting in 1959, male students who required personal assistance could live in a specially designed dormitory on campus.

60 Nugent, "Founder of the University of Illinois Disabled Students Program," 64.

61 Mary Lou Breslin, "Cofounder and Director of the Disability Rights Education and Defense Fund, Movement Strategist," 55, interview conducted in 1996–1998 by Susan O'Hara, Disability Rights and Independent Living Movement Oral History Series, Regional Oral History Office, Bancroft Library, University of California, Berkeley; Nugent, "Founder of the University of Illinois Disabled Students Program," 68–69.

62 Breslin, "Cofounder and Director of the Disability Rights Education and Defense Fund," 45–46.

63 Ibid., 54.

64 Ibid., 45.

65 Ibid., 55.

66 Fred Fay, "Community Organizer and Advocate for Equal Access and Equal Rights; Cofounder of Opening Doors, the Boston Center for Independent Living,

and the American Coalition of Citizens with Disabilities," 23, interview conducted in 2001 by Fred Pelka, Disability Rights and Independent Living Movement Oral History Series, Regional Oral History Office, Bancroft Library, University of California, Berkeley.

67 Ibid., 24–26.
68 Kitty Cone, "Political Organizer for Disability Rights, 1970s–1990s, and Strategist for Section 504 Demonstrations, 1977," 35, interview conducted from 1996 to 1998 by David Landes, Disability Rights and Independent Living Movement Oral History Series, Regional Oral History Office, Bancroft Library, University of California, Berkeley.
69 Breslin, "Cofounder and Director of the Disability Rights Education and Defense Fund," 47.
70 Fay, "Community Organizer and Advocate for Equal Access and Equal Rights," 16.
71 Nugent, *Design of Buildings to Permit Their Use by the Physically Handicapped*, 56.
72 American National Standards Institute, *ANSI 117.1–1961*.
73 Nugent, "Founder of the University of Illinois Disabled Students Program," 119.
74 McCullough and Farnham, *Space and Design Requirements*; Nugent, "Founder of the University of Illinois Disabled Students Program," 53.
75 American National Standards Institute, *ANSI 117.1–1961*.
76 *2010 Standards for Accessible Design*.
77 American National Standards Institute, *ANSI 117.1–1961*, 11.
78 American National Standards Institute, *ANSI 117.1–1980*.
79 American National Standards Institute, *ANSI 117.1–1961*, foreword.
80 Steinfeld and Schroeder, *Access to the Built Environment*, 111–12.
81 Nugent, *Design of Buildings to Permit Their Use by the Physically Handicapped*, 59.

CHAPTER 3. ELECTRIC MOMS AND QUAD DRIVERS
1 Ida Brinkman, "The Home and I," *Toomeyville Junior Gazette*, Winter 1958, 13.
2 Ibid., 13–14.
3 Ibid., 15.
4 "Happy Birthday," *Toomey J Gazette*, Fall–Winter 1959, 9.
5 Gerber, "Disabled Veterans," 904; Berkowitz, "The Federal Government and the Emergence of Rehabilitation Medicine," 530–31; Berns et al., *Spinal Cord Injury*.
6 The American National Standards Institute published *ANSI 117.1–1961* in 1961. While these standards were officially adopted for new construction in many states and municipalities, few accessible buildings and streetscapes were actually built in the 1960s. Features such as curb cuts, wheelchair ramps to public buildings, and accessible restrooms were not common sights in American cities until the mid-1970s, and in many locales were not widespread until new federal regulations were adopted in 1977, following nationwide protests by disability rights groups. Percy, *Disability, Civil Rights, and Public Policy*, 110.
7 Kline and Pinch, "Users as Agents of Technological Change"; Eglash, "Appropriating Technology."

8 Cohen, *A Consumer's Republic*, 193–290.

9 Others who have linked rights and identity movements to consumer culture include Weems, *Desegregating the Dollar*; Halter, *Shopping for Identity*; and Dávila, *Latinos, Inc.*.

10 Hamraie, *Building Access*, 104–7.

11 Veterans of World War II received unprecedented support through the 1944 GI Bill, including advanced prosthetic technologies, long-term rehabilitation treatment, and subsidies for automobile and housing costs.

12 Smith, *Patenting the Sun*; Oshinsky, *Polio*; Wilson, *Living with Polio*. Polio was special among other disabilities, starting with medical care. The National Foundation for Infantile Paralysis provided significant funding for polio treatment, creating, at some hospitals, a sharp divide between the polio wards and spaces for other patients. At Rancho Los Amigos, Los Angeles County's rehabilitation hospital, the NFIP funded a separate polio treatment campus, with, according to counselors, better food, better facilities, and better care. Lisa Livote, "Interview Notes for Roy Snelson," February 11, 1988, Papers of the Rancho Los Amigos Hospital.

13 Wilson, *Living with Polio*, 2.

14 For example, one widely cited survey of polio cases in the United States drew on family surveys in which families were questioned about the incidence of various communicable diseases. The only reported data in this survey were for "children of native white parents." Collins, "The Incidence of Poliomyelitis." More recent reviews of the prevalence and spread of the disease rely on these studies. Trevelyan, Smallman-Raynor, and Cliff, "The Spatial Dynamics of Poliomyelitis."

15 Rogers, "Race and the Politics of Polio."

16 This image of polio differed significantly from its associations around the turn of the twentieth century with poor and immigrant communities. Rogers, *Dirt and Disease*.

17 Smith, *Patenting the Sun*; Rose, *March of Dimes*.

18 "Happy Birthday"; masthead, *Toomey J Gazette*, 1967.

19 Masthead, *Toomeyville Jr Gazette*, August 1958.

20 The periodical was begun as *Paraplegia News* in January 1951; for 1952–1953 it went by the *Journal of Paraplegia*, and returned to the *Paraplegia News* in 1954.

21 Collections and analyses of polio survivors' oral histories include Wilson, *Living with Polio*; Sass, Gottfried, and Sorem, *Polio's Legacy*; and selections from the Disability Rights and Independent Living Movement Oral History Series of the Regional Oral History Office, Bancroft Library, University of California at Berkeley.

22 Joe Macrander, "Hospital-Based Group Business Projects," *Toomey J Gazette*, 1968; "Halt and Blind, Unbeatable Team," *Toomey J Gazette*, 1968.

23 Stiker, *A History of Disability*, especially 122–48.

24 Rusk, *New Hope for the Handicapped*, 95; Berns et al., *Spinal Cord Injury*, 9–13; Wilson, *Living with Polio*, 114–15, 154–55; Wilson, "And They Shall Walk."

25 Wilson, *Living with Polio*, 154; Diane and Bob Smith, "We Are Practically Independent . . . ," *Toomey J Gazette*, 1968; Brinkman, "The Home and I."

26 Wilson, "And They Shall Walk."

27 Rancho Los Amigos Hospital, *Annual Report, FY 1949–1950*, 6–7; "Chronology" (typescript, Downey, CA, n.d.), Papers of the Rancho Los Amigos Hospital; Los Angeles County Farm, *A Guide for New Patients*.

28 Landsberger et al., "Mobile Arm Supports," 78; Leifer, "Rehabilitative Robots," 9.

29 Ernie Bontrager, interview by Lisa Livote, February 24, 1988, Papers of the Rancho Los Amigos Hospital; Livote, "Interview Notes for Roy Snelson"; Furman, *Progress in Prosthetics*, 61.

30 Landsberger et al., "Mobile Arm Supports," 77.

31 Colleen Fliedner, "Interview Notes for Richard Daggett," October 31, 1985, 2, Papers of the Rancho Los Amigos Hospital.

32 Paul K. Longmore, "Disability Scholar and Activist, Historian of Early America," 9–10, interview conducted in 2006 by Ann Lage, Disability Rights and Independent Living Movement Oral History Series, Regional Oral History Office, Bancroft Library, University of California, Berkeley.

33 *Distribution and Use of Hearing Aids, Wheel Chairs, Braces, and Artificial Limbs, July 1958–June 1959*; Brandt and Pope, *Enabling America*, 2–3; "Disability Status: 2000—Census 2000 Brief," 2000, www.census.gov.

34 Bruck, *Access*, 144; Feeney, "Are Aids for the Disabled Consumer Goods?"

35 Bruck, *Access*, 147.

36 Mason, *Life Prints*, 23.

37 Catalog (Cleveland: Cleo Living Aids, 1981); Karp, *Choosing a Wheelchair*, 3–4; Belinda Bean and Susan Schapiro, "Consumer Warranty Law: Your Rights and How to Enforce Them" (Disability Rights Center, August 1977), 4–8, Deborah Kaplan Papers.

38 *Colson Ball-Bearing Rubber-Tired Steel Wheels* (Cleveland: Colson-Cleveland Co., n.d.).

39 "Wheelchair Lore," *Toomey J Gazette*, Spring 1965, 84.

40 Kamenetz, "Wheelchairs," 475; Karp, *Choosing a Wheelchair*, 4.

41 Guffey, *Designing Disability*, xx.

42 "Everest & Jennings Folding Wheel Chairs Bring Independence to the Handicapped," *Valor*, August 1950, 21.

43 "Everest & Jennings Wheel Chairs for Smoother Performance," *Valor*, August 1952, 10.

44 "Statement of Disability Rights Center before the Senate Subcommittee on Antitrust and Monopoly" (Disability Rights Center, April 16, 1978), 1–2, Deborah Kaplan Papers.

45 Details are scant on Fascole. Several publications mentioned it in the late 1950s and early 1960s, but it closed by 1963, when a new owner was indicted for defrauding mail-order customers. "Do It Yourself with X Tend," *Paraplegia News*, October 1956; "Now! You Don't Have to Reach or Stoop When You Use the

Fascole Reach-EZ-E!," 1958; "Man Held in Fraud on the Handicapped," *New York Times*, November 28, 1963, 51.

46   "Market Place," *Toomey J Gazette*, Fall–Winter 1959, 38.

47   "The Spokesman," *Toomey J Gazette*, Spring 1960, 6–7.

48   Goldstein, *Do It Yourself*; Sparke, *As Long as It's Pink*, 164–221.

49   Gelber, "Do-It-Yourself."

50   Clark, *The American Family Home*; Rome, *The Bulldozer in the Countryside*.

51   "$9,990 Levitt Houses Boast 70' Lots"; Polly Dunger, telephone conversation, July 19, 2009, notes in possession of author.

52   Garee, *Ideas for Making Your Home Accessible*, 5.

53   "Brainstorms," *Toomey J Gazette*, Fall–Winter 1959, 15–16.

54   "Wheelchairs: Accessories, New Models, Oddments and Endments," *Toomey J Gazette*, 1968, 60.

55   "Equipment," *Toomey J Gazette*, Spring 1961, 11.

56   Zona Roberts, "Counselor for UC Berkeley's Physically Disabled Students' Program, Mother of Ed Roberts," 63–65, interview conducted in 1994–1995 by Susan O'Hara, Disability Rights and Independent Living Movement Oral History Series, Regional Oral History Office, Bancroft Library, University of California, Berkeley.

57   Author conversation with Zona Roberts, Berkeley, CA, July 27, 2009.

58   "Homemaking," *Toomey J Gazette*, 1968, 16–27.

59   Ibid., 18.

60   Ibid., 21.

61   Ibid., 17.

62   Ibid., 19.

63   Marchand, *Advertising the American Dream*, 144–46.

64   Heloise Cruse, "Hints from Heloise," *Evening Independent*, March 21, 1970, sec. B, 4; March 28, 1969, sec. B, 2.

65   Heloise Cruse, "Hints from Heloise," *Ludington Daily News*, July 17, 1971, 3; Cruse, "Hints from Heloise," *Virgin Islands Daily News*, May 30, 1974, 10.

66   "Mouthsticks," *Toomey J Gazette*, Spring 1960, 8–9.

67   Meikle, *American Plastic*, 83–96; Friedel, "Scarcity and Promise."

68   Editorial, *Toomey J Gazette*, Fall–Winter 1959; "TJG Presents First International Exhibition of Paralyzed Artists—Featuring Mouthstick Painting," *Toomey J Gazette*, Spring 1960.

69   Wilson, *Living with Polio*, 137.

70   Phil Draper, "It's Accessible, It's Electric, It's Fascinating," in Daniels, *Going Where You Wheel on Telegraph Avenue*, 21.

71   Susan O'Hara, "1958–1988," 1988, Disabled Students Program Records, Bancroft Library, University of California, Berkeley; Edward V. Roberts, "The UC Berkeley Years: First Student Resident at Cowell Hospital, 1962," interview conducted in 1994 by Susan O'Hara, in Disability Rights and Independent Living Movement Oral History Series, *University of California's Cowell Hospital Residence Program*, 16.

72 Brinkman, "The Home and I," 15; "Wheelchairs: Accessories, New Models, Oddments and Endments," 60.
73 Vince La Michle, "The Home and I," *Toomey J Gazette*, Fall–Winter 1959, 17.
74 Franz, "Automobiles and Automobility," 54; Flink, *The Automobile Age*; Hounshell,
   From the American System to Mass Production.
75 "Quad Drivers," *Toomey J Gazette*, Spring 1965, 38–41.
76 "Special Driving Control Created for President Roosevelt," *Polio Chronicle* 3, no. 7
   (February 1934); Jim Benjaminson, "The Plymouth Cars of Franklin D. Roosevelt
   (and Eleanor)," accessed July 12, 2009, www.allpar.com.
77 For many of the elite patients at Warm Springs, self-driving was not a necessity
   given the prevalence of chauffers; still, the ability to drive oneself clearly had an
   appeal. "Home, Franklin: The President and Other Polios Become Their Own
   Chauffeurs," *Polio Chronicle*, October 1933. On Warm Springs in general, see
   Rogers, "Polio Chronicles."
78 Flink, *The Automobile Age*, 215.
79 Joe Jordan, "Hand Controlled," *Paraplegia News*, January 1951, 7.
80 Flink, *The Automobile Age*, 215.
81 Jordan, "Hand Controlled," 7.
82 "Equipment: A Fourteen Page Feature on Quad Driving, Wheelchairs, Remote
   Controls, Idea Parade," *Toomey J Gazette*, 1968, 54.
83 "Quad Drivers," 38–41.
84 Brinkman, "The Home and I," 15.
85 "Travel by Respos," *Toomey J Gazette*, Spring 1961, 18–19.
86 *You Too Can Drive!* (Wixom, MI: Gresham Driving Aids, n.d.); *Driving Aids and
   Accessories* (Winimac, IN: Braun Corporation, n.d.); Society of Automotive Engineers, *Vehicle Controls for Disabled Veterans*, 14.
87 J. Sinko, Steering Wheel Spinner, U.S. Patent 2,790,330, filed December 30,
   1953, and issued April 30, 1957; P. F. White, Steering Wheel Spinner, U.S. Patent
   2,561,961, filed November 23, 1948, and issued July 24, 1951; J. E. Wood, Steering
   Wheel Spinner, U.S. Patent 2,567,901, filed July 15, 1950, and issued September 11,
   1951. My thanks to Roger White of the NMAH for discussion of steering wheel
   knobs and references.
88 White, *Home on the Road*, 96.
89 Shell, *Polio and Its Aftermath*; Irvin, *Home Bound*.
90 Wilson, *Living with Polio*, 154–55; Longmore, *Why I Burned My Book*, 233.
91 Editorial, 1.

CHAPTER 4. BERKELEY, CALIFORNIA

1 Barbara Winslow and John Parman, "Report from Berkeley," *Progressive Architecture*, October 1977.
2 Zukas, "The History of the Berkeley Center for Independent Living"; Frieden, "IL:
   Movement and Programs"; Linton, "Series Introduction."

3   As I note in chapter 2, rehabilitation doctors such as Howard Rusk offered
    "Activities of Daily Life" as a measure of the extent of rehabilitation. Being able
    to climb stairs, eat alone, or get in and out of bed were examples he used of being
    "physically independent, capable of caring for [oneself] entirely." Rusk, *New Hope
    for the Handicapped*, 90.

4   Susan Pflueger and Edward Roberts distinguished between "traditional Indepen-
    dent Living services," such as provision of wheelchairs and orthopedic devices,
    and a holistic concept that included these physical supports along with a focus
    on "Consumer Rights." Pflueger and Roberts, *Independent Living*; Nancy Crewe
    and Irving Zola asserted more succinctly that "IL means allowing people with
    disabilities to live as they choose in their communities rather than confining
    them in institutions." Crewe and Zola, *Independent Living for Physically Disabled
    People*, ix.

5   As I've written in chapter 2, Nugent's goals of making the first national stan-
    dard adaptable to a wide variety of public settings made for a conservative and
    tentative design program. Nugent, *Design of Buildings to Permit Their Use by the
    Physically Handicapped*.

6   The Architectural Barriers Act was drafted in response to a report that existing
    codes "lack[ed] teeth" and had produced limited, and often conflicting, measures
    to require or encourage access. National Commission on Architectural Barriers
    to Rehabilitation of the Handicapped, *Design for All Americans*; however, seven
    years after the act's passage, the U.S. General Accounting Office found that only
    10 percent of federal sites had improved compliance with the ANSI guidelines,
    and none had followed them completely. Percy, *Disability, Civil Rights, and Public
    Policy*, 110.

7   Part of the reason for the Berkeley movement's renown is that it has been well
    documented, providing a counterbalance to the lack of disability-related re-
    sources in many historical collections. The Bancroft Library at the University of
    California at Berkeley holds the Disability Rights and Independent Living Move-
    ment Collection, and has made efforts to preserve this history, including an oral
    history project that significantly informs this chapter. Historical accounts of the
    emergence of the Berkeley movement include Shapiro, *No Pity*, 42–73; Charlton,
    Nothing about Us without Us, 113–14; Fleischer and Zames, *The Disability Rights
    Movement*, 37–43; and Nielsen, *A Disability History of the United States*, 162–64.

8   There is a variety of evidence of disabled students attending college throughout
    the twentieth century. In the 1940s and 1950s, rehabilitation literature docu-
    mented students attending local colleges or taking correspondence courses.
    Many schools, including the University of California at Berkeley had resources,
    although minimal, for wheelchair-using students. A UC Berkeley guide to campus
    from 1957 directed students to special parking areas and key-access elevators in
    academic buildings. "Report of the Assistance Service for the Handicapped Stu-
    dents" (typescript, University of California, Berkeley, September 1957), Disability

Rights and Independent Living Collection; Corbett OToole traces a history of disabled students at Berkeley, including students who came to UC ("Cal") from the nearby School for the Deaf and School for the Blind. OToole, *Fading Scars*, 76–78.

9 Brown, "Breaking Barriers."

10 Quoted in Kittay, "Dependency," 56.

11 Roberts, "Counselor for UC Berkeley's Physically Disabled Students' Program, Mother of Ed Roberts," 64; Roberts, "The UC Berkeley Years," 20.

12 "Guide to the Disabled Students' Program Records, 1965–" (Organizational Chronology, Berkeley, CA), accessed June 18, 2009, www.oac.cdlib.org; John Hessler noted that the dormitory could fit only twelve students, and thus proposed an expansion in 1969. John Hessler, "Draft Proposal to Expand Cowell Program," 1969, Michael Fuss Papers.

13 Herbert R. Willsmore, "Student Resident at Cowell, 1969–1970, Business Enterprises Manager at the Center for Independent Living, 1975–1977," interview conducted in 1997–1998 by Kathryn Cowan, in Disability Rights and Independent Living Movement Oral History Series, *University of California's Cowell Hospital Residence Program*, 182.

14 Hessler, "Draft Proposal to Expand Cowell Program."

15 Hessler had plans to attend the Sorbonne, which was completely inaccessible. According to Eric Dibner, Hessler and his attendants rented a villa outside Paris, where he conducted his studies from home. Eric Dibner, "Advocate and Specialist in Architectural Accessibility," interview conducted by Kathy Cowan in 1998, in Disability Rights and Independent Living Movement Oral History Series, *Builders and Sustainers of the Independent Living Movement*, vol. 3, 16–17.

16 Eric Dibner, "2424–2428 Dwight Way" (drawing, undated [ca. 1977]), 17, Eric Dibner Papers, 1973–1991.

17 Charles A. Grimes, "Attendant in the Cowell Residence Program, Wheelchair Technologist, and Participant/Observer of Berkeley's Disability Community, 1967–1990s," interview conducted in 1998 by David Landes, 24, in Disability Rights and Independent Living Movement Oral History Series, Regional Oral History Office, Bancroft Library, University of California, Berkeley.

18 The counselor, Lucile Withington, announced that some students would be dismissed for poor academic records. The students pushed back, publicizing their struggle to the local press and appealing to Withington's superiors. The department did not fire Withington, as the students demanded, but did transfer her to another assignment. Roberts called the conflict a kind of "training" for broader political struggles. Roberts, "The UC Berkeley Years," 25, 38. Withington herself observed the political significance of the conflict, recalling later that "it was almost negative psychology, because it brought them closer together, it gave them strength." Lucile Withington, "Department of Rehabilitation Counselor, Cowell Residence Program 1969–1971," interview conducted in 1998 by Sharon Bonney,

in Disability Rights and Independent Living Movement Oral History Series, *UC Berkeley's Cowell Hospital Residence Program*, 77–78, 86.

19 Shapiro, *No Pity*, 42–73; "History and Development of Physically Disabled Student Program" (typescript, University of California, Berkeley, Office of Student Activities, September 1974), Disabled Students Program Records, Disability Rights and Independent Living Collection.

20 "History and Development of Physically Disabled Student Program"; Hale Zukas, "CIL History" (typescript—notes and revisions, 1975), Hale Zukas Papers, 1971–1988.

21 "VOTE YES" (flyer, Berkeley, CA, 1969), Michael Fuss Papers.

22 Willsmore, "Student Resident at Cowell, 1969–1970," 162.

23 Krizack, "What about the Electric Wheelchair?"

24 Physically Disabled Students Program, "Staff Reports," 1970, Disability Rights and Independent Living Collection.

25 Technicians complained that wheelchair companies would not provide assistance because they were not a commercial retailer of the chairs. "Physically Disabled Students' Program" (mid-year report to Department of Health, Education and Welfare, Berkeley, CA, fiscal year 1971), Hale Zukas Papers, 1971–1988. The repair shop was set up at the university's Alumni House. Timothy R. Black, "Letter to Colleen Peixotto, Alumni House," October 27, 1970, Disability Rights and Independent Living Collection.

26 Physically Disabled Students Program, "Staff Reports."

27 Willsmore, "Student Resident at Cowell, 1969–1970," 192.

28 Rorabaugh, *Berkeley at War*, 31.

29 Turner, *From Counterculture to Cyberculture*, 11–12.

30 "Hear Ye, Hear Ye," *Berkeley Barb*, April 18, 1969, 2.

31 Rorabaugh, *Berkeley at War*, 162.

32 Ibid., 164–65.

33 Catherine Caulfield, "First Woman Student in the Cowell Program, 1968," interview conducted in 1994 by Susan O'Hara, in Disability Rights and Independent Living Movement Oral History Series, *University of California's Cowell Hospital Residence Program*, 139–40.

34 Allen, "The End of Modernism?," 366–68.

35 Ibid., 369; Mitchell, "The End of Public Space?," 108.

36 Berkeley City Council, regular meeting minutes, June 17, 1969, 6–7.

37 Resolution No. 43,814 N.S.: Adopting Specifications for Telegraph Avenue Reconstruction, Dwight Way to Bancroft Way, and Directing the Purchasing Agent to Advertise for Bids (1970), 22. The resolution called for bids that would include "cost of forming and constructing wheelchair ramps. . . . There are approximately 16 wheelchair ramps on this project."

38 Edythe Campbell, "Letter to Donald Lorence," October 15, 1970. Rolling Quad Donald Lorence wrote to the city council in October acknowledging the new ramps. Herbert Willsmore Collection.

39 California adopted a code requiring wheelchair access in 1974. Steinfeld and Schroeder, *Access to the Built Environment*, 63.

40 University of California, Berkeley, Office of Architects and Engineers, "Minutes: Reduction of Barriers to the Physically Handicapped," February 12, 1970, Disability Rights and Independent Living Collection.

41 Stew Albert, "Free for All," *Berkeley Barb*, May 25, 1969.

42 Allen, "The End of Modernism?," 366–67.

43 James Charlton is an early exception, as he situated independent living movements within the broader global push for liberation from capitalist and authoritarian forces. Charlton, *Nothing about Us without Us*, 131–32.

44 Siebers, *Disability Theory*, 179–82; Kittay, "Dependency," 55.

45 David Konkel, "First Blind Services Coordinator at the Physically Disabled Students' Program, UC Berkeley, 1970; Founding Member of the Center for Independent Living in Berkeley," interview conducted in 2000 by Fred Pelka, in Disability Rights and Independent Living Movement Oral History Series, *Blind Services and Advocacy*, 132–33.

46 Hale Zukas, "National Disability Activist: Architectural and Transit Accessibility, Personal Assistance Services," interview conducted in 1997–1998 by Kathryn Cowan, in Disability Rights and Independent Living Movement Oral History Series, *Builders and Sustainers of the Independent Living Movement*, vol. 3.

47 The first recorded CIL meeting occurred in the PDSP office on Durant Street. Hale Zukas, "First Meeting of the Potential Board of Directors" (typescript, Berkeley, June 1971), Hale Zukas Papers, 1971–1988; former attendant Carol Billings described the PDSP office's "communal feeling," with "walkies" and "crips" hanging out, sharing meals, and so forth. She also described CIL's origins in a "closet" within this office. Carol Fewell Billings, "Attendant and Observer in the Early Days of the Physically Disabled Students' Program and the Center for Independent Living, 1969–1977," in Disability Rights and Independent Living Movement Oral History Series, *Builders and Sustainers of the Independent Living Movement*, vol. 2.

48 Zukas, "First Meeting of the Potential Board of Directors"; "Meeting of the Board of the Center for Independent Living" (minutes, February 24, 1972), Hale Zukas Papers, 1971–1988. It is frequently reported that Ed Roberts was a founder of CIL. He was not, as he had left Berkeley for a job at the Office of Education in Washington, DC. He returned in 1973 and assumed the directorship of CIL until 1976, when Governor Jerry Brown appointed him director of rehabilitation for the state of California.

49 Zukas, "The History of the Berkeley Center for Independent Living."

50 Fleischer and Zames, *The Disability Rights Movement*, 39. Board members would be automatically accepted if they had "a permanent primary disability affecting mobility, sensory, or communication skills"; those with no disability would join with four sitting board members' signatures. All clients of CIL who had

received services for at least two months were eligible to vote in the organization's elections. "Bylaws of the Center for Independent Living" (typescript, 1972), Hale Zukas Papers, 1971–1988.

51 Zukas, "The History of the Berkeley Center for Independent Living."

52 "Bylaws of the Center for Independent Living"; "Meeting of the Board of the Center for Independent Living."

53 Cover, *Independent: A New Voice for the Disabled and Blind*, Fall 1974.

54 Berkeley City Council, regular meeting minutes, October 13, 1970. The city clerk responded, assuring him that "this situation will be corrected." Campbell, "Letter to Donald Lorence."

55 Ruth Grimes and Herbert R. Willsmore, untitled typescript, September 28, 1971, Hale Zukas Papers, 1971–1988.

56 Berkeley City Council, Resolution No. 44,866-N.S. (1972).

57 The 125 ramps included 119 identified by PDSP as highest priority, plus 6 requested by specific individuals, according to the resolution. Berkeley City Council, Resolution No. 45,605-N.S. (1973).

58 Berkeley City Council, Resolution No. 44,866-N.S., 2–3.

59 Ibid., 1–3. The Live Oak Acorns Recreation Program seems to be a short-lived recreational group connected to Live Oak Park in Berkeley. Ruth Grimes identified it as a source in her initial proposal for a wheelchair route, and it is mentioned as a destination for some clients of the Center for Independent Living in a 1974 document. Grimes and Willsmore, untitled typescript; Center for Independent Living, "Application for Revenue Sharing Funds from Alameda County" (typescript, Berkeley, CA, 1975), Hale Zukas Papers, 1971–1988.

60 Percy, *Disability, Civil Rights, and Public Policy*; Scotch, *From Good Will to Civil Rights*.

61 Zukas, "National Disability Activist," 140.

62 The guidelines made no specific reference to sidewalk design, but stated that when walkways crossed driveways or parking lots, "they should blend to a common level." American National Standards Institute, *ANSI 117.1–1961*, 8.

63 As of 1997, Zukas stated that a few curbs remained in Berkeley that followed his design: on Telegraph, on the corridor south of Dwight. Zukas, "National Disability Activist," 142.

64 Ibid., 141.

65 Email correspondence with Hale Zukas, July 2016; Nora Ames pointed out this conflict to me in May 2016.

66 Glenn Fowler, "A.I.A. Awards for '70 Given to 14 Entries," *New York Times*, May 31, 1970; Harold L. Willson, "Architectural Barriers Report on Activities" (Architectural Barriers Committee, Easter Seal Society of Contra Costa County, November 11, 1965), Harold L. Willson Papers; Harre DeMoro, "BART Provides for Crippled," *Oakland Tribune*, July 23, 1969, sec. A.

67 Of the forty-three people interviewed, only twenty had used the system; of these, five had used it only once. Eric Dibner, Hale Zukas, and Ken Stein, "The Impact

of BART on the Physically Disabled" (typescript, Spring 1975), Hale Zukas Papers, 1971–1988.

68 Ibid.

69 W. E. Brock, fire marshall, letter to Phil Draper, February 20, 1976, Hale Zukas Papers, 1971–1988.

70 John P. Kenealy, "Letter to Fire Marshall, City of Berkeley," March 11, 1976, Hale Zukas Papers, 1971–1988.

71 City of Berkeley, "Appeal by Center for Independent Living from Fire Marshal's Order to Vacate Fourth Floor of 2020 Milvia" (memorandum, May 18, 1976), Hale Zukas Papers, 1971–1988; "Public Hearing for C.I.L." (City of Berkeley memorandum, May 13, 1976), Hale Zukas Papers, 1971–1988.

72 Judith Heumann, "Pioneering Disability Rights Advocate and Leader in Disabled in Action, New York; Center for Independent Living, Berkeley; World Institute on Disability; and the U.S. Department of Education, 1960s–2000," interview conducted from 1998 to 2001 by Susan Brown, David Landes, and Jonathan Young, 285, in Disability Rights and Independent Living Movement Oral History Series, Regional Oral History Office, Bancroft Library, University of California, Berkeley.

73 Marty Brokaw, "There's a Feeling of Tolerance Here," in Daniels, *Going Where You Wheel on Telegraph Avenue*, 29–30.

74 Notably, there were attempts to bring CIL's message and services into poor and diverse communities such as Oakland. There was a short-lived East Oakland outpost of CIL that was developed in collaboration with the Black Panther Party; consensus among African American staff and affiliates of CIL is that it remained "at a distance" from the primary CIL, "plunked down" without deep community ties. Schweik, "Lomax's Matrix." Today CIL operates satellite offices in Oakland and Alameda.

75 Draper, "It's Accessible, It's Electric, It's Fascinating," 22.

76 Linton, "Series Introduction."

77 For example, Kitty Cone, who had left the more conservative University of Illinois in Urbana-Champaign in 1966 to work on civil rights causes, moved to the Bay Area in 1972 to work with the Socialist Workers' Party. When she connected with CIL and eventually became a staff member, she brought experience in organizing and left-leaning politics. Cone, "Political Organizer for Disability Rights."

78 Zukas, "National Disability Activist," 143.

79 See also Hamraie, *Building Access*, 123–24.

80 Dibner, "Advocate and Specialist in Architectural Accessibility," 63–65.

81 Frederick C. Collignon, "UC Professor of City and Regional Planning: Policy Research and Funding Advocacy," in Disability Rights and Independent Living Movement Oral History Series, *Builders and Sustainers of the Independent Living Movement*, vol. 3, 79–82.

82 Lifchez, *Design for Independent Living*, xx.

83 Disability Rights and Independent Living Movement Oral History Series, *Architectural Accessibility and Disability Rights*, 74.

84 Lifchez wrote that the architectural tendency to render access in abstract images and dimensions "transforms handicapped persons into objects, for example, into wheelchairs with measurable requirements." Lifchez, "Designing Supportive Physical Environments," 131.

85 Lifchez, *Design for Independent Living*, 144–47.

86 Ibid., 144.

87 He did highlight occasional examples, such as Charles Moore and Raymond Oliver's house for a blind man and his family of four. The house was also covered in Schmertz, "Two Houses by Charles Moore."

88 Lifchez, *Design for Independent Living*, 131.

89 The partnering schools struggled to integrate the curriculum, given a range of curricular and institutional circumstances. Lifchez noted a deep sense of disappointment as he and his collaborators observed the "negative stance" the profession began to take after the release of new federal regulations on access in 1977. Lifchez, *Rethinking Architecture*, 70.

90 Disability Rights and Independent Living Movement Oral History Series, *Architectural Accessibility and Disability Rights*, 81.

91 Daniels, *Ramps Are Beautiful*.

92 Ibid., 7.

93 Ibid., 26.

94 Michael Chacko Daniels, "'Our Ramp Is Beautiful,' Says Valentina Estes," in Daniels, *Ramps Are Beautiful*, 10–12.

95 Dolores Dixon, "I Can Easily Get My Mother Out on Our Ramp," in Daniels, *Ramps Are Beautiful*, 14–17.

96 Kenneth Mineau, "Questions for Users in Designing a Ramp," in Daniels, *Ramps Are Beautiful*, 34–36.

97 Ibid., 41–44.

98 Dibner, "Advocate and Specialist in Architectural Accessibility," 36.

99 Ibid., 24; Ken Stein, telephone conversation, July 18, 2016. See also Hamraie, *Building Access*, 95, 287–88, n. 1.

100 Even the existing historical markers can be misleading: a plaque mounted in downtown Berkeley claims to mark the first curb cut in the United States—a claim proven false by Steven Brown's research on Kalamazoo and Urbana-Champaign. As this chapter shows, downtown Berkeley was not even the first local site of curb access.

101 Frances Dinkelspiel, "Decades-Old Mural Could Derail Berkeley Apartment Project," *Berkeleyside*, November 25, 2014, www.berkeleyside.com.

CHAPTER 5. KNEELING TO THE DISABLED

1 Scotch, *From Good Will to Civil Rights*, 72–74; another provision of the 1973 Rehabilitation Act (Section 502) was to create the Architectural and Transportation Barriers Compliance Board, in part to explore the possibility of more widespread accessibility measures. Percy, *Disability, Civil Rights, and Public Policy*, 107–10.

2 Percy, *Disability, Civil Rights, and Public Policy*, 54.

3 Legislators had discussed alterations to the 1964 Civil Rights Act to include the category of disability, but no formal proposal or debate preceded Section 504 of the Rehabilitation Act. Scotch, *From Good Will to Civil Rights*, 43–44; Percy, *Disability, Civil Rights, and Public Policy*, 52; Fleischer and Zames, *The Disability Rights Movement*, 48; O'Brien, *Crippled Justice*, 107. In 1980 the conservative American Enterprise Institute claimed that one of the amendment's sponsors, Rep. Charles Vanick, confessed he had "no idea" that it would "become the most far reaching and costly civil rights law for the disabled ever enacted." Smith and Riggar, "Accessible Transportation," 13.

4 Scotch, *From Good Will to Civil Rights*, 99.

5 Fay, "Community Organizer and Advocate for Equal Access and Equal Rights," 35.

6 Percy, *Disability, Civil Rights, and Public Policy*, 68.

7 These groups included local organizations such as independent living centers, as well as veterans' and workers' groups. Nielsen, *A Disability History of the United States*, 165–69; Patterson, "Points of Access"; Jennings, *Out of the Horrors of War*.

8 Scotch, *From Good Will to Civil Rights*, 80–82.

9 Heumann, "Pioneering Disability Rights Advocate," 275.

10 Cone, "Political Organizer for Disability Rights," 96; Frank G. Bowe, "Letter to President Jimmy Carter," March 1977, Disability Rights and Independent Living Collection.

11 Shapiro, *No Pity*, 65–69. Protests have been documented at ten HEW offices across the country. In San Francisco the protest lasted from April 5 to April 30, 1977. Paul K. Longmore Institute on Disability, "Protesting across America," in *Patient No More*.

12 Ron Washington was another participant who had previously engaged with African American civil rights causes. Paul K. Longmore Institute on Disability, "Activist Ron Washington on the Section 504 Protests and Civil Rights," in *Patient No More*.

13 504 Emergency Coalition, untitled release, April 1977, Disability Rights and Independent Living Collection.

14 Nancy Hicks, "Handicapped Use Protests to Push H.E.W. to Implement '73 Bias Law," *New York Times*, April 11, 1977, sec. A.

15 Scotch, *From Good Will to Civil Rights*, 115.

16 Paul K. Longmore Institute on Disability, "Victory Speeches and Protest Songs," in *Patient No More*.

17 "WID Celebrates the First Ed Roberts Day in California," World Institute on Disability, April 30, 1977, www.wid.org.

18 National Research Council, *NRC Transbus Study*, 81.

19 Robert Lindsey, "2 Prototypes of 'Bus of Future' Delivered to Desert Test Area: Not a 'Face-Lifting,'" *New York Times*, March 29, 1974; Rohr, *Rohr Industries Transbus*; Truck and Coach Division, *The General Motors Transbus*; Booz Allen Research, *Human Factors Evaluation of Transbus by the Elderly*.

20 "Statement by Elliott M. Estes, President of General Motors" (press release, New York, July 12, 1978), General Motors Heritage Center Archive; National Research Council, *NRC Transbus Study*, 83–84.

21 Steven V. Roberts, "Putting a Price Tag on Equality: The Cost of Civil Rights Delays Threaten Project," *New York Times*, June 25, 1978, sec. Business & Finance.

22 The RTS models rode 29 inches off the ground with kneeling height of 24 inches, as opposed to the Transbus's specification of 22 inches with kneeling height of 18 inches. The main competitor to GM, Rohr, produced an initial prototype that went as low as 17 inches off the ground. Ralph Blumenthal, "U.S. Agency Rules New Buses Must Be Built 10 Inches Lower," *New York Times*, July 28, 1976, sec. Business & Finance.

23 AMC's official statement said that it withdrew due to "confusion" over regulations. Roberts, "Putting a Price Tag on Equality."

24 Fleischer and Zames, *The Disability Rights Movement*, 56–57; Clint Page, "Is the 10-Year Wait for a Good City Bus Coming to an End?," *Nation's Cities*, May 1977; National Research Council, *NRC Transbus Study*.

25 Some activists, concerned that government compromises on the mandate would invite new attacks on Section 504 regulations, saw the Transbus as a sine qua non of developing accessibility policies. Roberts, "Putting a Price Tag on Equality."

26 Paranchini, "Sic Transit Transbus," 34.

27 Smith and Riggar, "Accessible Transportation," 13.

28 "An Interview with Mayor Edward Koch," *Wall Street Journal*, March 10, 1981.

29 Zukas, "Why Disabled People Do Not Use BART."

30 Smith and Riggar, "Accessible Transportation," 15.

31 Ronald Smothers, "New Buses: New Hope to Disabled," *New York Times*, February 2, 1982, sec. B1.

32 "How Congress Can Move the Handicapped," *New York Times*, September 24, 1980, sec. Editorial.

33 "Must Every Bus Kneel to the Disabled?," *New York Times*, November 18, 1979, sec. Editorial.

34 "The $2,000 Subway Token," *New York Times*, June 23, 1984, sec. Editorial.

35 McKnight et al., "Transportation for the Mobility-Limited," 443.

36 C. Kenneth Orski, "Rethinking Transit," *New York Times*, February 14, 1981.

37 Orski, "Changing Directions of Public Transportation."

38 Clyde Farnsworth, "Reagan Signs Order to Curb Regulations," *New York Times*, February 18, 1981.

39 McCluskey, "Rethinking Equality and Difference," 877.

40 Johnson and Shaw, *To Ride the Public's Buses*, 3.

41 Surveying more than 200 accessibility-related protests of the 1970s to 1990s, Sharon Barnartt and Richard Scotch found that 127, or 61 percent, were focused on transportation. Barnartt and Scotch, *Disability Protests*, 75.

42 ADAPT changed its name after the passage of the ADA to American Disabled for Attendant Programs Today, acknowledging the lack of individual household support. Barnartt, "Social Movement Diffusion?"

43 Barnartt and Scotch, *Disability Protests*, 18–21.

44 "Ramp by Ramp: A Guide to Disability Rights Landmarks in Denver" (brochure, Denver, undated [after 1993]), http://adaptmuseum.net; L. A. Chung, "Cops Bust Disabled Protesters," *San Francisco Chronicle*, September 19, 1987; Peggy McCarthy, "Disabled to Protest Transit," *New York Times*, September 13, 1987, sec. Connecticut Weekly; "Disabled Protesters Arrested," *New York Times*, September 29, 1987.

45 Johnson and Shaw, *To Ride the Public's Buses*.

46 "ADAPT Cordially Invites You to an Uproar" (flyer, Denver, October 1983), http://adaptmuseum.net.

47 Johnson and Shaw, *To Ride the Public's Buses*, vii.

48 Americans with Disabilities Act of 1990, Pub. L. No. 101–336 (1990), www.ada.gov.

49 Orski, "Rethinking Transit."

50 MacLean, *Freedom Is Not Enough*, 230–35.

51 Graham, "Introduction," 6.

52 Percy, *Disability, Civil Rights, and Public Policy*, 89.

53 Berkowitz, "A Historical Preface to the Americans with Disabilities Act," 109.

54 National Council on Disability, *On the Threshold of Independence*.

55 Timothy B. Clark, "The Clout of the 'New' Bob Dole," *New York Times*, December 12, 1982, sec. Sunday Magazine.

56 Crystal Nix, "From a Wheelchair, Most Doors Are Closed," *New York Times*, May 21, 1986.

57 Peter H. Lewis, "Clever Design Can Assist Handicapped," *New York Times*, January 15, 1985; Paul Grimes, "Practical Traveler: For People with Disabilities," *New York Times*, June 8, 1986; Paul Grimes, "Practical Traveler: Making America Accessible," *New York Times*, June 15, 1986; Dennis Hevesi, "How Disabled People Clear Hurdles of Flying," *New York Times*, August 23, 1987, sec. Practical Traveler; "Air Carriers and the Disabled Struggle to Write New Rules," *New York Times*, September 8, 1987; Jacqueline Shaheen, "The Disabled Find Housing Options Severely Limited," *New York Times*, December 6, 1987, New Jersey edition; Joanne Lipmann, "Ads Featuring Disabled People Become a Little More Common," *Wall Street Journal*, September 7, 1989.

58 International Center for the Disabled, *The ICD Survey of Disabled Americans*.

59 National Council on Disability, *Toward Independence*.

60 Berkowitz, "A Historical Preface to the Americans with Disabilities Act," 108.

61 "Americans with Disabilities Act," Web video, *Call-In* (C-SPAN, May 17, 1990), www.c-spanvideo.org.

62 The greatest shortfall of the ADA, like Section 504 before it, came in its interpretation in court cases over employment. In many of these cases, including those before the Supreme Court, arguments dwelled on who could be considered

disabled, rather than the question of discrimination itself. O'Brien, *Crippled Justice*, 137–38, 163–68; Stein, Waterstone, and Wilkins, "Cause Lawyering for People with Disabilities," 1658–59.

63 Howard, *The Death of Common Sense*, 1, 112–13.

64 Ibid.

65 Davis, *Bending Over Backwards*, 124–25.

CHAPTER 6. FROM ACCESSIBLE TO UNIVERSAL

1 Commentary on the struggles between historic preservation and "handicapped access" can be found throughout the 1970s, 1980s, and 1990s, and intensified after the passage of the ADA. Examples include Campbell, "It's Accessible, but . . . Is It Architecture?" New York City's Landmarks Preservation Commission effectively blocked many accessibility renovation projects over their interference with historical architecture. David W. Dunlap, "Old Synagogue Denied Elevator Bid," *New York Times*, March 29, 1987; Leonard Kriegel, "New York City's Inhuman Dimension," *New York Times*, May 25, 1987.

2 Few articles in the architecture and design press covered accessibility with in-depth discussion of design strategies; likewise, few high-profile architects discussed their approaches to legally required disability access. One exception was coverage of Stanley Tigerman's school for the blind and David Niland's wheelchair-accessible house in the "Beyond Scale" special issue of *Design Quarterly*.

3 Mary Johnson, "Universal Man: Ron Mace Leads the Way to Design That Includes Everybody," *Mainstream*, August 1994, 27.

4 Mace recalled that his professors told him "not to try," as a person with a disability would never be able to perform the demanding work of the profession. Ostroff, Limont, and Hunter, *Building a World Fit for People*.

5 Mace first described Universal Design in his 1985 *Designers West* article "Universal Design." His life's work is fully chronicled in Hamraie, *Building Access*, especially chapter 6: "Barrier Work."

6 This argument can be found throughout the upbeat writing of home economists and rehabilitation specialists—for example, Lillian Gilbreth, who commented after designing a kitchen for the American Heart Association, "There wasn't a single thing in it which wouldn't be equally good for a person who had nothing in the world the matter with her except overweight." Lancaster, *Making Time*, 317. Likewise, the U.S. presidential report that recommended initial federal regulations on access asserted that "many improvements made to accommodate the handicapped also add to the safety and convenience of the able-bodied." National Commission on Architectural Barriers to Rehabilitation of the Handicapped, *Design for All Americans*, 6.

7 Mace, "Universal Design."

8 Story, Mueller, and Mace, *The Universal Design File*, 6.

9 McConnell, "Universal Design," 34.

10 Le Corbusier, "Type-Needs," 84–89.

11 Fondation Le Corbusier, "The Modulor and Modulor 2."

12 Makower, *Touching the City*, 166–68.

13 Hosey, "Hidden Lines," 103.

14 Ibid., 103–7.

15 Dreyfuss, *The Measure of Man*, 5.

16 Serlin, *Replaceable You*; Flinchum, *Henry Dreyfuss, Industrial Designer*.

17 Dreyfuss, *Designing for People*, 27.

18 Ibid., 26–27.

19 Serlin, *Replaceable You*, 53.

20 Dreyfuss, *The Measure of Man*.

21 Dreyfuss, *Designing for People*, 216.

22 Williamson, "Getting a Grip"; Delphia, "Ergonomics and Negative Space," 43–50.

23 "The Handicapped Majority," *Industrial Design*, May 1974, 25.

24 Diffrient, Tilly, and Bardagjy, *Humanscale 1/2/3*.

25 See also Hamraie, *Building Access*, 30–38.

26 Diffrient, Tilly, and Bardagjy, *Humanscale 1/2/3*, 4.

27 Diffrient, Bardagjy, and Polites, "Dimensions of Experience," 11.

28 Industrial Designers Society of America, *Industrial Design Excellence*; "Humanscale and Niels Diffrient," accessed December 4, 2016, www.humanscale.com.

29 Diffrient, Bardagjy, and Polites, "Dimensions of Experience," 11.

30 Mace and Laslett, *An Illustrated Handbook of the Handicapped Section of the North Carolina State Building Code*.

31 Ostroff, Limont, and Hunter, *Building a World Fit for People*.

32 Mace and Laslett, *An Illustrated Handbook of the Handicapped Section of the North Carolina State Building Code*, 4–5.

33 Ibid., 23.

34 Ibid., 17.

35 Ibid., 21.

36 Mandel, *Making Good Time*.

37 Guffey, "The Scandinavian Roots of the International Symbol of Access," 368.

38 Guffey, *Designing Disability*, 69; on Goldsmith's own campaign for an accessibility symbol, 81–93 and 101–10; and on the development and application of the International Symbol of Access, 121–37.

39 These architects' frankness in representing the disabled body seemed to forecast the more recent campaign #saytheword, which encourages media and others to use the word "disability" rather than euphemisms like "special needs" or "differently abled."

40 Articles include Richard Hollerith, "Viewpoint: Eliminating the Handicap," *Industrial Design*, March 1976, 54–55; and Rolf Faste, "New System Propels Design for the Handicapped," *Industrial Design*, July 1977, 51–55.

41 Hamraie, *Building Access*, 31–33.

42 Papanek, *Design for the Real World*, xxi.

43 Ibid., 154–83.

44 Ibid., 83.

45 Papanek, *Design for Human Scale*, 13–14.

46 Ibid., 15.

47 Clarke, "The Anthropological Object in Design," 75–76.

48 Moore and Conn, *Disguised.*

49 Ibid., 39–40.

50 Ibid., 160–61.

51 Burgstahler and Doe, "Disability-Related Simulations"; Olson, "How Disability Simulations Promote Damaging Stereotypes."

52 Moore and Conn, *Disguised*, 12–13.

53 Ibid., 161.

54 Liz Jackson identifies the distinction between "designing for" and "designing with" disability. Liz Jackson, "Zappos Created a Disability Line without Talking to Actual Disabled People," Extra Newsfeed, May 9, 2017, https://extranewsfeed.com; Liz Jackson, "We Are the Original Lifehackers," *New York Times*, May 30, 2018, sec. Opinion, www.nytimes.com.

55 Consumer historian Sam Binkley refers to the Cuisinart as one of the ultimate products of the yuppie 1980s, a product that took appliances from kitchen tools to "cooking experiences." Binkley, *Getting Loose*, 74.

56 Barbara Allen Guilfoyle, "After Cuisinart, the Deluge," *Industrial Design*, May 1978, 44; "Selected Objects," *Julia Child's Kitchen at the Smithsonian National Museum of American History*, accessed April 15, 2010, http://americanhistory.si.edu.

57 The company asked for "quality of form and detailing." Industrial Designers Society of America, *Industrial Design Excellence, 1980–1985*, 178. Harrison had researched disability for more than a decade as a professor, leading his students in projects in collaboration with rehabilitation specialists as well as a full-scale, wheelchair-accessible model house constructed for the International Lead-Zinc Research Organization. See Williamson, "Getting a Grip."

58 Industrial Designers Society of America, *Industrial Design Excellence, 1980–1985*; Hiesinger and Marcus, *Landmarks of Twentieth-Century Design.*

59 Marc Harrison, curriculum vitae, 1985, Marc Harrison Papers, Ser. I, Box 8, Hagley Museum and Library.

60 John Wall, "U.S. Design—With Old-World Elan," *Washington Times*, February 10, 1986, sec. Insight.

61 Williamson, "Getting a Grip," 224.

62 Marc Harrison, "Questionnaire for Katonah Gallery," November 1983, Marc Harrison Papers, Ser. I, Box 8.

63 Marc Harrison, "Food Processor (1)," 1978, Marc Harrison Papers, Ser. II, MD 99, H; Marc Harrison, "Food Processor (2)," 1978, Marc Harrison Papers, Ser. II, MD 99, H.

64 "The Food Processor Revolution: Act II," *New York*, November 13, 1978; "Cuisinart Model CFP-9: Good as It Was, It's Better Now" (advertisement, 1976), Marc Harrison Papers, Ser. I, Box 4; Craig Claiborne, "She Demonstrates How to Cook Best with New Cuisinart," *New York Times*, January 7, 1976, sec. Food Day.

65 Marc Harrison, "Questionnaire for Katonah Gallery," November 1983, Marc Harrison Papers, Ser. I, Box 8.

66 Harrison included the design story of the Cuisinart in materials for an exhibition at the Katonah Gallery in 1983, as well as for an entry in the Industrial Designers Society of America's *Industrial Design Excellence, 1980–1985* (McLean, VA: Design Foundation, 1985), 178.

67 Story, Mueller, and Mace, *The Universal Design File*, 11–12; "UD Case Study—Oxo," accessed March 18, 2008, www.design.ncsu.edu; Walter Nicholls, "Getting a Grip: How OXO Invented Hand-Friendly Kitchen Tools," *Washington Post*, October 27, 1999, sec. F; Pilar Guzman, "Handles with Care," *One*, 2000.

68 "UD Case Study—Oxo"; Jackson, "We Are the Original Lifehackers"; Sam Farber, telephone communication, February 2, 2008.

69 Guzman, "Handles with Care," 142.

70 Farber, telephone communication.

71 "Gadgets You Can Grip Are Tools You Can Use" (OXO Good Grips, ca. 1990), Division of Medicine and Science, National Museum of American History.

72 Mueller, "The Case for Universal Design"; Herbst, "Nobody's Perfect."

73 Story, Mueller, and Mace, *The Universal Design File*, 90.

74 Madeline Drexler, "A Universal Handle," *Boston Globe Magazine*, December 12, 1993.

75 Ibid.; Florence Fabricant, "Food Stuff," *New York Times*, January 20, 1999, sec. Style.

76 *Unlimited by Design* (New York: Cooper-Hewitt, National Design Museum, Smithsonian Institution, 1998).

77 *Universal Kitchen*, poster, 1998, Marc Harrison Papers.

78 Ibid.

79 Samuels, "Limited to Design?"

CHAPTER 7. BEYOND RAMPS

1 Russell, *Beyond Ramps*.

2 Ibid., 109.

3 For example, the largest accrediting body in American architectural education mentions the design of "sites, facilities, and systems that are responsive to relevant codes and regulations, and include the principles of life-safety and accessibility standards." National Architectural Accrediting Board, *2014 NAAB Conditions for Accreditation*, 16.

4 Hamraie describes a certain kind of "critical friction" in the products of design work that acknowledged the complexity of inequality: "beyond their functional value, they also drew attention to the failures of existing material arrangements." *Building Access*, 116.

5 Grigely, "Beautiful Progress to Nowhere"; see also Cachia, "Beautiful Progress to Somewhere?"

6 Kuppers, *Disability Culture and Community Performance*, 18.

7 Cogdell, *Eugenic Design*; Gorman, "Educating the Eye."

8 Lewis, "Crip"; McRuer, *Crip Theory*.

9 Hamraie, "Universal Design and the Problem of 'Post-Disability' Ideology."

10 Heskett, *Design*, 2.

11 Gilbert and Schantz, *The Paralympic Games*.

12 Karp, *Choosing a Wheelchair*, 4–9; for more on disabled persons as inventors, see Ott, "The Sum of Its Parts."

13 "Bob Hall. Racing Wheelchair (1986)," accessed August 1, 2013, www.moma.org; Huber, "Boston."

14 Karp, *Choosing a Wheelchair*, 4.

15 Christopher Lyon and Hilarie Sheets, "Designs for Independent Living," *MoMA*, no. 47 (April 1, 1988): 5.

16 Shapiro, *No Pity*, 211–36.

17 Karp, *Choosing a Wheelchair*, 6.

18 Lyon and Sheets, "Designs for Independent Living."

19 *The Museum of Modern Art Catalog* (New York: Museum of Modern Art, 1992).

20 Rosemarie Garland Thomson cites Mullins as a figure of disability made "exotic" in fashion culture, as well as someone who casts "disability as a career advantage," in "Seeing the Disabled," 360–63, 374, n. 26.

21 Johnette Howard, "She's Got Legs," *Sports Illustrated for Women*, Fall 1997.

22 Aimee Mullins, "My 12 Pairs of Legs," 2009, www.ted.com.

23 "No. 13 | Alexander McQueen: Savage Beauty | The Metropolitan Museum of Art, New York," *Alexander McQueen: Savage Beauty*, accessed February 7, 2014, http://blog.metmuseum.org.

24 Mullins includes clips of Cremaster in her TED talk; some parts are also viewable on YouTube. Mullins, "My 12 Pairs of Legs"; Sobchack, "A Leg to Stand On," 297.

25 Mullins, "My 12 Pairs of Legs."

26 "No. 13 | Alexander McQueen: Savage Beauty"; Kahn, "Catwalk Politics."

27 Sobchack, "A Leg to Stand On."

28 Bespoke Innovations, accessed December 12, 2013, bespokeinnovations.com; Rajagopal, "Ready for Prime Time."

29 Summit, "Designing with the Body."

30 "3D Systems Acquires Bespoke Innovations," May 24, 2012, www.3dsystems.com; josh.odell, "A Leg That Fits: Making Natasha's 3D-Printed Prosthetic in Two Weeks," July 29, 2014, www.3dsystems.com.

31 House Committee on Veterans' Affairs, *Providing Automobiles*, 19.

32 Attfield, *Wild Things*, 15.

33 Dunne and Raby, *Speculative Everything*, 33–34; Paola Antonelli, "States of Design 04: Critical Design," *Domus*, no. 949 (July 2011): 86–93.

34 Anthony Dunne and Fiona Raby, "Critical Design FAQ," 2007, www.dunneandraby.co.uk.

35 Pullin, *Design Meets Disability*.

36 Ibid., 49.

37 Ibid., 23–28.

38 Ibid., 191.

39 In a similar recent project, Sara Hendren designed an "alterpodium" with Amanda Cachia that allows Cachia to obtrusively set up her own podium at academic events. Cachia, "The Alterpodium."

40 Sara Hendren, "About Sara Hendren," *Abler*, March 5, 2014, http://ablersite.org.

41 Poole, "The Accessible Icon Project Revamps Familiar Isotype."

42 "New Handicapped Sign Rolls into New York City," *All Things Considered*, National Public Radio, July 7, 2013, www.npr.org.

43 Ibid.

44 Sara Hendren, "The Edited City, 2.0," April 14, 2011, http://sarahendren.net.

45 Poole, "The Accessible Icon Project Revamps Familiar Isotype."

46 Kyle Vanhemert, "How a Guerrilla Art Project Gave Birth to NYC's New Wheelchair Symbol," *Co.Design*, June 6, 2013, www.fastcodesign.com, comments section.

47 Sara Hendren, "Against Re-Branding; Against Placebo Politics," March 5, 2014, http://ablersite.org.

48 Image description by Park McArthur.

49 Russeth, "Park McArthur."

50 "Park McArthur at Essex Street."

51 Cachia, "Beautiful Progress to Somewhere?"

52 Johnson and McRuer attribute the term to Lisa Duggan, and its spread to "the ephemera of conference chatter, social networking, and other queer gatherings." Johnson and McRuer, "Cripistemologies," 130.

53 McRuer and Johnson, "Proliferating Cripistemologies."

54 Thomson, "Seeing the Disabled"; Thomson, *Staring*; Millett-Gallant, *The Disabled Body in Contemporary Art*.

55 Colligan, "Is There Such a Thing as Crip Fashion Justice?"

CONCLUSION

1 *White House Design for All Showcase* (Washington, DC: White House, 2016), www.whitehouse.gov (archived page).

2 "South by South Lawn," accessed October 3, 2016, www.whitehouse.gov.

3 Titchkosky, *The Question of Access*, 4.

BIBLIOGRAPHY

ARCHIVES
California Social Welfare Archives, University of Southern California
Papers of the Rancho Los Amigos Hospital
City of Berkeley County Clerk
Disability Rights and Independent Living Collection, Bancroft Library
Eric Dibner Papers
Disabled Students Program Photograph Collection
Disabled Students Program Records
Michael Fuss Papers
Deborah Kaplan Papers
Herb Willsmore Papers
Harold L. Willson Papers
Hale Zukas Papers
Division of Medicine and Science, National Museum of American History
Ehrman Medical Library, New York University Medical Center Library
Rusk Institute of Rehabilitation Medicine Archive
General Motors Heritage Center Archive
Graduate Theological Seminary
Berkeley Free Church Collection
Hagley Museum and Library
Marc Harrison Papers
Thomas Lamb Papers
William Pahlmann Papers
Schlesinger Library, Radcliffe Institute for Advanced Study
Mary Elizabeth Switzer Papers
Smithsonian Institution Libraries Special Collections
Cooper-Hewitt, National Design Museum Library
National Museum of American History Library

MUSEUM COLLECTIONS
Cooper-Hewitt, National Design Museum
DisAbility History Museum
Hagley Museum and Library
Metropolitan Museum of Art

Museum of Modern Art
National Museum of American History, Smithsonian Institution

PERIODICALS
Berkeley Barb, 1969–1975
The Independent: A New Voice for the Disabled and Blind, 1974–1975
Industrial Design/ID, 1945–1990
New York Times, 1945–2017
Paraplegia News, 1951–1974
Polio Chronicle, 1931–1934
Toomey J Gazette, 1958–1969
Valor, 1950–1953
Wall Street Journal, 1978–2008
Washington Post, 1973–2010

U.S. GOVERNMENT PUBLICATIONS
Americans with Disabilities Act of 1990, Pub. L. No. 101–336 (1990). www.ada.gov.
Booz Allen Research. *Human Factors Evaluation of Transbus by the Elderly.* Washington, DC: Urban Mass Transportation Administration, Department of Transportation, 1976.
Bostrom, James A., and Ronald L. Mace. *Adaptable Housing: A Technical Manual for Implementing Adaptable Dwelling Unit Specifications.* Raleigh, NC: Barrier Free Environments, Inc. for the U.S. Department of Housing and Urban Development, 1987.
Distribution and Use of Hearing Aids, Wheel Chairs, Braces, and Artificial Limbs, July 1958–June 1959. Health Statistics from the U.S. National Health Survey. Washington, DC: U.S. Department of Health, Education, and Welfare, 1961.
General Accounting Office. *Further Action Needed to Make All Public Buildings Accessible to the Physically Handicapped.* FPCD-75–166. Washington, DC: U.S. General Accounting Office, 1975.
House Committee on Veterans' Affairs. *Artificial Limb Program.* Hearings before the Committee on Veterans' Affairs, 80th Congress, 2nd Session, 1948.
———. *Providing Automobiles or Other Conveyances for Certain Disabled Veterans.* Hearings before the Committee on Veterans' Affairs, 80th Congress, 1st Session, 1947.
———. *Providing Housing Units for Paraplegic and Certain Other Service-Connected Disabled Veterans.* Hearings before the Committee on Veterans' Affairs, 80th Congress, 1st Session, 1947.
House Subcommittee on Aid to Physically Handicapped. *Aid to Physically Handicapped.* Hearings before the Committee on Labor, 79th Congress, 1st Session, Part 15: Amputees, 1945.
National Commission on Architectural Barriers to Rehabilitation of the Handicapped. *Design for All Americans: Message from the President of the United States.* Washington, DC: U.S. Government Printing Office, 1968.

National Council on Disability. *On the Threshold of Independence: Progress on Legislative Recommendations from "Toward Independence."* Washington, DC: National Council on Disability, 1988. www.ncd.gov.

———. *Toward Independence: An Assessment of Federal Laws and Programs Affecting Persons with Disabilities—With Legislative Recommendations*. Washington, DC: National Council on Disability, 1986. www.ncd.gov.

Paralyzed Veterans of America. "Legislative Program." March 31, 1965. Records of the Veterans Administration, RG 15. National Archives and Records Administration I, Washington, DC.

Rankin, John. "Authorizing the Payment by the Administrator of Veterans' Affairs of the Purchase Price of Automobiles or Other Conveyances Purchased by Certain Disabled Veterans: Report." 79th Congress, 2nd Session, July 27, 1946. Washington, DC: U.S. Congressional Serial Set.

Redkey, Henry. *Rehabilitation Centers in the United States*. Washington, DC: Office of Vocational Rehabilitation, U.S. Department of Health, Education, and Welfare, 1952.

Reister, Frank. *Medical Statistics in World War II*. Washington, DC: Office of the Surgeon General, Department of the Army, 1975.

Rogers, Edith Nourse. "Authorizing the Payment by the Administrator of Veterans' Affairs of the Purchase Price of Automobiles or Other Conveyances Purchased by Certain Disabled Veterans: Report." 80th Congress, 1st Session, June 2, 1947. Washington, DC: U.S. Congressional Serial Set.

Servicemen's Readjustment Act of 1944 (Public Law 386, 78th Cong., June 22, 1944) with Amendments prior to August 11, 1948: The Act Providing for Vocational Rehabilitation of Disabled Veterans. House Committee Print No. 371. Washington, DC: U.S. Government Printing Office, 1948.

Smithsonian: A Guide for Disabled People. Washington, DC: Smithsonian Institution and President's Committee on Employment of the Handicapped, 1980.

Steinfeld, Edward, and Steven Schroeder. *Access to the Built Environment: A Review of Literature*. Washington, DC: U.S. Department of Housing and Urban Development, Office of Policy Development and Research, 1979.

2010 Standards for Accessible Design. Washington, DC: Department of Justice, 2010. www.ada.gov.

War Department. *Helpful Hints to Those Who Have Lost Limbs*. War Department Pamphlet 8–7. Washington, DC: U.S. War Department, 1944.

ARTICLES

Allen, Peter. "The End of Modernism?" *Journal of the Society of Architectural Historians* 70, no. 3 (September 2011): 354–74.

Antonelli, Paola. "States of Design 04: Critical Design." *Domus*, no. 949 (July 2011): 86–93.

Barnartt, Sharon N. "Social Movement Diffusion? The Case of Disability Protests in the U.S. and Canada." *Disability Studies Quarterly* 28, no. 1 (January 31, 2008). http://dsq-sds.org.

Baynton, Douglas C. "Disability and the Justification of Inequality in American History." In *The New Disability History: American Perspectives*, edited by Paul K. Longmore and Lauri Umansky, 33–57. New York: New York University Press, 2001.

———. "'These Pushful Days': Time and Disability in the Age of Eugenics." *Health and History* 13, no. 2 (January 1, 2011): 43–64.

Berkowitz, Edward D. "The Federal Government and the Emergence of Rehabilitation Medicine." *Historian* 43, no. 4 (Winter 1981): 530–45.

———. "A Historical Preface to the Americans with Disabilities Act." *Journal of Policy History* 6, no. 1 (1994): 96–119.

Boris, Eileen. "Contested Rights: The Great Society between Home and Work." In *The Great Society and the High Tide of Liberalism*, edited by Sidney M. Milkis and Jerome M. Mileur, 115–45. Amherst: University of Massachusetts Press, 2005.

Boris, Eileen, and Jennifer Klein. "Organizing Home Care: Low-Waged Workers in the Welfare State." *Politics and Society* 34, no. 1 (March 2006): 81–107.

Brown, Steven E. "Breaking Barriers: The Pioneering Disability Students Services Program at the University of Illinois, 1948–1960." In *The History of Discrimination in U.S. Education: Marginality, Agency, and Power*, edited by Eileen Tamura, 165–92. New York: Palgrave Macmillan, 2008.

Burgdorf, Marcia Pearce, and Robert Burgdorf. "A History of Unequal Treatment: The Qualifications of Handicapped Persons as a 'Suspect Class' under the Equal Protection Clause." *Santa Clara Lawyer* 15, no. 4 (Summer 1975): 855–910.

Burgstahler, Sheryl, and Tanis Doe. "Disability-Related Simulations: If, When, and How to Use Them in Professional Development." *Review of Disability Studies* 1, no. 2 (2004): 4–17.

Cachia, Amanda. "The Alterpodium: A Performative Design and Disability Intervention." *Design and Culture* 8, no. 3 (2016): 311–25.

———. "Beautiful Progress to Somewhere?" In *The Incorrigibles: Perspectives on Disability Visual Culture in the 20th and 21st Centuries*, 79–83. Birmingham, U.K.: mac for DASH Arts, 2016.

Campbell, Robert. "It's Accessible, but . . . Is It Architecture?" *Architectural Record*, August 1991: 42–44.

Cartwright, Morse A. "Re-Education of the Returned Soldier and Sailor." *Annals of the American Academy of Political and Social Science* 227 (May 1943): 111–21.

Chung, L. A. "Cops Bust Disabled Protesters." *San Francisco Chronicle*, September 19, 1987.

Clark, Daniel A. "'The Two Joes Meet. Joe College, Joe Veteran': The G.I. Bill, College Education, and Postwar American Culture." *History of Education Quarterly* 38, no. 2 (Summer 1998): 165–89.

Clarke, Alison. "The Anthropological Object in Design: From Victor Papanek to Superstudio." In *Design Anthropology: Object Culture in the 21st Century*, edited by Allison Clarke, 74–87. Vienna: Springer, 2011.

Colligan, Sumi. "Is There Such a Thing as Crip Fashion Justice?" Paper presented at Society for Disability Studies, San Jose, CA, June 17, 2011.

Collins, Selwyn D. "The Incidence of Poliomyelitis and Its Crippling Effects, as Recorded in Family Surveys." *Public Health Reports (1896-1970)* 61, no. 10 (March 8, 1946): 327–55.

Covalt, Donald A. "The Medical Rehabilitation Program in the Veterans Administration." *Occupational Therapy and Rehabilitation* 25, no. 4 (August 1946): 123–27.

Cowan, Ruth Schwartz. "The Consumption Junction: A Proposal for Research Strategies in the Sociology of Technology." In *The Social Construction of Technological Systems: New Directions in the Sociology and History of Technology*, edited by Wiebe E. Bijker, Thomas Parke Hughes, and Trevor J. Pinch, 261–80. Cambridge: MIT Press, 1987.

Delphia, Rachel. "Ergonomics and Negative Space: Thomas Lamb's Wedge-Lock Handle." In *The Utility of Emptiness*, edited by Uli Marchsteiner, 43-50. Barcelona: Museu de les Arts Decoratifs, 2008.

Diffrient, Niels, Joan Bardagjy, and Nicholas Polites. "Dimensions of Experience: Understanding and Measuring Human Experience in the Designed Environment." *Design Quarterly* 96 (January 1, 1975): 1–43.

Dilnot, Clive. "The State of Design History—Part I: Mapping the Field." In *Design Discourse: History, Theory, Criticism*, edited by Victor Margolin, 213–32. Chicago: University of Chicago Press, 1989.

Edwards, Martha L. "Constructions of Physical Disability in the Ancient Greek World: The Community Concept." In *The Body and Physical Difference: Discourses of Disability*, edited by David T. Mitchell and Sharon L. Snyder, 35-50. Ann Arbor: University of Michigan Press, 1997.

Eglash, Ron. "Appropriating Technology: An Introduction." In *Appropriating Technology: Vernacular Science and Social Power*, vii–xii. Minneapolis: University of Minnesota Press, 2004.

Feeney, R. J. "Are Aids for the Disabled Consumer Goods?" In *The Use of Technology in the Care of the Elderly and the Disabled: Tools for Living*, edited by Jean Bray and Sheila Wright, 253–56. Westport, CT: Greenwood, 1980.

Franz, Kathleen. "Automobiles and Automobility." In *Material Culture in America: Understanding Everyday Life*, edited by Shirley Teresa Wajda and Helen Sheumaker, 53–56. Santa Barbara, CA: ABC-CLIO, 2008.

Friedel, Robert. "Scarcity and Promise: Materials and American Domestic Culture during World War II." In *World War II and the American Dream*, edited by Donald Albrecht and Margaret Crawford, 42–89. Washington, DC: National Building Museum, 1995.

Frieden, Lex. "IL: Movement and Programs." *American Rehabilitation*, August 1978, 6–9.

Fritsch, Kelly. "Beyond the Wheelchair: Rethinking the Politics of Disability and Accessibility." *Briarpatch Magazine*, March 10, 2014. https://briarpatchmagazine.com.

Funk, Robert. "Disability Rights: From Caste to Class—The Humanization of Disabled People." In *Law Reform in Disability Rights: Articles and Concept Papers, B1–B21*. Berkeley: Disability Rights Center, 1981.

Gelber, Steven M. "Do-It-Yourself: Constructing, Repairing and Maintaining Domestic Masculinity." *American Quarterly* 49, no. 1 (1997): 66–112.

Gerber, David A. "Disabled Veterans, the State, and the Experience of Disability in Western Societies, 1914–1950." *Journal of Social History* 36, no. 4 (Summer 2003): 899–916.

———. "Heroes and Misfits: The Troubled Social Reintegration of Disabled Veterans in *The Best Years of Our Lives.*" *American Quarterly* 46, no. 4 (December 1994): 545–74.

Gilbreth, Lillian. "Building for Living." In *A Nationwide Report on Building Happy, Useful Lives for the Handicapped: A Record of the 1950 Convention*, 48–50. Chicago: National Society for Crippled Children and Adults, 1951.

Gillette, Howard. "Washington: Symbol and City." *Journal of American History* 79, no. 1 (1992): 208–12.

Gorman, Carma. "Educating the Eye: Body Mechanics and Streamlining in the United States, 1925–1950." *American Quarterly* 58, no. 3 (2006): 839–68.

Graham, Hugh Davis. "Introduction." *Journal of Policy History* 6, no. 1 (1994): 1–11.

Grigely, Joseph. "Beautiful Progress to Nowhere." *Parallel Lines*, 2011. www.parallel linesjournal.com.

Guffey, Elizabeth. "The Scandinavian Roots of the International Symbol of Access." *Design and Culture* 7, no. 3 (2015): 357–76.

Hamraie, Aimi. "Universal Design and the Problem of 'Post-Disability' Ideology." *Design and Culture*, August 19, 2016, 1–25.

———. "Universal Design Research as a New Materialist Practice." *Disability Studies Quarterly* 32, no. 4 (September 2012). http://dsq-sds.org.

Herbst, Laura. "Nobody's Perfect." *Popular Science*, January 1997, 64–66.

Herschbach, Lisa. "Prosthetic Reconstructions: Making the Industry, Re-Making the Body, Modelling the Nation." *History Workshop Journal* 44 (Autumn 1997): 22–57.

Hilleary, J. F. "Buildings for All to Use: The Goal of Barrier-Free Architecture." *American Institute of Architects Journal* 51 (March 1969): 40–50, 82, 84.

Hosey, Lance. "Hidden Lines: Gender, Race, and the Body in Graphic Standards." *Journal of Architectural Education* 55, no. 2 (November 2001): 101–12.

Howard, Johnette. "She's Got Legs." *Sports Illustrated for Women*, Fall 1997, 82–90.

Huber, Joseph. "Boston: The 100th Marathon and the Wheelchair Athlete." *Palestra: Forum of Sport, Physical Education and Recreation for Those with Disabilities 12, no. 2* (1996): 33–37.

Jennings, Audra. "'An Emblem of Distinction': The Politics of Disability Entitlement, 1940–1950." In *Veterans' Policies, Veterans' Politics: New Perspectives on Veterans in the Modern United States*, edited by Stephen R. Ortiz, 94–118. Gainesville: University Press of Florida, 2012.

Johnson, Mary. "Universal Man: Ron Mace Leads the Way to Design That Includes Everybody." *Mainstream*, August 1994, 18–27.

Johnson, Merri Lisa, and Robert McRuer. "Cripistemologies: Introduction." *Journal of Literary and Cultural Disability Studies* 8, no. 2 (2014): 127–47.

Kahn, Nathalie. "Catwalk Politics." In *Fashion Cultures: Theories, Explorations and Analysis*, edited by Stella Bruzzi and Pamela Church Gibson, 114–27. New York: Routledge, 2013.

Kamenetz, Herman L. "Wheelchairs." In *Orthotics Etcetera*, edited by Sidney Licht, 474–77. Baltimore: Waverly, 1966.

King, Karen J., and Rebecca Ingraham. "Inclusive Design." In *Architectural Graphic Standards*, edited by Andy Pressman, 873–931. New York: John Wiley and Sons, 2007.

Kittay, Eva. "Dependency." In *Keywords for Disability Studies*, edited by Rachel Adams, Benjamin Reiss, and David Serlin, 54–57. New York: New York University Press, 2014.

Kline, Ronald, and Trevor Pinch. "Users as Agents of Technological Change: The Social Construction of the Automobile in the Rural United States." *Technology and Culture* 37, no. 4 (October 1, 1996): 763–95.

Krizack, Mark. "What about the Electric Wheelchair? Smithsonian Online Exhibit on Disability Rights Leaves a Gap on Technology." *Disability World*, no. 3 (July 2000). www.disabilityworld.org.

Kudlick, Catherine J. "Disability History: Why We Need Another 'Other.'" *American Historical Review* 108, no. 3 (June 2003): 763–93.

Landsberger, S., P. Leung, V. Vargas, J. Shaperman, J. Baumgarten, Y. L. Yasuda, E. Sumi, D. McNeal, and R. Waters. "Mobile Arm Supports: History, Application, and Work in Progress." *Topics in Spinal Cord Injury Rehabilitation* 11, no. 2 (2005): 74.

Le Corbusier. "Type-Needs: Type-Furniture." In *The Theory of Decorative Art: An Anthology of European and American Writings, 1750–1950*, edited by Isabelle Frank, 84–89. New Haven: Yale University Press, 2000.

Leifer, Larry. "Rehabilitative Robots." *Robotics Age*, June 1981, 4–15.

Lewis, Victoria Ann. "Crip." In *Keywords for Disability Studies*, edited by Rachel Adams, Benjamin Reiss, and David Serlin, 46–48. New York: New York University Press, 2014.

Lifchez, Raymond. "Designing Supportive Physical Environments." In *Independent Living for Physically Disabled People*, edited by Nancy M. Crewe and Irving Kenneth Zola, 130–53. San Francisco: Jossey-Bass, 1983.

Linton, Simi. "Series Introduction." In *University of California's Cowell Hospital Residence Program for Physically Disabled Students, 1962–1975: Catalyst for Berkeley's Independent Living Movement, i–vi*. Berkeley: Regional Oral History Office, Bancroft Library, University of California, Berkeley, 2000. www.oac.cdlib.org.

Longmore, Paul K., and David Goldberger. "The League of the Physically Handicapped and the Great Depression: A Case Study in the New Disability History." *Journal of American History* 87, no. 3 (December 1, 2000): 888–922.

Mace, Ronald. "Universal Design: Barrier Free Environments for Everyone." *Designers West*, November 1985, 147–52.

McCluskey, Martha T. "Rethinking Equality and Difference: Disability Discrimination in Public Transportation." *Yale Law Journal* 97, no. 5 (April 1988): 863–80.

McConnell, Vicki. "Universal Design: Including People with Physical Disabilities." *Plastics Design Forum*, August 1993, 32–38.

McDaid, Jennifer Davis. "'How a One-Legged Rebel Lives': Confederate Veterans and Artificial Limbs in Virginia." In *Artificial Parts, Practical Lives: Modern Histories of Prosthetics*, edited by Katherine Ott, David Serlin, and Stephen Mihm, 119–46. New York: New York University Press, 2002.

McKnight, Claire, Marcia Walsh, Leonard Robins, and Ashish Sen. "Transportation for the Mobility-Limited: An Analysis of Current Options." *Policy Analysis* 6, no. 4 (1980): 441–65.

McRuer, Robert, and Merri Lisa Johnson. "Proliferating Cripistemologies: A Virtual Roundtable." *Journal of Literary & Cultural Disability Studies* 8, no. 2 (2014): 149–69.

Mitchell, Don. "The End of Public Space? People's Park, Definitions of the Public, and Democracy." *Annals of the Association of American Geographers* 85, no. 1 (March 1995): 108–33.

Mueller, James. "The Case for Universal Design: If You Can't Use It, It's Just Art." *Ageing International*, March 1995, 19–23.

Nieusma, Dean. "Alternative Design Scholarship: Working toward Appropriate Design." *Design Issues* 20, no. 3 (Summer 2004): 13–24.

Niland, David. "A House Remade." In "Beyond Scale: Two Projects for the Physically Handicapped." Special issue, *Design Quarterly* 105 (1978).

"$9,990 Levitt Houses Boast 70' Lots." *Architectural Forum*, October 1951.

Olson, Toby. "How Disability Simulations Promote Damaging Stereotypes." *Braille Monitor*, January 2014. https://nfb.org.

Onkst, David H. "'First a Negro . . . Incidentally a Veteran': Black World War Two Veterans and the G.I. Bill of Rights in the Deep South, 1944–1948." *Journal of Social History* 31, no. 3 (Spring 1998): 517–43.

Orski, C. Kenneth. "Changing Directions of Public Transportation in the United States." *Built Environment* 8, no. 3 (1982): 156–66.

Ott, Katherine. "Disability Things: Material Culture and American Disability History, 1700–2010." In *Disability Histories*, edited by Susan Burch and Michael Rembis, 119–35. Champaign: University of Illinois Press, 2014.

Page, Clint. "Is the 10-Year Wait for a Good City Bus Coming to an End?" *Nation's Cities*, May 1977, 4–6.

Paranchini, Allan. "Sic Transit Transbus." *Reason*, July 1980, 34–37.

"Park McArthur at Essex Street." *Contemporary Art Daily*, January 27, 2014. www.contemporaryartdaily.com.

Parsons, John G. "The Public Struggle to Erect the Franklin Delano Roosevelt Memorial." *Landscape Journal: Design, Planning, and Management of the Land* 31, no. 1 (February 16, 2013): 145–59.

Patterson, Lindsey. "Points of Access: Rehabilitation Centers, Summer Camps, and Student Life in the Making of Disability Activism, 1960–1973." *Journal of Social History* 46, no. 2 (2012): 473–99.

Poole, Buzz. "The Accessible Icon Project Revamps Familiar Isotype." *Print*, June 6, 2013. www.printmag.com.

Puaca, Laura Micheletti. "The Largest Occupational Group of All the Disabled: Home-makers with Disabilities and Vocational Rehabilitation in Postwar America." In *Disabling Domesticity*, edited by Michael Rembis. New York: Palgrave Macmillan, 2016.

Rajagopal, Avinash. "Ready for Prime Time." *Metropolis*, April 2013. www.metropolis mag.com.

Ratto, Matt, and Robert Ree. "Materializing Information: 3D Printing and Social Change." *First Monday* 17, no. 7 (June 27, 2012). http://firstmonday.org.

Rogers, Naomi. "Polio Chronicles: Warm Springs and Disability Politics in the 1930s." *Asclepio, Revista de Historia de la Medicina y de la Ciencia* 61, no. 1 (June 2009): 143–74.

———. "Race and the Politics of Polio: Warm Springs, Tuskegee, and the March of Dimes." *American Journal of Public Health* 97, no. 5 (2007): 784–95.

Rose, Sarah F. "The Right to a College Education? The GI Bill, Public Law 16, and Dis-abled Veterans." *Journal of Policy History* 24, no. 1 (2012): 26–52.

Rusk, Howard. "Rehabilitation: The Third Phase of Medicine." *Canadian Medical As-sociation Journal* 61 (December 1949): 603–7.

Russeth, Andrew. "'Park McArthur: Ramps' at Essex Street." *Gallerist NY*, January 22, 2014. http://galleristny.com.

Samuels, Robert. "Limited to Design?" *New Mobility: The Magazine for Active Wheel-chair Users*, January 1999. http://newmobility.com.

Sauerborn, Paula J. "Advances in Upper Extremity Prosthetics in the United States dur-ing World War II and Early Post–World War II Era." *Journal of Facial and Somato Prosthetics*, 1998, 93–104.

Schmertz, Mildred F. "Two Houses by Charles Moore." *Architectural Record* 161, no. 7 (1977): 109–16.

Schweik, Susan. "Homer's Odyssey: Multiple Disability and *The Best Years of Our Lives*." In *Civil Disabilities: Citizenship, Membership, and Belonging*, edited by Beth Linker and Nancy J. Hirschmann, 22–43. Philadelphia: University of Pennsylvania Press, 2015.

———. "Lomax's Matrix: Disability, Solidarity, and the Black Power of 504." *Disability Studies Quarterly* 31, no. 1 (January 2011www.dsq-sds.org.

"Shoulder-Operated Artificial Arms and Hands." *Scientific American* 114, no. 2 (Janu-ary 15, 1916): 77.

Smith, Edward R., and T. F. Riggar. "Accessible Transportation: Human Rights . . . versus . . . Costs." *Journal of Rehabilitation* 54, no. 2 (April 1988): 13–17.

Sobchack, Vivian. "A Leg to Stand on: Prosthetics, Metaphor, and Materiality." In *The Object Reader*, edited by Fiona Candlin and Rayford Guins, 279–96. New York: Routledge, 2009.

Stein, Michael Ashley, Michael E. Waterstone, and David B. Wilkins. "Cause Lawyering for People with Disabilities." Edited by Samuel R. Bagenstos. *Harvard Law Review* 123, no. 7 (2010): 1658–1703.

Summit, Scott. "Designing with the Body." *Innovation: The Journal of the Industrial Designers Society of America*, Summer 2012, 10–11.

tenBroek, Jacobus. "The Right to Live in the World: The Disabled in the Law of Torts." *California Law Review* 54, no. 2 (May 1966): 841–919.

Thomson, Rosemarie Garland. "Seeing the Disabled: Visual Rhetorics of Disability in Popular Photography." In *The New Disability History: American Perspectives*, edited by Paul K. Longmore and Lauri Umansky, 335–74. New York: New York University Press, 2001.

Trevelyan, Barry, Matthew Smallman-Raynor, and Andrew D. Cliff. "The Spatial Dynamics of Poliomyelitis in the United States: From Epidemic Emergence to Vaccine-Induced Retreat, 1910–1971." *Annals of the Association of American Geographers* 95, no. 2 (June 2005): 269–93.

Upton, Dell. "White and Black Landscapes in Eighteenth-Century Virginia." *Places: A Quarterly Journal of Environmental Design* 2, no. 2 (1984): 59–72.

Vanhemert, Kyle. "How a Guerrilla Art Project Gave Birth to NYC's New Wheelchair Symbol." *Co.Design*, June 6, 2013. www.fastcodesign.com.

Williamson, Bess. "Access." In *Keywords for Disability Studies*, edited by Rachel Adams, Benjamin Reiss, and David Serlin, 14–17. New York: New York University Press, 2014.

———. "Getting a Grip: Disability and American Industrial Design of the Late Twentieth Century." *Winterthur Portfolio* 46, no. 4 (Winter 2012): 213–36.

Wilson, Daniel J. "And They Shall Walk: Ideal versus Reality in Polio Rehabilitation in the United States." *Asclepio, Revista de Historia de la Medicina y de la Ciencia* 61 (July 2009): 175–92.

Zimmerman, Muriel. "Accent on Progress." *IPMR: A Chronicle of Independence*, Fall 1955, 19–22.

Zukas, Hale. "The History of the Berkeley Center for Independent Living (CIL)." *Independent Living Institute*, 1975. www.independentliving.org.

———. "Why Disabled People Do Not Use BART." *Independent: A New Voice for the Disabled and Blind* 1, no. 3 (Winter 1974): 12.

BOOKS

Adas, Michael. *Dominance by Design: Technological Imperatives and America's Civilizing Mission*. Cambridge: Belknap, 2006.

American National Standards Institute. *ANSI 117.1–1961: American National Standard Specifications for Making Buildings and Facilities Accessible to, and Usable by, the Physically Handicapped*. New York: American National Standards Institute, 1961.

———. *ANSI 117.1–1980: American National Standard Specifications for Making Buildings and Facilities Accessible to and Usable by Physically Handicapped People*. New York: American National Standards Institute, 1980.

Attfield, Judy. *Wild Things: The Material Culture of Everyday Life*. Oxford: Berg, 2000.

Barnartt, Sharon N., and Richard K. Scotch. *Disability Protests: Contentious Politics, 1970–1999*. Washington, DC: Gallaudet University Press, 2001.

Berns, S. Harry, Edward W. Lowman, Howard A. Rusk, and Donald A. Covalt. *Spinal Cord Injury: Rehabilitation Costs and Results in 31 Successive Cases Including a Follow-Up Study*. Rehabilitation Monograph, XIII. New York: Institute of Physical Medicine and Rehabilitation, New York University-Bellevue Medical Center, 1957.

Binkley, Sam. *Getting Loose: Lifestyle Consumption in the 1970s*. Durham: Duke University Press, 2007.

Boatwright, Roger Bates. "The Social Adjustment of Eleven World War II Veterans to Paraplegia." M.A. thesis, Southern Methodist University, 1952.

Brandt, Edward N., and Andrew MacPherson Pope, eds. *Enabling America: Assessing the Role of Rehabilitation Science and Engineering*. Washington, DC: National Academy Press, 1997.

Bruck, Lilly. *Access: The Guide to a Better Life for Disabled Americans*. New York: David Obst Books, 1978.

Canaday, Margot. *The Straight State: Sexuality and Citizenship in Twentieth-Century America*. Princeton: Princeton University Press, 2009.

Charlton, James I. *Nothing about Us without Us: Disability Oppression and Empowerment*. Berkeley: University of California Press, 1998.

Clark, Clifford Edward. *The American Family Home, 1800–1960*. Chapel Hill: University of North Carolina Press, 1986.

Cogdell, Christina. *Eugenic Design: Streamlining America in the 1930s*. Philadelphia: University of Pennsylvania Press, 2004.

Cohen, Lizabeth. *A Consumers' Republic: The Politics of Mass Consumption in Postwar America*. New York: Knopf, 2003.

Crewe, Nancy M., and Irving Kenneth Zola, eds. *Independent Living for Physically Disabled People*. San Francisco: Jossey-Bass, 1983.

Daniels, Michael, ed. *Going Where You Wheel on Telegraph Avenue: An Evaluation of Accessibility on the Avenue Using a Model Applicable Anywhere*. Berkeley: Center for Independent Living, 1984.

———. *Ramps Are Beautiful: The Architecture of Independence*. Berkeley: Center for Independent Living, 1982.

Dávila, Arlene M. *Latinos, Inc.: The Marketing and Making of a People*. Berkeley: University of California Press, 2001.

Davis, Lennard J. *Bending Over Backwards: Disability, Dismodernism, and Other Difficult Positions*. New York: New York University Press, 2002.

Day, Clarence. *The Crow's Nest*. New York: Knopf, 1921.

Deaver, George, and Eleanor Brown. *Physical Demands of Daily Life: An Objective Scale for Rating the Orthopedically Exceptional*. New York: Institute for the Crippled and Disabled, 1945.

Deetz, James. *In Small Things Forgotten: The Archaeology of Early American Life*. Garden City, NY: Anchor/Doubleday, 1977.

Diffrient, Niels, Alvin R. Tilly, and Joan C. Bardagjy. *Humanscale 1/2/3: A Portfolio of Information, 1. Sizes of People, 2. Seating Considerations, 3. Requirements for the Handicapped and Elderly*. Cambridge: MIT Press, 1974.

Disability Rights and Independent Living Movement Oral History Series. *Architectural Accessibility and Disability Rights in Berkeley and Japan*. Berkeley: Regional Oral History Office, Bancroft Library, University of California, 2004.

———. *Blind Services and Advocacy and the Independent Living Movement in Berkeley*. Berkeley: Regional Oral History Office, Bancroft Library, University of California, 2000.

———. *Builders and Sustainers of the Independent Living Movement in Berkeley*. Vols. 1–4. Berkeley: Regional Oral History Office, Bancroft Library, University of California, 2000.

———. *Massachusetts Activists and Leaders in the Disability Rights and Independent Living Movement*. Berkeley: Regional Oral History Office, Bancroft Library, University of California, 2004.

———. *UC Berkeley's Cowell Hospital Residence Program: Key Administrators and California Department of Rehabilitation Counselors*. Berkeley: Regional Oral History Office, Bancroft Library, University of California, 2000.

———. *University of California's Cowell Hospital Residence Program for Physically Disabled Students, 1962–1975: Catalyst for Berkeley's Independent Living Movement*. Berkeley: Regional Oral History Office, Bancroft Library, University of California, 2000.

Dreyfuss, Henry. *Designing for People*. New York: Grossman, 1974.

———. *The Measure of Man: Human Factors in Design*. New York: Whitney Library of Design, 1960.

Driving Aids and Accessories. Winimac, IN: Braun Corporation, n.d.

Dunne, Anthony, and Fiona Raby. *Speculative Everything: Design, Fiction, and Social Dreaming*. Cambridge: MIT Press, 2013.

Ellcessor, Elizabeth. *Restricted Access: Media, Disability, and the Politics of Participation*. New York: New York University Press, 2016.

Fallan, Kjetil. *Design History: Understanding Theory and Method*. Oxford: Berg, 2010.

Faries, John Culbert. *Three Years of Work for Handicapped Men: A Report of the Activities of the Institute for Crippled and Disabled Men*. New York: Institute for Crippled and Disabled Men, 1920.

Fleischer, Doris Zames, and Frieda Zames. *The Disability Rights Movement: From Charity to Confrontation*. Philadelphia: Temple University Press, 2001.

Flinchum, Russell. *Henry Dreyfuss, Industrial Designer: The Man in the Brown Suit*. New York: Cooper-Hewitt, National Design Museum, Smithsonian Institution and Rizzoli, 1997.

Flink, James J. *The Automobile Age*. Cambridge: MIT Press, 1988.

Fondation Le Corbusier. "The Modulor and Modulor 2." In *LC Online Paket*. Berlin: Birkhäuser- De Gruyter, 2000.

Fuad-Luke, Alastair. *Design Activism: Beautiful Strangeness for a Sustainable World*. London: Earthscan, 2009.

Furman, Bess. *Progress in Prosthetics: A Summary under Sponsorship of the Prosthetics Research Board of the National Academy of Sciences*. Washington, DC: Office of Vocational Rehabilitation, 1962.

Gallagher, Hugh Gregory. *FDR's Splendid Deception*. New York: Dodd, Mead, 1985.

Garee, Betty. *Ideas for Making Your Home Accessible*. Bloomington, IL: Accent Special Publications, 1979.

Garvey, Ellen Gruber. *The Adman in the Parlor: Magazines and the Gendering of Consumer Culture, 1880s to 1910s*. New York: Oxford University Press, 1996.

Gerber, David A., ed. *Disabled Veterans in History*. Ann Arbor: University of Michigan Press, 2000.

Gilbert, Keith, and Otto J. Schantz. *The Paralympic Games: Empowerment or Side Show?* Aachen: Meyer & Meyer Verlag, 2008.

Goldstein, Carolyn. *Do It Yourself: Home Improvement in 20th-Century America*. Washington, DC, and New York: Princeton Architectural Press for the National Building Museum, 1998.

Gordon, Linda. *Pitied but Not Entitled: Single Mothers and the History of Welfare, 1890–1935*. New York: Free Press, 1994.

Grier, Katherine C. *Culture and Comfort: Parlor Making and Middle-Class Identity, 1850–1930*. Washington, DC: Smithsonian Institution Press, 1997.

Gritzer, Glenn, and Arnold Arluke. *The Making of Rehabilitation Medicine: A Political Economy of Medical Specialization, 1890–1980*. Berkeley: University of California Press, 1985.

Guffey, Elizabeth. *Designing Disability: Symbols, Space, and Society*. New York: Bloomsbury, 2017.

Halter, Marilyn. *Shopping for Identity: The Marketing of Ethnicity*. New York: Schocken, 2000.

Hamraie, Aimi. *Building Access: Universal Design and the Politics of Disability*. Minneapolis: University of Minnesota Press, 2017.

Heskett, John. *Design: A Very Short Introduction*. New York: Oxford University Press, 2005.

———. *Toothpicks and Logos: Design in Everyday Life*. Oxford, UK: Oxford University Press, 2002.

Hiesinger, Kathryn B., and George H. Marcus, eds. *Design since 1945*. Philadelphia: Philadelphia Museum of Art, 1983.

———. *Landmarks of Twentieth-Century Design: An Illustrated Handbook*. New York: Abbeville, 1993.

Hounshell, David A. *From the American System to Mass Production, 1800–1932: The Development of Manufacturing Technology in the United States*. Baltimore: Johns Hopkins University Press, 1984.

Howard, Philip K. *The Death of Common Sense: How Law Is Suffocating America*. New York: Random House, 1994.

Industrial Designers Society of America. *Industrial Design Excellence, 1980–1985*. McLean, VA: Design Foundation, 1985.

Institute for the Crippled and Disabled. *Rehabilitation Trends: Midcentury to 1956*. New York: Institute for the Crippled and Disabled, 1956.

International Center for the Disabled. *The ICD Survey of Disabled Americans: Bringing Disabled Americans into the Mainstream, a Nationwide Survey of 1,000 Disabled People*. New York: L. Harris and Associates, 1986.

Irvin, Cass. *Home Bound: Growing up with a Disability in America*. Philadelphia: Temple University Press, 2004.

Isaacson, Walter. *Steve Jobs*. New York: Simon and Schuster, 2011.

Jennings, Audra. *Out of the Horrors of War: Disability Politics in World War II*. Philadelphia: University of Pennsylvania Press, 2016.

———. "With Minds Fixed on the Horrors of War: Liberalism and Disability Activism, 1940–1960." Ph.D. diss., Ohio State University, 2008.

Johnson, Mary, and Barrett Shaw. *To Ride the Public's Buses*. Louisville, KY: Advocado Press, 2001.

Kafer, Alison. *Feminist, Queer, Crip*. Bloomington: Indiana University Press, 2013.

Karp, Gary. *Choosing a Wheelchair: A Guide for Optimal Independence*. Cambridge: O'Reilly, 1998.

Kessler, Henry Howard. *The Knife Is Not Enough*. New York: Norton, 1968.

Kuppers, Petra. *Disability Culture and Community Performance: Find a Strange and Twisted Shape*. Houndmills: Palgrave Macmillan, 2011.

Lancaster, Jane. *Making Time: Lillian Moller Gilbreth, A Life beyond "Cheaper by the Dozen."* Boston: Northeastern University Press, 2004.

Latour, Bruno. *We Have Never Been Modern*. Cambridge: Harvard University Press, 1993.

Lebovich, William L. *Design for Dignity: Studies in Accessibility*. New York: Wiley and Sons, 1993.

Lifchez, Raymond. *Design for Independent Living: The Environment and Physically Disabled People*. New York: Whitney Library of Design, 1979.

———. *Rethinking Architecture: Design Students and Physically Disabled People*. Berkeley: University of California Press, 1987.

Linker, Beth. *War's Waste: Rehabilitation in World War I America*. Chicago: University of Chicago Press, 2011.

Longmore, Paul K. *Why I Burned My Book and Other Essays on Disability*. Philadelphia: Temple University Press, 2003.

Los Angeles County Farm. *A Guide for New Patients*. Downey, CA: Los Angeles County Farm, 1929.

Mace, Ronald L., and Betsy Laslett, eds. *An Illustrated Handbook of the Handicapped Section of the North Carolina State Building Code: Including a Reprint of General Construction, Volume 1, Section 11x, Making Buildings & Facilities Accessible to & Usable by the Physically Handicapped and Dec. 1973 Amendments: For the Governor's Study Committee on Architectural Barriers and the North Carolina Department of Insurance*. Raleigh: North Carolina Dept. of Insurance, Special Office for the Handicapped, 1974.

MacLean, Nancy. *Freedom Is Not Enough: The Opening of the American Workplace*. New York: Russell Sage, 2006.

Makower, Timothy. *Touching the City: Thoughts on Urban Scale*. AD Primers. Chichester, England: Wiley, 2014.

Mandel, Mike. *Making Good Time: Scientific Management, the Gilbreths Photography and Motion Futurism*. Santa Cruz, CA: M. Mandel, 1989.

Marchand, Roland. *Advertising the American Dream: Making Way for Modernity, 1920–1940*. Berkeley: University of California Press, 1985.

Margolin, Victor. *Design Discourse: History, Theory, Criticism*. Chicago: University of Chicago Press, 1989.

———. *The Politics of the Artificial: Essays on Design and Design Studies*. Chicago: University of Chicago Press, 2002.

Marks Adjustable Folding Chair Co. *The Marks Improved Adjustable Folding Chair: Combining a Parlor, Library, Smoking, Reclining or Invalid Chair, Lounge, Bed, and Child's Crib*. New York: The Company, 1880.

Marks, George Edwin. *Manual of Artificial Limbs: . . . An Exhaustive Exposition of Prosthesis*. New York: A. A. Marks, 1907.

Mason, Mary Grimley. *Life Prints: A Memoir of Healing and Discovery*. New York: Feminist Press at the City University of New York, 2000.

McCullough, Helen E., and Mary B. Farnham. *Space and Design Requirements for Wheelchair Kitchens*. Urbana: University of Illinois Agricultural Experiment Station, 1960.

McRuer, Robert. *Crip Theory: Cultural Signs of Queerness and Disability*. New York: New York University Press, 2006.

Meikle, Jeffrey L. *American Plastic: A Cultural History*. New Brunswick: Rutgers University Press, 1995.

———. *Design in the USA*. Oxford History of Art. Oxford: Oxford University Press, 2005.

Millett-Gallant, Ann. *The Disabled Body in Contemporary Art*. Basingstoke: Palgrave Macmillan, 2012.

Mittelstadt, Jennifer. *From Welfare to Workfare: The Unintended Consequences of Liberal Reform, 1945–1965*. Chapel Hill: University of North Carolina Press, 2006.

Moore, Pat, and Charles Paul Conn. *Disguised: A True Story*. Waco, TX: Word Books, 1985.

National Architectural Accrediting Board. *2014 NAAB Conditions for Accreditation*. Washington, DC: National Architectural Accrediting Board, 2014.

National Research Council. *NRC Transbus Study*. Washington, DC: National Academy of Sciences, 1979.

Nielsen, Kim. *A Disability History of the United States*. Boston: Beacon, 2012.

Nugent, Timothy J. *Design of Buildings to Permit Their Use by the Physically Handicapped: A National Attack on Architectural Barriers*. Washington, DC: National Academy of Sciences–National Research Council, 1967.

O'Brien, Ruth. *Crippled Justice: The History of Modern Disability Policy in the Workplace*. Chicago: University of Chicago Press, 2001.

Oshinsky, David M. *Polio: An American Story*. New York: Oxford University Press, 2005.

Ostroff, Elaine, Mark Limont, and Daniel Hunter. *Building a World Fit for People: Designers with Disabilities at Work*. Boston: Adaptive Environments Center, 2002.

OToole, Corbett Joan. *Fading Scars: My Queer Disability History*. Fort Worth, TX: Autonomous Press, 2015.

Ott, Katherine, David Serlin, and Stephen Mihm, eds. *Artificial Parts, Practical Lives: Modern Histories of Prosthetics*. New York: New York University Press, 2002.

Papanek, Victor J. *Design for Human Scale*. New York: Van Nostrand Reinhold, 1983.

———. *Design for the Real World: Human Ecology and Social Change*. New York: Pantheon, 1972.

Paralyzed Veterans of America. *An Oral History of the Paralyzed Veterans of America*. Washington, DC: Paralyzed Veterans of America, 1985.

Parker, Alfred E. *The Berkeley Police Story*. Springfield, IL: Charles C. Thomas, 1972.

A People's Park Chronology. Berkeley: Demic Publishing, 1969.

Percy, Stephen L. *Disability, Civil Rights, and Public Policy: The Politics of Implementation*. Tuscaloosa: University of Alabama Press, 1989.

Pflueger, Susan, and Edward V. Roberts. *Independent Living*. Washington, DC: Institute for Research Utilization, 1977.

Phillips, Lisa, Rosemarie Haag Bletter, and David A. Hanks, eds. *High Styles: Twentieth-Century American Design*. New York: Whitney Museum of American Art in association with Summit Books, 1985.

Pullin, Graham. *Design Meets Disability*. Cambridge: MIT Press, 2009.

Pursell, Carroll W. *Technology in Postwar America: A History*. New York: Columbia University Press, 2007.

Rancho Los Amigos Hospital. *Annual Report, FY 1949–1950*. Downey, CA: Rancho Los Amigos Hospital, 1950.

Rogers, Naomi. *Dirt and Disease: Polio before FDR*. New Brunswick: Rutgers University Press, 1992.

Rohr. *Rohr Industries Transbus: Final Report*. Bethesda, MD: Booz Allen Applied Research, 1975.

Rome, Adam Ward. *The Bulldozer in the Countryside: Suburban Sprawl and the Rise of American Environmentalism*. Cambridge, UK: Cambridge University Press, 2001.

Rorabaugh, W. J. *Berkeley at War: The 1960s*. New York: Oxford University Press, 1989.

Rose, David. *March of Dimes: Images of America*. Charleston, SC: Arcadia, 2003.

Rose, Sarah F. *No Right to Be Idle: The Invention of Disability, 1840s-1930s*. Chapel Hill: University of North Carolina Press, 2017.

Rusk, Howard A. *A Functional Home for Easier Living Designed for the Physically Disabled, the Cardiac, and the Elderly*. New York: New York University–Bellevue Medical Center, Institute of Physical Medicine and Rehabilitation, 1959.

———. *New Hope for the Handicapped: The Rehabilitation of the Disabled from Bed to Job*. New York: Harper, 1949.

———. *A World to Care For: The Autobiography of Howard A. Rusk, M.D.* New York: Random House, 1972.

Rusk, Howard A., and Eugene J. Taylor. *Living with a Disability*. Garden City, NY: Blakiston, 1953.

Russell, Emily. *Reading Embodied Citizenship*. New Brunswick: Rutgers University Press, 2011.

Russell, Marta. *Beyond Ramps: Disability at the End of the Social Contract: A Warning from an Uppity Crip*. Monroe, ME: Common Courage Press, 1998.

Sass, Edmund, George Gottfried, and Anthony Sorem, eds. *Polio's Legacy: An Oral History*. Lanham, MD: University Press of America, 1996.

Schweik, Susan M. *The Ugly Laws: Disability in Public*. New York: New York University Press, 2009.

Scotch, Richard K. *From Good Will to Civil Rights: Transforming Federal Disability Policy*. 2nd ed. Philadelphia: Temple University Press, 2001.

Scott, James C. *Seeing Like a State: How Certain Schemes to Improve the Human Condition Have Failed*. New Haven, CT: Yale University Press, 1998.

Serlin, David Harley. *Replaceable You: Engineering the Body in Postwar America*. Chicago: University of Chicago Press, 2004.

Shapiro, Joseph P. *No Pity: People with Disabilities Forging a New Civil Rights Movement*. New York: Times Books, 1993.

Shell, Marc. *Polio and Its Aftermath: The Paralysis of Culture*. Cambridge, MA: Harvard University Press, 2005.

Siebers, Tobin. *Disability Aesthetics*. Ann Arbor: University of Michigan Press, 2010.

———. *Disability Theory*. Ann Arbor: University of Michigan Press, 2008.

Simon, Herbert. *The Sciences of the Artificial*. Cambridge: MIT Press, 1969.

Skocpol, Theda. *Protecting Soldiers and Mothers: The Political Origins of Social Policy in the United States*. Cambridge, MA: Belknap, 1992.

Smith, Jane. *Patenting the Sun: Polio and the Salk Vaccine*. New York: Anchor, 1990.

Society of Automotive Engineers. *Vehicle Controls for Disabled Veterans*. Detroit: S.A.E. War Engineering Board, 1945.

Sparke, Penny. *As Long as It's Pink: The Sexual Politics of Taste*. London: Pandora, 1995.

Stiker, Henri-Jacques. *A History of Disability*. Ann Arbor: University of Michigan Press, 1999.

Story, Molly Follette, James L. Mueller, and Ronald L. Mace. *The Universal Design File: Designing for People of All Ages and Abilities*. Raleigh, NC: Center for Universal Design, 1998.

Thomson, Rosemarie Garland. *Extraordinary Bodies: Figuring Physical Disability in American Culture and Literature*. New York: Columbia University Press, 1997.

———. *Staring: How We Look*. Oxford: Oxford University Press, 2009.

Titchkosky, Tanya. *The Question of Access: Disability, Space, Meaning*. Toronto: University of Toronto Press, 2011.

Truck and Coach Division, General Motors Corporation. *The General Motors Transbus: Final Report*. Bethesda, MD: Booz Allen Applied Research, 1975.

Turner, Fred. *From Counterculture to Cyberculture: Stewart Brand, the Whole Earth Network, and the Rise of Digital Utopianism*. Chicago: University of Chicago Press, 2006.

Weatherford, Doris. *American Women during World War II: An Encyclopedia*. New York: Routledge, 2010.

Weems, Robert E. *Desegregating the Dollar: African American Consumerism in the Twentieth Century*. New York: New York University Press, 1998.

Weller, Allen S. *100 Years of Campus Architecture at the University of Illinois*. Urbana: University of Illinois Press, 1968.

White, Roger B. *Home on the Road: The Motor Home in America*. Washington, DC: Smithsonian Institution Press, 2000.

Wilson, Daniel J. *Living with Polio: The Epidemic and Its Survivors*. Chicago: University of Chicago Press, 2005.

Wilson, Robert G. "Need for and Development of Aids for Handicapped People." M.S. thesis, Illinois Institute of Technology, 1952.

Winner, Langdon. *The Whale and the Reactor: A Search for Limits in an Age of High Technology*. Chicago: University of Chicago Press, 1986.

Woodham, Jonathan M. *Twentieth Century Design*. Oxford History of Art. Oxford: Oxford University Press, 1997.

Wright, Mary Einstein. *Mary and Russel Wright's Guide to Easier Living*. New York: Simon and Schuster, 1951.

INTERNET SOURCES

Abler. http://ablersite.org.

All Par. Allpar.com.

Berkeleyside. http://berkeleyside.com.

Bespoke Innovations. http://bespokeinnovations.com.

Brown, Steven. "The Curb Ramps of Kalamazoo: Discovering Our Unrecorded History," 1999. www.independentliving.org.

Center for Universal Design, North Carolina State University. http://cud.ncsu.edu.

C-SPAN Archive. http://cspanvideo.com.

Disability Rights and Independent Living Movement Oral History Series. Regional Oral History Office, Bancroft Library, University of California. http://oac.cdlib.org/.

Dunne and Raby. www.dunneandraby.co.uk.

EveryBody: An Artifact History of Disability in America. Smithsonian National Museum of American History, 2014. http://everybody.si.edu.

Google patents. http://patents.google.com

"History of ADAPT." http://adaptmuseum.org.

"History—UC Berkeley." http://berkeley.edu.

Humanscale. http://humanscale.com.

Institute for Human-Centered Design. http://humancentereddesign.org.

Paul K. Longmore Institute on Disability. *Patient No More*. http://longmoreinstitute.sfsu.edu.

National Public Radio. http://npr.org.

TED. http://ted.com.

3D Systems. www.3Dsystems.com.

United Nations Convention on the Rights of Persons with Disabilities. United Nations
     Division for Social Policy and Development: Disability, 2007. www.un.org.
U.S. Census. www.census.gov.
White House. www.whitehouse.gov.
World Institute on Disability. www.wid.org.

FILMS
Diary of a Sergeant. Vol. 1. Uncle Sam Movie Collection. Washington, DC: Chudwig
     Group, 2002.
Stanton, Andrew. *WALL-E.* Disney/Pixar, 2008.
United States Army. Signal Corps. *Meet McGonegal.* War Department, 1944.
Wyler, William. *The Best Years of Our Lives.* HBO Home Video, 1997.

INDEX

Bold page references indicate figures.

ABOUT THE AUTHOR

Bess Williamson is Associate Professor of Art History, Theory, and Criticism at the School of the Art Institute of Chicago.

CRIP: NEW DIRECTIONS IN DISABILITY STUDIES

General Editors: Michael Bérubé, Robert McRuer, and Ellen Samuels

Committed to generating new paradigms and attending to innovative interdisciplinary shifts, the Crip: New Directions in Disability Studies series focuses on cutting-edge developments in the field, with interest in exploratory analyses of disability and globalization, ecotheory, new materialisms, affect theory, performance studies, postcolonial studies, and trans theory.

Crip Times: Disability, Globalization, and Resistance
Robert McRuer

Accessible America: A History of Disability and Design
Bess Williamson

CPSIA information can be obtained
at www.ICGtesting.com
Printed in the USA
JSHW041042191221
21388JS00001B/18